The
# Book of
# Friendship

# The
# Book of
# Friendship

by

## JOSIE BARNARD

virago

VIRAGO

First published in Great Britain in 2011 by Virago Press

A CIP catalogue record for this book
is available from the British Library.

ISBN 978-1-84408-548-4

Typeset in Ehrhardt by M Rules
Printed and bound in Great Britain by
Clays Ltd, St Ives plc

Papers used by Virago are from well-managed forests
and other responsible sources.

MIX
Paper from
responsible sources
FSC® C104740

Virago Press
An imprint of
Little, Brown Book Group
100 Victoria Embankment
London EC4Y 0DY

An Hachette UK Company
www.hachette.co.uk

www.virago.co.uk

*For Louis and Ynys*

# Contents

PART THREE: ONWARDS AND UPWARDS

# Introduction

Friendship is strange. Out of the sea of acquaintances and strangers, how do we make our friends? When do they appear in our lives? 'We cannot tell the precise moment when friendship is formed,' wrote the eighteenth-century essayist Samuel Johnson. 'As in filling a vessel drop by drop, there is at last a drop which makes it run over; so in a series of kindnesses there is at last the one which makes the heart run over.'

It often feels hard to explain. On the one hand, friends are crucial to us. On the other, they can seem like an awful lot of effort. In a soliloquy about the passing of time and the pointlessness of living, Bernard, a character in Virginia Woolf's novel *The Waves*, says, 'I have lost friends, some by death ... others by sheer inability to cross the street.'

Some leave you feeling lazy. Yet there are friends for whom you'd do anything. There doesn't seem to be any logic to it. 'Friendship my oxygen,' says the novelist Michèle Roberts. The American philosopher and poet Ralph Waldo Emerson wrote of his friends: 'The great God gave them to me. By oldest right, by the divine affinity of virtue with itself, I find them, or rather, not I, but the Deity in me.'

But friends can be so unpredictable.

At the start of the 2008 teen film *Angus, Thongs and Perfect Snogging*, the protagonist Georgia arrives at a party dressed as a stuffed olive because she and her fourteen-year-old pals had agreed to come as hors d'oeuvres – one as a vol au vent, one as a cocktail sausage. But her friends bottled out and didn't tell her. The film opens with Georgia standing aghast in the middle of the party, fat and green with her head made up to look like a bit of pimento, staring at her friends, who all look glamorous. Yet these same friends also help Georgia devise a 'snogging scale', get a boyfriend and throw the best party in Eastbourne.

And yes, notebook at my side I did watch *Angus, Thongs and Perfect Snogging* from start to finish. I also read pivotal essays on friendship by philosophers including Kant and Kierkegaard. I found myself listening rather too intently to other people's conversations in the changing room at my local swimming pool. I made my way systematically through works by psychologists and sociologists, historians, biographers and critics in the British Library. In second hand shops I happened across books such as *Mutual Aid* by the Russian anarchist Peter Kropotkin, crumpled and annotated. TV programmes like *Glee* held a new fascination.

Indeed, at times it felt as if everything I did was part of my research. Nipping out for coffee with a mate was not so simple any more. It's not that my friends were my research. But inevitably I thought about friendship while I was with them. If I mentioned to a close friend or someone I hardly knew that I was writing a book on friendship, more often than not their eyes would light up and they'd say: *You must include such and such a book/writer/song/artist.* And I'd find myself scrabbling for pencil stubs and making notes on table napkins.

It was exciting, but also a bit alarming. Friendship was turning out to be such a vast subject.

It soon became clear that I could not be comprehensive. I had to stop trying to be. Obviously, some texts demand attention: Aristotle's *Nicomachean Ethics*, for example. Aristotle says a great many astute, wise things about friendship. And he uses phrases that have left moral philosophers squirming for more than two millennia. He said that 'friendships of excellence' were the only type worth having, and that they were only available to male aristocrats. From the Enlightenment on, Aristotle was charged with elitism. Still more problematic, though, was his assertion that only those who were 'self-sufficient' could have truly worthwhile friendships. To achieve self-sufficiency, Aristotle said, one must be 'a friend to oneself most of all'. 'The good person,' he stated, 'must be a self-lover.'

And this one small word, 'self-lover', proved a terrible stumbling-block. A self-lover is surely selfish, which makes friendship something achieved at the expense of the greater good and therefore indefensible.

Yet Aristotle was a fierce champion of friendship. 'No one would choose to live without friends, even if he had all other goods.' For his shrewd *and* for his controversial observations, Aristotle became a leaping-off point. And I decided that, if they shed light on the same aspect of friendship, figures as diverse as Joyce Grenfell and Émile Zola, Cicero and The

Spice Girls, could be grouped together. Suddenly it felt a bit like throwing a party. It didn't have to be linear. It *shouldn't* be linear.

I talked to eighteen-year-old Clem and nineteen-year-old Arianna about texting versus Facebook. I looked at the clothes and activities depicted in the sixteenth-century Flemish artist Pieter Bruegel the Elder's painting *Children's Games*. I thought about the fact that in Lancashire cotton mills, workers would keep communicating with their friends over the noise of the looms using sign language and lip reading. I considered the ways things have changed in the relatively recent past for mothers. In 1935, one new mother who called herself 'Ubique' was so desperately isolated that she wrote to the letters page of *Nursery World* magazine: 'Can any mother help me?' Many women now who join ante-natal classes stay friends with that same group for decades. Mumsnet.com allows new mothers kept awake by colicky babies to give each other support from opposite ends of the country at 3 a.m.

I took facts and opinions, others' and my own. I selected, I shaped. I realised I was on a journey, but not up a mountain that has a definitive summit. In fact, there's no one peak to conquer. This book is an exploration. I go down side alleys, I discover coves and glades. But there are truths to be found along the way. 'Of the things which wisdom provides for the blessedness of one's whole life, by far the greatest is the possession of friendship,' said the Greek philosopher Epicurus. Plato said that he would rather have a single companion than all Darius's gold.

Money doesn't buy us happiness anyway, we know that.

Indeed, books like *Affluenza* by Oliver James show that a commitment to accumulating it actually takes us individually and nationally into debt.

Families are more fractured nowadays. Figures from the UK's Office for National Statistics show that almost half of all marriages in England and Wales will end in divorce. Aunts and uncles often live hundreds of miles away. The roles men and women play in society continue changing. It is not only women who tend children. As mothers increasingly hold down high-powered jobs, the househusband gains ground. It has been assumed for decades now that women are innately better at friendships, specifically at friendships that are more about empathy and sharing intimacies, while men's friendships are about going out and doing things together. Women fighting to become barristers find it necessary to develop the kinds of friendships that used to be confined to gentlemen's clubs and the golf course. Men trying to ferry children between classes and after-school clubs find that a busy domestic schedule is barely feasible without a network of fellow parents. Many people choose not to have children at all.

Our society is now infused with a fear of moral collapse. But stating simply that rethinking friendship might be a significant part of the answer is something we balk at in the twenty-first century.

The answer is not to suddenly acquire more friends, or to narrow too many friends down to one, or to dismiss Facebook on the grounds that it's simply not possible to have 352. But there are dos and don'ts of friendship, and in this book, ranging as it does through history and through disciplines and exploring representations of friendship in fiction, I will point to ways of making the most of what you have.

More than ever in our fractured society, friendship is, as Friedrich Nietzsche described it, 'a problem worthy of a solution'.

# PART ONE

# BEGINNINGS

'The meeting of two personalities is like the contact of two chemical substances: if there is any reaction, both are transformed.'

Carl Jung

# 1

# Opening Gambit

As a child, I found friendships alluring and confusing, even frightening. What would it be like to have someone you could trust like that? My upbringing was socially and geographically isolated. I felt I couldn't 'do' friendships. Travelling in on the school bus, standing in the playground, watching television: around me, everyone seemed simply to have them, with no effort. I was sombre and bespectacled. Then to my delight, at infant school, a girl called Dawn invited me back for tea, a meal that featured a stack of Mother's Pride cut in triangles and spread with bright-red jam. The return invitation saw Dawn in our somewhat ramshackle house out on the moor, a few mouthfuls into a plate of cassoulet, choking on a bay leaf because she had been too embarrassed to ask why there was a piece of foliage in her food and had tried to swallow it. That was the end of that alliance, and perhaps the start of my interest in trying to work out this elusive, potent thing called friendship.

From playground to grave, friendships play critical roles

in all our lives. They define and can even replace relationships with siblings and parents; they can last decades longer than most modern marriages.

It is like being released as a child into a sweet shop, with extra pocket money. You can *choose*, and not just one, either. You can have loads of friends, of a whole variety of types – close friends whose shoulders you can cry on; casual friends with whom you can get drunk and crash parties; friends who aid your health by also enjoying golf or badminton, and who, handily, play to a similar standard; friends you have to nurture because they might prove advantageous at work; friends who live down the road and take in a package if you are out and save you having to go and collect it from the post office later; friends you've known since nursery, with whom you don't even have to speak and in whose presence you feel immediately comforted and understood. And so on, up ladders, down snakes, all over the place.

A 'best' friend can play a dramatic part in your life. They will be the first person you go to in tears if your boyfriend dumps you. They might be your bridesmaid. They will cancel meetings and travel hundreds of miles to be there at your anniversary party. But the kinds of friendships that develop in bingo halls or on the bowling green, over a pint at lunchtime or over the heads of toddlers at playgroup, are vital too. Studies repeatedly show that just these kinds of casual social ties are measurably good for your health. They lower blood pressure, heart rate and cholesterol to such a degree that not having friends can be as detrimental to your health as smoking or being overweight.

His examination of friendship proved controversial later,

but Aristotle was adamant. True friendships, he said, were the highest order of relationships possible in society, and his opinion has been held not only in Ancient Greece but by key thinkers all over the world for centuries. 'Of a perfect society friendship is the peak,' wrote the sixteenth-century French essayist Michel de Montaigne. A few years later across the Channel in Elizabethan England, the philosopher and statesman Francis Bacon declared, 'Without true Friends the world is but a wilderness.' The Roman writers and statesmen Cicero and Seneca wrestled with the subject, as did the twelfth-century Cistercian abbot Aelred of Rievaulx, and the Italian theologian Thomas Aquinas a hundred years later. The German philosopher Immanuel Kant (1724–1804) described friendship as 'the whole end of man, through which he can enjoy his existence'.

Kant said that we all try to make ourselves good in order to deserve friendship, and ultimately that is good for society. But he was well aware that friendship comes with problems. He also warned, in the same essay, 'Even to our best friend we must not reveal ourselves in our natural state as we know it ourselves. To do so would be loathsome.' And whether friendship is morally defensible or not, 'loathsome' is a pretty off-putting label.

In 1846, in his essay 'You Shall Love Your Neighbour', Søren Kierkegaard proposed that 'self-love' on its own is bad enough, but that friendship is an appalling magnification of self-love. When two people become friends, it is no longer 'I–other' as separate entities, he said, but 'I–other–I' united in a single, huge, even more selfish self. Friendship, Kierkegaard declared, is a sin. 'It is the weakness of man which renders him social,' wrote Jean-Jacques Rousseau in his didactic novel *Émile*; 'it is our common miseries which carry our hearts towards humanity.'

It would be easier if we could think of friendship as either totally bad or purely good. It can be messy and perverse. After the narrator of Richard Ford's novel *The Sportswriter* has trekked to Sarasota on a wild goose chase for his dead friend Walter, he says: 'What's friendship's realest measure? I'll tell you. The amount of precious time you'll squander on someone else's calamities and fuck-ups.' Gore Vidal said, 'Whenever a friend succeeds, a little something in me dies.' The closer the friend, the more painful it can be if they suddenly get huge wealth or just the kind of job *you* wanted. Yet you can experience the sharpest stab of jealousy and still, genuinely, love your friend dearly. Once that feeling has subsided, you'll almost certainly do the decent thing and go out and buy them flowers. By the time you get to their place, happiness for them will have taken over.

Friendship is glorious. But the day-to-day realities of it can also be peculiar.

Sitting down with a cup of tea and a bun one day recently, I decided to search my mind and see which favourite moments with friends popped up. One was when I'd just finished my turn working a morning at the cooperative crèche we joined when our son was six months old. Almost all the other children and parents had left. Tchaikovsky's *Nutcracker* came on the radio. And, between the washing lines strung like bunting across his living-room, the remaining fellow parent suddenly launched into his own version of the Dance of the Sugar Plum Fairy. The other odd moment that suddenly occupied me was a summer afternoon from several years ago on a beach in Dorset when a long-time friend and I were making our way to the sea across stones the size of dinosaur's eggs – only, when I turned to check her progress, she'd just realised her swimming costume was twisted and she was stuck in a rather uncompromising position trying to pull it back in place.

I have wept in some friends' arms, I have cracked open champagne with others. Why was it these two rather low-key moments that surfaced? I think they both represent points at which I felt that we – me and a new friend; me and an old friend – had suddenly become a few shades more relaxed with each other. Though I didn't tell either of them that these moments mattered to me, at the time or later.

'I go to my friend, we walk on the grass, / And the hours and moments like minutes pass,' wrote the poet Stevie Smith in 'The Pleasures of Friendship', drawing attention to the way time can lose its hold when you're with a friend. An hour can shrink, and a moment expand, and this can be unsettling. Perhaps, in a café, I'm ready for a second cup of tea, but my companion is putting their coat on to go. Have I offended them? Friendships are ripe for misunderstandings.

In an exchange of letters between the poet Alexander Pope and the Anglo-Irish clergyman and satirist Jonathan Swift, Pope wrote in August 1723: 'I really thought you would know yourself to be so certainly entitled to my Friendship, that 'twas a possession.' By this time, the two men had been separated by the Irish Sea for the better part of a decade. Pope couldn't pretend that he had been sitting alone in London pining over Swift. Indeed, he stressed that 'My Friendships are increas'd by new ones.' Swift was not appeased, writing back in September, 'Your Notions of Friendship are new to me; I believe every man is born with his quantum, and he can not give to one without Robbing another.'

John Lennon and Paul McCartney sang about how much easier it is to get by 'With a Little Help from My Friends'.

The film director Jean Renoir wrote in a letter to Janine Bazin dated 12 June 1974: 'Don't think that this is a letter. It is only a small eruption of a disease called friendship.'

Yet we just can't stop ourselves going back for more. In George Orwell's and Margaret Atwood's futuristic novels *Nineteen Eighty-four* and *The Handmaid's Tale*, friendship is considered so dangerous by the authorities that it is banned. In Atwood's, it is punishable by death. In both books, the protagonists risk their lives for snatches of it.

But how *should* we value it?

A young woman who works at a local grocery shop told me she spends every New Year's Eve with the same female friend, at home, over dinner. I was impressed, and, I'll admit, a little embarrassed for her. The thought crossed my mind: Didn't she get invited to parties? They may not be true friends individually, but at least being at a party shows you have lots.

When I was in my early twenties, an elderly relative gave me a piece of advice that she clearly considered a gem. I should never simply *see* a friend, she said. I should not merely *hang out*, but must always do something else as well – for example, go to an art show – because whereas I would forget the friend, I would never forget the show. By contrast, the Scottish tradition of Hogmanay makes friends pivotal.

At the stroke of midnight on New Year's Eve, friends and neighbours rush round to each other's houses with presents. Coal might be taken to symbolise warmth, or a 'black bun' to represent a hope that your friend has abundant food in the months to come. According to the part of Hogmanay known as 'first-footing', whichever friend arrives first sets the luck for the rest of the year.

In the eighteenth century a tradition of 'friendship balls', or 'witches balls', evolved, probably in the Nailsea Glass-works factory near Bristol. These items were made at the ends of shifts. They featured lots of different colours. The idea was that they would hang in your window and the refracting light would attract evil spirits into the ball and keep them trapped there. But it's no good just buying a friendship ball for yourself. Its power comes when it has been given to you by a friend.

# 2
# Wild Things

Children's friendships are mesmerising to watch, not least because they often seem to happen by magic. On a fine summer's day on almost any beach, children from disparate families come together to build sandcastles as if they have been friends for ever. Without having to negotiate or give each other instructions they know just when to whoop and dance and when to dig furiously, which sections of ramparts to repair to stop water breaking through and which turrets to decorate, then at what point to trample the whole construction delightedly, as sea water starts to splash around their feet.

In Jean Vigo's film *Zéro de Conduite* (1933), in the opening scene a boy waits in a carriage of the train that will take him to boarding school. He looks sullen. Slumped down in the seat, alone, he is clearly bored. Then his friend turns up. The atmosphere changes immediately. They don't even bother talking. They just start showing each other tricks. One blows up a pair of balloons and positions them as breasts. The other clenches a feather between his buttocks so it sticks out from his trousers like a tail. Their pranks are not even particularly imaginative or daring. But the director doesn't feel there is any need for narrative drive or plot development here. The camera keeps rolling as the friends show each other silly tricks. Nothing else happens for several minutes. The sheer joy on the boys' faces is captivating.

We all know that feeling. With friends, we can be wild.

Bruegel's *Children's Games* presents a veritable chaos of children's friendships. The sombre sixteenth-century coats and long skirts don't appear to impede the children much at all. Between the houses, in a square in the foreground of the painting and all the way up a street behind, you see line games, circle games, pair games; girls and boys are tumble-turning, leap-frogging, rolling hoops; a group astride a balustrade wield riding crops; participants in a tug-of-war ride piggy-back. Think of the shenanigans the children in Enid Blyton or the *Harry Potter* books get up to. The joy is in the anarchy.

When I was four and living in a terrace in Leeds, the slightly older girl next door invited me to crawl to the back of her dad's tool shed with her and share her stolen jelly, straight from the packet. It was a revelation. All the fuss adults went to, diluting the stuff with pints of water. They were so wrong. After eating six raw cubes in quick succession, I felt only slightly sick.

The things friends encourage us to do are often unnerving, and thrilling. When I went up to secondary school a brand-new friend persuaded me to leave the grounds one break-time, and down by the weir, in the wild flowers at the edges, she told me what a condom was used for. At first I didn't believe her; the idea seemed absurd. She brought one out, ripping open the packet to show me. And then I *knew* the sex education teacher had taught us nothing. But then she demonstrated that condoms also make great water bombs. Having just discussed the gory details of sexual intercourse with due sobriety, we were suddenly filling condoms from a stream and exploding them on a stretch of concrete path, giggling insanely.

It's all about pushing boundaries. But with friends you can do it as if by accident, as part of the exuberance.

Clare, the main character in Audrey Niffenegger's 2004 novel *The Time Traveller's Wife*, is basically a good girl. But in an early scene, when she's eleven, at a classmate's birthday party attended by the entire fifth grade she experiments with what's OK – and what may not be. They all do. They play truth-and-dare, they talk about potential boyfriends, they do a ouija board. Wriggling in their sleeping bags on the pink carpet, that is what they're there for: to break rules. The party girl brings out peppermint schnapps. It doesn't cross Clare's mind to say no. Whether or not she likes the drink is barely relevant. It is alcoholic. She savours the way it feels – like 'Vicks VapoRub in my chest'.

It's not just about breaking rules, though. Indeed, the thrill of that is likely to be quite short-lived. Once you've got away with something, then what? The wildness that comes with children's friendships is often about experiencing to the full new *sensations*.

In volume 5 of the manga (comic book) series *MÄR* by Nobuyuki Anzai, one rather sugar-sweet character with big eyes, Snow, is at first a Cinderella figure. She is shy. But then a single word of support from her new glamorous friend, Queen, and suddenly Snow is fearless. She feels as if she can control the universe, rip it up if she wants to. She picks 'FROZEN EARTH!!!' as her attack and charges into the wargames, leaping, kicking, punching. With a friend backing her, sounds like BWOOM!, PAK! and ZSSSH! explode on the page around her. Snow laughs in the face of Fugi the wind weaver.

We can feel crippled by awareness of our own inadequacies one minute, transformed by friendship the next. In twenty-first-century manga books, it turns cowardly girls into martial arts experts.

But the transformative powers of friendship have been celebrated for millennia.

In 1852, the novelist Émile Zola and the painter Paul Cézanne met as boys aged twelve and thirteen at the Collège Bourbon in Aix-en-Provence, where they famously saved each other. They were both outcasts. Paul was illegitimate; when Émile arrived from Paris, his family was destitute. It wasn't only that big, stubborn Paul had the guts to intervene and stop the other boys bullying Émile, though. Together, in the holidays and at weekends, they were able to leave Aix and do exactly what they wanted. Their biographers devote long, lyrical passages to the boys' rambling excursions up the spectacular Mont Sainte-Victoire. And much is made of the ways in which Émile and Paul's boyhood friendship gave them the courage to pursue their artistic dreams. Zola wrote later of how, during those Mont Sainte-Victoire forays, he and Paul were united by 'the awakening of a superior intelligence in the midst of the brutal mob of dreadful dunces who beat us'. The mountain later featured repeatedly in Cézanne's work. Their friendship also simply freed them to be children.

The boys would stuff books into their satchels. They read Homer, Virgil and Victor Hugo to each other. And out on Mont Sainte-Victoire they did typical boys' stuff: forged paths through brambles, jumped into streams, lit fires and cooked bits of meat on twigs. They joined hunting expeditions, not because they were good shots (even with practice they didn't become good shots). They just enjoyed the feel of slinging big guns and dirty game bags over their shoulders. They were 'scamps', Zola remembered, 'wearing out trousers on school benches ... We had a need of fresh air, of sunshine, of paths lost at the bottoms of ravines and of which we took possession as conquerors.'

One of the brilliant things about friendship is that it incorporates so many possibilities for wildness, all at once. It frees you to be silly, and to play at being older at the same time.

In her essay about Joyce Grenfell, *Joyce by Herself and Her Friends*, Virginia Graham says that she and the comedienne knew each other from the age of five. But it was not till their teens that they were pulled close, by Christian Science. Graham says that between the wars Christian Science was 'an unorthodox religion', one which 'in those un-ecumenical days entailed a certain amount of gentle persecution'. Yet together they committed to it, and could feel simultaneously reckless and mature for doing so. Every week, before going to the local matinée, over baked beans or Welsh rarebit at Lyons Corner House 'we would air our doubts and convictions, nodding wisely, like very old owls, as we pondered on the Creation, or later in the meal, between sucks at our Strawberry Nut Sundaes, on eternity.'

The nineteenth-century poet Leigh Hunt also found that friendship allowed him to be wild in a manner that was childish and earnest at the same time. It seems he was ambitious as a boy. His early friends included Thomas Barnes, who went on to become an editor of *The Times*. One of the masters he befriended at his school, Christ's Hospital, ensured that he went on to study at Cambridge. Nonetheless, although he loved learning, Hunt still escaped school at weekends with his friends whenever he could. He wrote later, 'What pleasant days have I not passed with Barnes, and other schoolfellows, bathing in the New River, and boating on the Thames! He and I began to learn Italian together; and anybody not within the pale of the enthusiastic might have thought us mad, as we went shouting the beginning of Metastasio's Ode to Venus, as loud as we could bawl, over the Hornsey fields.'

And as everyone knows, Leigh Hunt wasn't remotely unusual for wanting to let off steam by simply bellowing. Many young people before and after have harboured the desire to make a kerfuffle with friends for the heck of it.

The historian G. M. Trevelyan notes that at Cambridge University in the 1600s wealthy students wore clothes featuring ruffs, velvet and silk, carried swords and rapiers, played cards and dice, and went out to watch bear-baiting and cock-fighting, even though all these things were strictly forbidden by their college. 'Early in Elizabeth's reign,' says Trevelyan, 'parson Harrison complained that "gentlemen or rich men's sons often bring the Universities into much slander. For, standing upon their reputation and liberty, they ruffle and roist it out, exceeding in apparel, and riotous company.'"

In Mark Twain's *The Adventures of Tom Sawyer*, Tom fully intends to be an upright citizen, attending Sunday School, painting his Aunt Sally's fence. But with his school-mate Joe Harper he also tortures ticks with pins in class. That feels exciting, but Tom is drawn most of all to the boy he has been told *not* to play with: the son of the town drunk, Huckleberry Finn.

The appeal of the bad boy is visceral. Huck doesn't even go to school. His cast-off adults' clothes are 'in perennial bloom and fluttering with rags. His hat was a vast ruin with a wide crescent lopped out of its brim.' Most alluring of all, 'Huckleberry came and went at his own free will. He slept on door-steps in fine weather, and in empty hogsheads in wet ... he could go fishing or swimming when and where he chose, and stay as long as it suited him; nobody forbade him to fight; he could sit up as late as he pleased.' His routine activities include slinking off with a dead cat (a 'pretty stiff' one) at midnight, because a witch has told him that if he does so, and if he can find the grave of someone just buried and wicked, when a devil comes to the graveyard to collect the sinner, he can send the cat after the devil and any warts after the cat – and the sufferer will be cured of his warts.

It's not unusual for adults and children alike to be drawn to friends who make them feel free to be wild. When Virginia Woolf first met the upper-class Vita Sackville-West, she wrote excitedly in her diary of the free and easy supple-jointedness of the aristocracy – 'no inhibitions, no false reserves; anything can be said'. For Virginia, another big attraction was Vita's physical presence. She spoke of her legs 'running like slender pillars up into her trunk, which is that of a breastless cuirassier'. Virginia thought her Amazonian: 'all about her is virginal, savage'.

In *Paper Houses: A Memoir of the 70s and Beyond*, Michèle Roberts recalls her days in London when, straight out of university, she started 'groping' her way towards feminism and left-wing politics. It was with friends that she began to shed her nerves. With them, she ended up one night at a party in Stoke Newington in the house of the man who ran the International Socialists, going to bed at 3 a.m. on top of 'scattered heaps of leaflets and posters'. She joined a commune in Holloway and with her new friends hired a flat-back lorry and turned it into a carnival float, a 'boudoir on wheels', to take to a CND festival.

In the musical *Grease*, friends step in to help the main characters find their resolve with a sparky melody and a sassy two-step. In the 1978 film version, Olivia Newton-John's blonde, pristine Sandy daren't curl her hair or wear sexier clothes until one of the girls in the cool gang, the Pink Ladies, offers assistance. Jeff Conaway's character Kenickie could just get on and customise his car – he believes with a little work in the garage it could be turned into a top-grade sports car. But it is not until his friends, John Travolta's Danny and the T-Birds, agree to pitch in with spanners and wrenches that suddenly it seems he really will be able to turn his 'hunk o' junk' into 'Greased Lightning'.

You can do it on your own. But how much more fun, how much more *possible* it is to flout convention with friends.

Two of the most popular and long-running British comic strips, the *Beano*'s 'Bash Street Kids' and *Bunty*'s 'The Four Marys', both chart the antics of groups of friends who egg each other on to naughtiness. The Bash Street Kids are a motley crew featuring the leader Danny, who wears a skull and cross-bones on his jumper, short-sighted 'Erbert, ugly Plug, Smiffy and Toots. Their socks are always falling down; they've perpetually got catapults in their pockets or their hands in sweet jars; half the time, they stuff their homework in a dustbin. The Four Marys are a bit more staid. They attend a girls-only boarding school, St Elmo's. One of the Marys is working-class, and a bit worried about being looked down on. Sometimes their studies cause them angst.

But in both comic strips, a key function of the friends is to help each other resist or undermine figures of authority, whether it's the prim housemistress Miss Creef in 'The Four Marys' or the fat caretaker and the lanky, mortar-board-wearing teacher in 'The Bash Street Kids'.

In the 2006 film *High School Musical*, it's more complicated. Zac Efron's character Troy is helped by his friends to audition for the lead part in the school show – but only after they've colluded with the 'geeks' to sabotage his chances by fixing up a covert video link so that Troy's singing partner Gabriella can watch him denouncing her live. Sometimes the wildness of friendship comes at your expense.

Week after week, this aspect is emphasised in *Glee*, the all-singing, all-dancing American TV series in which teenage members of a high school glee club fight for trophies in singing competitions while negotiating their feelings of jealousy, guilt and rage. In one episode Kurt, who fancies

Finn, tells Rachel, who also fancies Finn, that Finn likes girls who wear tight clothes and lots of make-up – except, Finn has already told him expressly that those are just the kind of girls he hates. Rachel dresses up to seduce Finn, and is humiliated. She finds out that Kurt set her up. *He* is humiliated.

Whatever the internal ructions, by the end of each episode, one way or another, the glee club members have pulled together. The loyalty that comes with their friendship always wins out.

But meantime, the story lines show only too clearly that friendship opens you up to betrayal. It involves loyalty, and risk.

# 3

# Risk-taking

Friendship is about risk-taking. Particularly when we're children, we look to friends to help us start breaking away. Home can be safe and staid. In however small a way, friendship gives us the excuse to rebel.

A crucial thing about these early rebellions against home is that they often *happen* at home. It is only really a rebellion if your family knows about it. If a friend has been chosen in order to provoke, the friend has to be pushed in family members' faces. The daughter of a sheep farmer might suddenly seek out friends in a group of animal rights activists, concluding that it is essential to bring them home for dinner. The son of a left-wing couple decides that his soulmates all reside in the local branch of the Young Conservatives, and that they must have their next hustings in his family living-room.

And this slightly perverse home-based rebellion isn't something that's peculiar to the twenty-first century by any means.

In Tudor England, the future 'boy king' Edward VI was

educated at home. He clearly relished the chances for domestic rebellion that his friends gave him. His father, Henry VIII, decided that Edward needed maths and grammar, and to learn how to socialise as well. So Henry picked over a dozen well-born boys and shipped them into the palace to serve as his son's classmates under the tutor Richard Cox when Edward was seven.

Edward had perhaps a greater need to aim regular kicks at authority than most of us, and more difficulty. He was the heir to the throne, and pretty well everything he did was monitored. For a child who wasn't yet into double figures, he bore a phenomenal weight of responsibility. In the classroom, he gained a version of freedom. He let other boys practise their signatures in the margins of his schoolbooks. Of the sons of the nobles his father provided him with, Edward chose to become the close friend of just one, Barnaby Fitzpatrick, the son of an obscure Irish peer. The Protestant preacher Thomas Lever implored Edward to avoid Barnaby's company. But Lever's disapproval clearly just made his company more appealing. He and Edward got into scrapes. Barnaby acted as Edward's 'proxy for correction', getting whipped on Edward's behalf when the prince was naughty.

Although worlds away in terms of class and setting, in nineteenth-century Lancashire a young working-class woman, Cissie Foley, behaved in a strikingly similar manner. She was a 'setter on' in a spinning mill. She had plenty of other places she could go with her friends, but she found that the best place to distance herself from her family was at the kitchen table.

Having made some new friends in a class on the poetry of Robert Browning, she brought them back for tea, repeatedly. Her sister Alice wrote about it years later in her memoir *A Bolton Childhood*. Her hurt and anger still come across when she describes Cissie's friends as 'a quartet of "fuss-pots"' who ate too much of her anxious mother's home-made currant bread and patronised her into the bargain, while Cissie was 'sedulously imbibing socialistic ethics and culture'. The discussions, which 'ranged round politics, men, votes for women and culture', were all the more stimulating for Cissie because they excluded Alice and their mother.

It can be alarming to find that it's you who have been drafted in by the rebel, though. I had to slink out of back doors a couple of times after being encouraged by new friends to loudly voice my atheist and pacifist views – once in the kitchen of a schoolmate whose father was a vicar, and another time in the living-room of a girl whose entire family, it seemed, was in the army. Sometimes, it is even a family member who becomes the friend providing the escape from family. Stephen Spender presents himself in his autobiography as a timid teenager whose first big rebellious friendship was with his grandmother. She encouraged Stephen's interest in the arts, taking him to plays and painting exhibitions, against his father's wishes. Spender names his grandmother Hilda Schuster as one of his most important early friends. Friends don't have to be your age.

Like Spender, I too reached across the age gap for dangerous and rebellious friendship – though all within limits. When I was fourteen, I knew I wanted to go away on my own on holiday. One Friday I got my dad to put me on a

National Express coach to go and stay with my Great-aunt Agnes in Wiltshire. Even though it was she who, at a rare family gathering, had suggested I visit her, when I actually got to her house at 4 p.m. she looked baffled, then snapped, 'Well, what do you want to drink?', gesturing towards a trolley loaded with bottles of spirits.

I didn't know what they all were. She brightened. 'You could get into terrible trouble at parties. Men could take advantage of you. I'll have to teach you.' And for the rest of the evening, for as long as I could remain upright she gave me glass after glass of different types of alcohol, and made me repeat the names of every one. The next day, at noon, she asked me what I'd like to drink. Head throbbing, I couldn't remember a single one – and we started all over again.

I think the only concrete facts I came away from my Great-aunt Agnes's with were that port tastes like fruit juice but is lethal, and if you really do want fruit juice you have to fetch it yourself, as vodka has no taste so can be used by cads who'll spike it. Yet that visit was formative.

A great deal of the wildness we get up to with friends is useful and important.

The house where I spent most of my childhood was at the top of a dead-end road that stopped in moorland. A farmer's son called John lived at the top of a road on the other side of the hill. Sometimes he would walk over to call on us, sometimes my brother and sister and I would go to him. Often all four of us, having collected a couple more children along the way, would negotiate the land between. Many of the games we played took place in a disused barn in the middle of a field some distance from any roads or houses. A particular favourite of ours was to climb up to the first-floor rafters, where we'd take turns daring each other to walk across one of the beams. Arms out for balance, one foot in front of the other, the tussle between a desire to impress and fear of the drop made for precarious progress.

If one talks of an act of friendship, one generally means an act of generosity. What was being given out generously here was encouragement to do something dangerous. If one of us did fall, another could have gone for help. And the fact is, none of us did. I was rubbish at hockey – on my school report, in the box for 'sport' I always got a grade D and the comment, 'Tries hard'. But I could get across that beam with aplomb, and cheers.

The environmental psychologist Roger Hart also enjoyed a lot of freedom to play out with his friends while he was growing up in suburban Sussex in the 1970s. And like me, he values the opportunities unsupervised childhood friendships gave him for risk-taking. In his paper *Children's Experience of Place: A Developmental Study*, he describes playing a game of 'tracking' with the 'Old Mill Close gang'. In the process of running and dropping the twigs and stones that the other team were to follow, he and his mates went a bit further afield than usual.

At the end of Carfield Avenue I came across a busy main street which I knew I could not cross. I knew I was out of my territory yet things seemed familiar. With fascination I looked down the road and to my amazement I saw the village library. Suddenly I realized I had mentally conquered a large area of space for I knew how to reach this library by a completely different route. I had visited the library a number of times but always by walking with one of my family along Stapleford Lane. Now I realized that these two roads formed part of a giant circle.

With his peers he could feel at once that he had support, and that he had independently 'conquered' a new bit of the world.

# 4

# Tribal

The desire to be in with an in-crowd, *any* in-crowd, can be visceral.

The writer Elizabeth Bowen was an only child. In her memoir, she remembers how an invitation to a party could set her in such a state of excitement that 'I was often unable to eat my dinner; my throat tightened, my heart thumped.' Her parents would get so concerned that they'd send her off to her room to rest for an hour. And she savoured even that part of the ritual.

On arrival, stepping through the doorway of a house that had been transformed for the children's pleasure, she'd drink in every detail: 'flowers banked up out of harm's way, fur rugs expectantly rolled back and big chintz sofas in retreat against the walls'. It was both a joy and an endurance test to stay still in the pent-up silence of the entrance hall. 'A rustle of fidgeting (like the wind in corn) could be heard as one was led past the drawing-room door to lay off one's coat and shawls in a room above.' And then, once inside the party room, 'the fellow-guests, the children, are metamorphosed: in their lacy dresses or dark suits they are the *beau monde*. You may have often met them; you may have known them; you may have pulled their hair. Or they may be strangers: it is indifferent. In the hot, lit, packed room full of beating hearts, with its psychic orchestra soundlessly tuning up, everything is subsidiary to "the party".'

Of course, the place where you always see throngs of mates is school, but the fact of seeing them every day won't necessarily do much to reduce the intensity of the feelings. In Benjamin Disraeli's autobiographical novel *Coningsby*, when the blue-eyed, curly-haired protagonist arrives at Eton, he finds the chance to order his own breakfast exciting. But the sight of so many potential friends sends him into raptures. The halls, glades and avenues, however beautiful, are nothing on their own. It's 'the stirring multitude, the energetic groups', 'the emulation and the affection', 'the daring exploit and the dashing scrape' that make his heart race. 'At school, friendship is a passion,' said Disraeli. 'It entrances the being; it tears the soul.' It is striking that he is not interested in singling out any individual friendships. He celebrates friendship as an experience, as an *aspiration*.

There is a desperation, as a schoolchild, to be accepted. We just want to embed ourselves in the group. And this has always been true.

In the sixteenth century the letters home of one German schoolboy, fourteen-year-old Friedrich VIII Behaim, quickly gained that desperate edge. He did seem to be missing his family or finding his lessons problematic. Medieval parents who stumped up for a son's education did so in the hope that he would nurture relationships with students who might turn out to be fruitful future associates. What Friedrich wanted was to be included by his peers then and there.

He kept coming back to it. To his mother on 11 September 1578: 'I also ask you to send me a blood-letting lancet, so that I can be bled. The other students have their own special lancets.' He asked her to let him move out of the official college lodgings. For this request, on 27 August 1579, he wrote one of his longest, most wily letters. He spoke of the financial savings she'd make: she'd have less to pay for his firewood. 'The servants hang around here all day and I can get nothing done,' he declared. Furthermore, 'when I was last in chapel, someone stole my schilling from my locked trunk, and also several books from my comrades.'

But then, in mid-flow, he suddenly blurts out: 'I also do not want to stay in the college any longer.' All his friends had gone to live in lodgings in the town. His mother refused his request. She was worried about what he'd do under these friends' sway. She sent various panicky warnings, including an instruction that regardless of what his friends might do, Friedrich should *not* 'venture behind any castle', areas frequented by prostitutes.

But he was a long way from home. And in any case, maybe his mother was wrong to be so apprehensive. Being part of an 'in-crowd' is not always entirely bad, by any means.

In Muriel Spark's *The Prime of Miss Jean Brodie*, set in 1930s Edinburgh, the girls who are assigned Miss Brodie as their teacher are thrilled because Miss Brodie doesn't only teach them art history and the Classics – she also tells them personal details about her love life. And she doesn't discourage them from becoming a tight 'in-group'. Indeed, she practically insists on it: 'All my pupils are the crème de la crème'; her girls become the admired 'Brodie set'.

In the 2009 film *St Trinian's II: The Legend of Fritton's Gold*, when the headmistress, Rupert Everett's Miss Fritton, learns that the ring they need to find the treasure has been stolen, she invokes Henry V's St Crispin's Day call to action. 'We few, we happy few, we band of sisters!' Miss Fritton cries from the school's grand central staircase. 'For she who sheds her blood with me shall be my sister!' If they can find it, the treasure will help the school. Miss Fritton wants the girls to unite to make weapons. She's proud to see one lot wielding lacrosse sticks like swords, and another lot lined up and pulling back the elastic of their catapults ready to fire bits of chewed gum. Rebellious or outright illegal activities, if carried out as a group to help the group, are quite justified in Miss Fritton's view of things.

And for the individuals involved, the experience of getting up to no good together can make for a tighter bond. Indeed, in Thomas Hughes' *Tom Brown's Schooldays* the pull of the group is portrayed as not just exhilarating but healthy and character-forming. This autobiographical novel is largely based on the author's time at Rugby School in the 1830s. Hughes wrote it when his young son was due to go off to board there himself.

There is a level at which the book is an instruction manual: one of Hughes' messages is that you must stick with your friends no matter what. Like the parents of Friedrich VIII Behaim, he saw school as an investment in future contacts.

The class of 1855 would be an old boys' network in 1885. Hughes undoubtedly wanted his son to mix with the 'right sort'.

There are initiation tests in the novel, some of them quite nasty. The narrative makes clear that they are standard practice. At any good boarding school, the book seems to suggest, a new boy should get the blanket treatment. A dozen of the big boys grab one off a bed, chuck the new boy in and bundle him up. 'Once, twice, thrice and away!' – the blanket goes up and down 'like a shuttlecock', with an extra sense of achievement for the big boys if the whole package hits the ceiling. The only indication that the test has gone too far is if bones get broken.

A new boy can hide or whinge pathetically until he's let off. But Hughes doesn't advise it. Any new boy has to accept that he will be handled roughly, and he must accept it if he doesn't want to become an outcast. The trick with the blanket is to stay still while it's going on – that way you get less hurt. Most important of all, if you don't cry you gain your contemporaries' respect. And there will be fights, bloody ones, says Hughes. But if they are in defence of friends, you have to throw yourself right in. Friends will help by rubbing your hands and bringing sponges to freshen you up.

Similarly out on the sports fields: facing the opposition in a rugby match, you may not want to run straight at a row of hefty lads whose aim is to stop you getting the ball. Even if it is counterintuitive to put your head down and try to 'struggle now right through the scrummage', you must do exactly that, 'chancing all hurt for the glory of the School-house'. There's gallantry when the unfortunate Diggs has to sell his possessions off and Tom and East buy key pieces in order to give them back. There's a whiff of Arthurian legend about the Saturday nights when the older boys drink beer and the new boys are placed on tables to sing.

All this may be identifiable as a stage that children go through, though the hoops to be jumped through today are often quite different from those that Tom Brown was faced with. Nevertheless, it is important to get it right. The more cosseted a young child's home life, the harder it can be. Learning how to negotiate busy social situations is a serious business, and primary schools can be intimidating. It's handy if an interim group can be found, and playgroups serve that purpose. The child psychoanalyst D. W. Winnicott pointed to Cubs and Brownies as perfect places for a child to 'find a working relationship between ideas that are free and behaviour that needs to become group-related'. The movement spawned by Lieutenant-General Robert Baden-Powell in 1907 still gives children uniforms, which bring a clear sense of belonging.

I'd thought the toggles that Brownies have to wear silly until I wore them myself aged seven. And making pom-poms by winding bits of wool round circles of card acquired a sudden importance when I was doing it in a Scout hut with a row of other Brownies in order to earn a badge. Cubs and Brownies, Scouts and Guides allow children to feel *in*, and they deliver healthy lessons in how to socialise. Cooperation is a key factor. The original Scout Law, outlined in Baden-Powell's book *Scouting for Boys*, states: 'A Scout is Loyal', 'A Scout's Duty is to be Useful and to Help Others', and 'A Scout is a Friend to All.'

In their paper 'The Development of Subjective Group Dynamics', the psychologists Dominic Abrams and Adam Rutland say the desire to embed oneself in a group is experienced most keenly in 'middle childhood', between the ages of about seven and eleven. The child has begun to understand that he or she is not, after all, the centre of the universe. Joining the in-crowd is a way of simultaneously accepting that reality and denying it. If children can position themselves within a group that is at least at the centre of the school playground, they can maintain a robust ego even as they acknowledge the existence and rights of their peers.

There's a wide variety of benefits. Belonging to an in-group helps establish, as Abrams and Rutland put it, 'coherence and meaning for the self'; it can boost self-esteem enormously. In addition, new arrivals will find that in-groups 'demand rapid compliance', and the authors suggest that this is 'an early lesson in the value of consensus'. Ideally, with the help of an in-group a child will move from being egocentric to being a fierce group member to being an individual who is able to respect the needs of others within the group. But the process is fraught.

The new rules that in-groups invent for themselves are often cobbled together from patchy information.

Mary McCarthy's novel *The Group* follows eight Vassar graduates who have arrived to make their way in 1930s New York. Gossiping over nose-powdering or while snacking on tinned minced clams on toast feels thrilling. The tightness of the group generates an atmosphere of daring. Each can break the mould because her friends will back her up.

When Kay gets married, she decides there's no need for formalities such as wedding lists drafted by parents. She simply invites her friends herself. 'The sense of an adventure was strong.'

But they're making the rules up as they go along. In the 1930s, the Pill wasn't on the market; sex before marriage was still highly controversial. The women's talk of intercourse and contraception results in some things being half-understood.

Dottie Renfrew decides losing her virginity is a priority. First, she takes another member of the group along with her when she goes to get a 'Dutch cap' fitted. But knowing about cutting-edge contraceptive methods is only part of it. At the doctor's, 'she had nearly choked on "douche" and "birth control" as it was'. In a seedy attic room, after the man she chose has done the deed, he whips back the sheets. He's a near-stranger. All she wants is to be able to grab the sheets back and cover herself. And the physical humiliation of being 'laid bare' is not the end of it. The extent of her ignorance is exposed too. He has to explain the term 'coitus interruptus' and why there's a trace of blood on the towel.

Dottie is young, she's vulnerable. She lets the group empower her to do things she's not ready for. But sometimes we only embrace membership of an in-group as a way of making the best of a bad job.

In the comedy television series *Misfits* (2009–10), the teenage characters Nathan, Kelly, Simon, Alisha and Curtis become a group because they find themselves doing community service together. Their orange jumpsuits and the tasks that they find demeaning such as cleaning graffiti off walls tie them to each other in the eyes of the world. They're linked because they've all broken the law. They don't like their new group status, initially. It's only when a freak electrical storm gives them superpowers that their in-group status becomes exciting and they become real friends.

It's rare that there's just the one in-group in a young person's life. There are often conflicting in-groups all vying for dominance. In the *St Trinian's* film, when the cool tearaway rock star Roxy arrives, the Chavs, the Emos and the Geeks all want her in their gangs.

A key danger of in-groups that Abrams and Rutland identify in their paper is that for an in-group to be truly 'in', there must also be an 'out-group'. Friendships within in-groups often rest on belittling and excluding others. There are other complications, including a quirk they call 'the black sheep effect', whereby if a member of a rival group rejects that group, the members of the group he or she joins will treat 'the black sheep' better than its own existing members. The black sheep becomes vital, because 'a deviant from an out-group may help to reinforce the in-group's validity while undermining that of the out-group'. Although, Abrams and Rutland say, the ripples of instability can last long after that initial celebration of the new member. 'The presence of a deviant group member is itself a signal that the psychological validity of the group is under threat and should therefore provoke a reaction to restore that validity.' And the kinds of reactions they're talking about include existing members being turned on and ousted themselves.

In-groups come with possibilities of dramatic flare-ups. William Golding gives us a particularly chilling exploration of those possibilities in *Lord of the Flies*. He puts the characters in an extreme situation. A plane transporting a group of boys crashes, and they are stranded on an island. As they hack their way through the undergrowth exploring, one of the boys, the chorister Jack, sees the possibilities on the island for hunting pigs. However Ralph, while not disputing the appeal of this, suggests that if they are to be rescued, they must build a fire so that the smoke can be seen, so that they can get back to civilisation. Ralph is chosen as leader. And precisely because there had been a spark between them, Jack begins to hate Ralph.

Golding presents only too plausibly a scenario in which a group of boys forms a blood-thirsty tribe that hunts down Ralph with intent to kill, even though most of the tribe members had previously liked him. Now under Jack's charismatic leadership, the tribe fails to move on to 'become sensitive to the particular attributes of individuals', as Abrams and Rutland put it, and instead stays stuck firmly in the 'in-group favouring' mode, on a path to self-destruction.

It is particularly unnerving to watch Jack, who starts as a harmless if boisterous choirboy, turn from merely teasing his friend Piggy to hunting and finally killing him. It's not only the 'bad' guys who can let the thrill of power and control lead them to do things that they know are morally questionable or downright wrong.

In the film *Rebel without a Cause*, the central character, teenager Jim Stark played by James Dean, arrives in a new town and has to prove himself to his peers, which includes accepting challenges to switchblade knife fights. He is confused, but basically a decent kid. It is so important to him to be accepted that he also agrees to join a 'chickie' game, in which drivers race their cars towards a seaside cliff and jump out at the last minute. One boy gets his sleeve stuck on the door handle, and plunges to his death.

*Lord of the Flies* and *Rebel without a Cause* are fiction. More horrific, of course, are the real instances of in-groups that have brought with them disaster and death.

Details of the Hitler Youth, when they emerged, were terrifying. Richard Grunberger points out in *A Social History of the Third Reich* that it was 'the largest organization for young people ever to exist in the Western world'. The idea behind the Hitler Youth was to form children, boys and girls, into a tight band that would police each other and the adults around them. At its meetings, there were plenty of fun, life-affirming activities such as sports and singing. But their slogan was 'We are born to die for Germany.' Membership came with rigorous military training. Aged between ten and fourteen, a *Pimpf* at his first meeting might find himself berry-gathering in the hedgerows with his new friends. The initiation test, with these same friends, featured pseudo-war games (*Geländeübungen*). 'Ideally,' says Grunberger, 'the *Pimpf* was to experience the whole genesis of modern weapons from blowpipes and clubs through swords and pikes right up to small-bore rifles.' This was friendship with firepower. And the growth of the Hitler Youth was extraordinary. Membership was just over a hundred thousand in 1932. Three years later it had increased by thirty-five times. And joining the Hitler Youth was not compulsory until 1936.

Children were attracted to these compelling friendship groups, and the power they gave them. 'The mother of a ten-year-old Hitler Youth, who had asked her son to play with the little girl from next door,' says Grunberger, 'was given the answer: "It's out of the question. I'm in uniform."'

Although the very acquisition of swords, pikes and small-bore rifles pushed friendship out of adults' guiding hands and on to its own track, these children with guns were only just into double figures. The twin messages – that they should be utterly loyal to fellow party members and be ready to fight when commanded to do so – left them confused. They were being trained to attack an enemy they didn't encounter. Sometimes they turned on the other children, those the organisation had given them, supposedly, as friends and comrades. Grunberger reports: 'A sentry at Grimma in Saxony shot a ten-year-old *Pimpf* who had failed to memorize the password. Questioned by the police, the fourteen-year-old murderer stated that he had felt compelled to use his revolver when confronted with a spy who had infiltrated the camp.' Hitler Youth units often became, as Grunberger puts it, 'armed bands waging furious internecine warfare with air guns, and youngsters would limp home to distraught parents, with sprained limbs and other scars of battle.'

Gangs have always existed. But more recently there has been an alarming rise of gang culture and 'postcode wars'. Girls form gangs. You periodically see newspaper articles about them; for example, it was reported in January 2011 that four girls in Bridlington aged between sixteen and nineteen had terrorised another girl. The violence involved 'hair-pulling'. Criminologists including Susan Batchelor and Michele Burman say there's no doubt that girl gangs exist. And many of them get involved with a lot more than 'hair-pulling'. But the consensus is that girls tend to look to gangs more for self-affirmation and friendship.

The big, growing problem is with boys' gangs. In 1995, when he went to the aid of a pupil who was being attacked, headmaster Philip Lawrence was stabbed to death by a gang member, who was fifteen years old. In 2000, ten-year-old Damilola Taylor was stabbed as he walked home from Peckham library; four youths, all under eighteen and members of a gang known as the Peckham Boys, were tried for manslaughter.

In his paper 'Reluctant Gangsters: Youth Gangs in Waltham Forest', John Pitts notes that in the 1990s one of the Metropolitan Police's superintendents researched the numbers of youth gangs nationally. Although he elicited a 91.45 per cent response rate from UK police forces, only sixteen of them identified gangs in their areas, and this yielded a national total of only seventy-two. Yet 'within eight years [in 2006] the Metropolitan Police had identified 169 youth gangs in London alone, many using firearms in furtherance of their crimes and estimated to have been responsible for around 40 murders and 20% of the youth crime in the capital'.

The depth of children's need to be accepted in a group is profound; the things they will do to get or maintain that acceptance, far-reaching.

# 5

# Control Freaks

The poster for the 1953 film *The Wild One* features Marlon Brando wearing his trademark sneer and black biker's jacket. In the film, a roving gang of motorcyclists led by Brando's character Johnny terrorise a small town. The bikers are nomadic. Their loyalty to each other is paramount.

At one point Johnny is asked, 'What are you rebelling against?'

He famously answers, 'What've you got?'

There isn't any real motive for dragging the main street and frightening the residents. The details don't matter as long as he's with his friends and against authority.

Recently I spotted in the local shopping centre a sixteen-year-old boy who I knew a bit when he was at primary school. He used to sport a lopsided fringe and a big grin, running about, swinging across the monkey bars or playing football. The other day he was by a photo booth surrounded by mates, and working so hard to keep his face appropriately cool that I found him unnerving. If he'd been on his own, he'd probably just have nodded a hello. As it was, he turned away quickly when he saw me.

No wonder young people's friendships often provoke a desire in adults to control them, or even suppress them. In the late seventeenth century the philosopher John Locke advocated tightening the rein on such friendships. He argued that children were not, as was believed, empty vessels waiting to be filled with adults' ideas about morality. In fact, he said, they had minds of their own. If this was true, then children were capable not only of making friends themselves, but of choosing their friends and deciding how to conduct their friendships. The concept was alarming.

Schools were hotbeds of friendships. In *Some Thoughts Concerning Education* (1693), Locke suggests that a boy's friendships, if ungoverned, are potentially so worrying that it might be better for loving parents not to send him away to school at all. Rather, they should keep him at home as much as possible and try to become his best, his 'only sure Friends'. For out of sight, 'how is it possible to keep him from the contagion of rudeness and vice, which is everywhere so in fashion?' Instead, Locke says, in the confines of their home parents should talk to their sons, for 'Nothing cements and establishes Friendship and Good-will, so much as *confident Communication.*'

'Vice,' Locke cautions, 'ripens so fast now-a-days, and runs up to seed so early in young people, that it is impossible to keep a lad from spreading the contagion, if you will venture him abroad in the herd and trust to chance, or his own inclination, for the choice of his company at school.'

Perhaps capitalising on fears about friendship that Locke

had stimulated, in the mid-eighteenth century the first publisher of books specifically for children, John Newbery, ingeniously positioned himself as both the children's and the parents' friend. *A Little Pretty Pocket-Book* included two enticing 'letters from Jack the Giant-killer' and drawings of children having fun 'playing games including cricket and 'Base-Ball', while sombrely, the foreword advised those who wanted a 'virtuous son' to 'Take heed what company you intrust him with'. And Locke's notion that parents could influence their children's friendships, using books and education, held good for some time.

Whereas Locke was equivocal about the idea of teaching boys at home, the Victorian writer Elizabeth M. Sewell was was firm in her view about girls. Any parent who sent their daughter away to be educated was putting her in grave danger. She explained in 1865 in *Principles of Education*:

The aim of education is to fit children for the position in life which they are thereafter to occupy. Boys are to be sent out into the world to buffet with its temptations, to mingle with bad and good, to govern and direct. The school is the type of life they are hereafter to lead. Girls are to dwell in quiet homes, amongst a few friends; to exercise a noiseless influence, to be submissive and retiring. There is no connection between the bustling mill-wheel life of a large school and that for which they are supposed to be preparing. This alone is a sufficient reason for supposing, even on a cursory glance, that to educate girls in a crowd is to educate them wrongly.

And the idea that friends were an unhealthy distraction

from domestic duties infiltrated Victorian children's literature. Susan Coolidge's novel *What Katy Did* suggests that
the heroine has everything she needs within her family home's
four walls. As well as five siblings, Aunt Izzie and a loving
father, there is also a 'neat, dapper, pink-and-white' neighbour
called Cecy, of whom Katy's father Dr Carr approves
and who regularly calls round. Yet Katy insists on looking elsewhere for more exciting interactions. 'Poor Katy!
Her propensity to fall violently in love with new people was
always getting her into scrapes. Ever since she began to
walk and talk "Katy's intimate friends" had been one of
the jokes of the household.'

Katy becomes obsessed with her flamboyant, sentimental classmate, Imogen Clark. Dr Carr and Aunt Izzie deeply disapprove.

Imogen's real name was Elizabeth. She was rather a pretty
girl, with a screwed-up, sentimental mouth . . . Imogen was
a bright girl, naturally, but she had read so many novels
that her brain was completely turned. It was partly this
that made her so attractive to Katy, who adored stories,
and thought Imogen was a real heroine of romance.

An accident confines Katy to a wheelchair. Imogen doesn't
visit for two years, and when she does, she talks entirely about
herself. 'All the time [Katy] found herself taking the measure
of Imogen, and thinking, "Did I ever really like her? How
queer! Oh, what a wise man papa is!"' The narrative focus is
on her sudden deep understanding that her father was right
after all: all the friends a girl needs can be found right here
on her own front doorstep. Of course, despite Sewell's

warnings and the wariness of authors such as Coolidge, girls' schools *were* founded. But their atmosphere was very different. Existing boys' schools embraced the chance for pupils to, as Sewell put it, 'mingle with bad and good' in bustling institutions.

When the first girls' schools opened, staff worked hard to suppress the girls' friendships. Frances Power Cobbe had quite a shock when she arrived at an exclusive establishment in Brighton. She had come from rural Ireland where, in the 1820s in the countryside outside Dublin, she had enjoyed a very free early childhood. Her mother was ill. Her father was busy. Until she was in her teens, Frances was left to roam the family's 360-acre estate, making friends with whoever she pleased out of the farmholders and their children as well as the three male and eight female servants. Indeed, her biographer Sally Mitchell says that it was 'from Irish servants that Fan learned the outgoing warmth and garrulous friendliness that so many acquaintances noted'.

It was precisely this 'warmth and garrulous friendliness' that alarmed her father. Since it was now too late for governesses, Mr Cobbe sent Frances, at the age of fourteen, to a particularly exclusive school for girls, no. 32 Brunswick Terrace in Brighton. He wrote that it was 'a necessity ... much to be regretted ... but her welfare required it'. Mitchell comments, 'Presumably that meant turning the tomboy into a young lady, getting an adolescent out of the house, and providing her with social connections.' But any idea that she would gain social connections was particularly misguided.

At the school, Frances and the other girls had to memorise a verse of scripture while dressing in the morning. There was little fun to be had here, and the schedule seemed designed to suppress any chance of it. The girls would recite verbs in French, Italian or German while marching along Brighton esplanade, before dressing for dinner, 'in full evening attire of silk or muslin, with gloves and kid slippers,' says Mitchell, who also notes: 'If she had any close friends at school or if she ever encountered a schoolmate in adult society, no evidence survives.' And it wasn't only that Frances failed to hit it off with any of the two dozen other girls who'd been sent there too. Such exclusive ladies' schools, for daughters of MPs and country gentlemen, were more like medieval apprenticeships. But their essence was competition not for a job, but for a husband.

In *A History of Women's Education in England*, June Purvis points out that at such schools the girls had strange relationships with the teachers, who they had to kiss goodnight and address as 'Aunt'. 'The pupils also had to practise entering a crowded room and removing an empty teacup without rattling it.' This wasn't about making friends, it was about learning to become invisible amongst husbands' friends and families.

A Mrs Hugh Fraser attended one such boarding school: 'We were taught how to write notes to our equals, invitations, acceptances; inquiries for invalids, characters of servants, letters to our elders, and letters to strangers who we were supposed not to have met; letters to tradesmen – in the rigid third person.' There'd be no helping another girl to write, for instance, an especially important letter. She was a rival – any friendship could endanger one's future prospects.

However, it was only a matter of time before girls, aware of the kinds of friendships that boys enjoyed, began to want that kind of camaraderie for themselves.

Frances Mary Buss was the daughter of a dissolute father and a mother who set up a school out of necessity, to keep the family going. When Miss Buss started a school herself, the North London Collegiate, in 1850, it was innovative for two reasons. It was specifically for middle-, not upper-class girls. And, she decided, 'good' girls and friendships *were* in fact compatible. Indeed, she made camaraderie central to her school's ethos.

The NLC didn't all at once give girls the kind of raucous rough-and-tumble that Thomas Hughes depicts boys enjoying at school in *Tom Brown's Schooldays*. The school may have been for the daughters of 'Professional Gentlemen of limited means, Clerks in public and private offices, and Persons engaged in Trade and other pursuits', but it was still Victorian Britain. Decorum remained a high priority: pupils couldn't walk more than three abreast down corridors.

But the inaugural issue of the school journal *Our Magazine* declared a determination to encourage a certain *esprit de corps*. Students weren't made to feel as if they were in competition with each other for husbands. At a less progressive school previously, the future writer and educationalist Molly Hughes was embarrassed by the fact that she couldn't afford expensive clothes. 'Now at the North London I sensed at once a different atmosphere. No one asked where you lived, how much pocket-money you had, or what your father was – he might be a bishop or a rat-catcher.'

Miss Buss told her students, 'We want an active interest in the well-being of others.' The sewing club, the Dorcas Society, made five or six hundred items of clothing a year to give to local charities. And although the sewing itself was hard work, pupils including Molly found it fantastically enjoyable. For while they sewed, the girls were allowed to chat. It was a quiet kind of camaraderie that the girls developed over a needle and thread. But NLC initiatives such as the Dorcas Society signalled important changes.

Competitive sport was central at boys' schools – in *Tom Brown's Schooldays*, football and cricket in particular. Importance is attached to the lessons the boys learn on the pitch about how to forge new alliances with team-mates without jeopardising friendships that have been established previously in the dorms. One of the highlights of Frances Power Cobbe's holidays was the games of cricket she played with her brothers when they were home from school. Whether competitive sport was appropriate or not, girls could see for themselves how much fun it was and the extra dimension it added to friendship.

Dorothea Beale, the principal of Cheltenham Ladies' College which opened in 1854, had been resolutely against any kind of organised outdoor sport. However, as more girls' boarding schools sprang up – St Leonards in Fife in 1877, Roedean in 1885 in Brighton – this prejudice began to break down. In 1888, notes Purvis, St Leonards' headmistress Miss Louisa Innes Lumsden went personally to the National Association for Social Science to argue the case for giving her pupils team sports. They taught boys to obey and command, she said, and 'to gain patience, good temper, toleration, and the power to stand a beating good humouredly and to fight for the side and not for self. It is training of this sort that I wish to secure for girls.' Gradually, sports including cricket, lacrosse and hockey reached girls' schools.

Winifred Peck, who was at Wycombe Abbey in Buckinghamshire in the 1890s, recalled with particular relish the rush to get changed and assemble on the lacrosse or hockey field, or on the cricket pitch in the summer, by two o'clock: 'To many of us this was the centre, the highlight of the day ... Part of the fun came from the games dress – short tunics and baggy bloomers, with tam-o-shanters which always fell off. But what freedom, what glory, to scamper about after one ball or another in sun or rain or wind as one of a team, as part of the school.'

But staff in girls' schools didn't want to unleash too much friendship. At the turn of the century they still keenly sought ways of keeping it under control. By the time Elizabeth Bowen went to board at Downe House in Sussex aged twelve in 1914, ways of encouraging an acceptable kind of camaraderie were even built into her school's lunchtimes. 'Competitive sociability and team spirit were rather well united at my school by the custom of picking up tables. The first day of term seven seniors shut themselves up and, by rotative bidding, each picked up from the rest of the school a team of about eight for her table at meals,' she explains in *The Mulberry Tree*. 'The object of each team was to make the most conversation possible, and to be a success: girls were therefore picked with a view to chattiness, desirability, tact, table manners, resource and charm.' Girls had to have a forceful enough personality to be able to make good conversation, which would benefit the whole group: 'It was a great thing to be at the head of the most patently animated table in the dining-room. Many of us have grown up to be good hostesses.'

But things are very different today, surely. We see growing numbers of increasingly feisty portrayals of women's friendship on television in the twenty-first century – don't we? The cultural critic Diane Negra argues that contemporary portrayals of women's social lives in the media still warn women off friendship. However much comradeship and assertiveness mainstream 'chick flicks' depict at first, most, she says, build to an epiphany that sees the heroine prioritising heterosexual romance and/or motherhood.

I had a chat with the artist Jessica Voorsanger, whose work examines celebrity culture. 'Pretty much all TV female friendships are about being evil, catty and back stabbing,' she says.

> Even reality shows like *Big Brother* seem hell-bent now on making sure at least a couple of women in each series end up ganging up horribly on one of the other housemates. Just think of Jade Goody and S Club's Jo O'Meara in the 2007 *Celebrity Big Brother*. They behaved appallingly to Shilpa Shetty; there's no doubt, they came across as racist in ways that are not remotely OK. But the show creates a situation in which that kind of behaviour is encouraged. And then the press lambasts them.

Negra notes with disappointment in her book *What a Girl Wants?* (2009) that even the TV serial *Sex and the City* ends with Carrie deciding her friends aren't enough and she should move to New York with her boyfriend.

But in 2004, in issue 39 of the University of Colorado's online journal *Genders*, Negra wrote about the kinds of things that made *Sex and the City* so popular in the first place. With inexhaustible chutzpah, Carrie, Miranda, Charlotte and Samantha had endless shoes, fantastic sex, top careers and unassailable female friendships for over a decade. In one episode entitled *All or Nothing*, having settled into her new apartment and enjoyed an evening with her girlfriends, Samantha yells out: 'You see us, Manhattan? We have it all!' *Sex and the City* ran for six seasons, pulling in between five and seven million viewers for most episodes; it spawned two feature film versions. When the journalist Candace Bushnell started writing 'Sex and the City' as a column in the 1990s for the *New York Observer*, she had no clue that it would become so massive.

Friendship is something that won't be boxed. It wriggles.

Teachers at Elizabeth Bowen's school thought they had it taped. Versions adults might think of as wholesome could be encouraged through sport and such practices as 'picking up tables'. But children have break-times. Outside, they devise their own extracurricular activities. At boarding school, there is all that time in the dorm. Although Bowen's school encouraged 'competitive sociability' over lunch, as night closed in staff worked fervently to suppress friendships.

The dormitory arrangements were strict. Bowen remembers: 'Great friends were not put together and were not allowed into each other's bed-rooms.' However, 'it was always possible to stand and talk in the door, with one toe

outside'. Naturally, the ban only provoked assignations. There
was a water tap outside the bedrooms, where the girls could
legitimately go to fill hot-water bottles. The head herself
would come and disperse any group she found. But she
couldn't be there every minute. 'Girls of a roving disposition
with a talent for intimacy were always about this passage.
A radiator opposite this tap was in demand in winter; one
could lean while one talked and warm the spine through the
dressing-gown. The passage was dim-lit, with wobbly gas
brackets, and it was always exciting to see who got there
first.'

Even on the lawn by the old mulberry tree, round the
mound on which Shakespeare plays were acted, 'We girls
were for ever masticating some foreign substance, leaves of
any kind, grass from the playing fields, paper, india rubber,
splits from pencil-ends or the hems of handkerchiefs.'

The need to fit in is strong. But it comes hand in hand
with an equally urgent desire to stand out. 'The ever difficult business of getting oneself across was most pressing
of all at this age: restricted possessions, a uniform dictated
down to the last detail and a self-imposed but rigid emotional snobbishness shutting the more direct means of self-
expression away. Foibles, mannerisms we therefore exaggerated
most diligently.' Bowen describes how dormitory decorations
were at once bold statements and interchangeable. 'Photos
of relatives, sometimes quite distant but chosen for their good
appearance, the drawings of Dulac, Medici prints and portraits
of Napoleon, Charles I, Rupert Brooke, Sir Roger Casement
or Mozart lent advertising touches of personality to each cubi-
cle's walls.'

Stuffed toys had their place, too: 'Several dormitory beds with their glacial white quilts were encumbered all day and shared nightly with rubbed threadbare teddy bears, monkeys or in one case a blue plush elephant ... A good deal of innocent fetishism came to surround these animals; the mistress of the blue elephant used to walk the passages, saying: "You must kiss my elephant."' This is an image that doesn't seem so innocent to me. The idea of the blue elephant's 'mistress' roaming the passages and insisting that other girls kiss her stuffed toy makes for a somewhat disturbing picture – because even as the girl's action purports to be about connecting with her friends, there is something very self-regarding about it.

# 6

# Narcissism

Some friendships are largely, if not entirely, about boosting one person's status.

I have a couple of friends who always want to meet near their home or place of work. They laugh as they call themselves control freaks. When challenged, they will agree to travel somewhere that is not so convenient for them. But their first instinct is to stay put and have others travel to them.

Some friends are perpetually in trouble. There is always a crisis going on for them. Is this the opposite of narcissistic? Are they always in need of help because they are so short of ego? Another way of looking at it is that their endless problems make them the centre of friends' attention. I'd like to say that I'm always innocent of both these traits. But I'm not. Friendships reveal a need to nurture oneself, even the friendships that involve getting immersed in a group. Gaining a clan's protection is about preserving yours truly.

Young children and teenagers make friendship bracelets for one another, out of embroidery thread, generally in vibrant colours. Surely these just indicate generosity? Even the simple ones involve five to seven different-coloured lengths of 'embroidery floss'; you use cardboard, Sellotape and scissors to help your fingers weave and knot and loop the threads. Making them requires dexterity and pretty extensive patience. You will only dedicate yourself to a micro-macramé task like this if you *really* like the person you are planning to give it to.

But then, once it is on your friend's wrist, the bracelet is on display. It is public. To honour the work and skill that go into making a friendship bracelet, the recipient is supposed to wear it until the cords deteriorate and it falls off of its own accord. That means wearing it through baths, through the night, during skipping games, while hands are rummaging in crisp packets or holding fizzy drinks that splash.

This is an important part of the symbolism. Friendship bracelets may get mucky – indeed, they *will* get mucky. But as long as they have been made with enough love and attention, they will stay on valiantly. And there is a level at which the gift turns your friend into a possession. The bracelet becomes a sort of declaration of ownership, like a collar.

Do all friendships stem from narcissism? When Aristotle dissected friendship in the *Nicomachean Ethics*, he identified three types of friendship: 'utility-based', 'pleasure-based', and 'friendships of excellence'. He dismissed the first two types because they are about self-gratification. 'Utility-based' friendships spring from a desire for gain (these are the kinds of friendships that will help you get a job or gain a promotion), and 'pleasure-based' friendships are about fun (going out and getting drunk and enjoying yourself, for example). Aristotle said only the third type, 'friendships of excellence', are worth having; and to have these, the attachment had to be so strong that the parties would as soon harm themselves as they would their friend. Each had to be so highly evolved morally and spiritually that he would die for the other.

The Roman statesman and philosopher Seneca agreed. 'For what purpose, then, do I make a man my friend?' he asks in *Epistolae Morales*. 'In order to have someone for whom I may die, whom I may follow into exile, against whose death I may stake my own life.' In the Book of Ruth, Naomi suffers famine, her husband dies and both her sons too. Planning to return to her people, she tells her daughters-in-law not to risk the journey. But Ruth responds: 'Do not press me to leave you or to turn back from following you! Where you go, I will go; where you lodge, I will lodge; your people shall be my people, and your God my God. Where you die, I will die – there will I be buried' (Ruth 1:16).

But this is high drama. It puts oneself and the phenom-enal sacrifices one is prepared to make centre stage. Kierkegaard railed against the narcissism that he said drives friendship. He gave his essay about friendship (1846) an instruction as a title: 'You Shall Love Your Neighbour'. He says friendship involves passion: 'the praise of erotic love and friendship belongs to paganism'. Like erotic love, friendship 'self-ignites', making people prone to fits of jealousy. 'Love and friendship are the very height of self-feeling.'

Although, is it necessarily a bad thing if self-feeling, if narcissism, plays a key part in friendship?

In the 1960s D. W. Winnicott pointed out that children

who grow up to be good at friendships are precisely the ones who have been helped as infants to become comfortable with themselves. The first critical lesson in friendship is learning to cope with separation from the mother. Once the infant can trust that the mother's love will stay intact even if her attention is withdrawn, he has, as Winnicott puts it, 'integrated from within'. That is, the child has secured a sense of self that will keep him buoyant without his (or her) mother. And as long as the child has safely integrated from within, in the wider world he or she can play with other children without feeling the need to be subsumed in those other children in order to be included. Narcissism is absolutely at the centre. Indeed, suggests Winnicott, it is the children who come to friendship with low self-esteem who are bad at it.

Certainly, it is easy to come up with examples of children who didn't have the kind of secure family background Winnicott describes and whose friendships suffered accordingly. The novelist John Steinbeck's childhood was marked by his father's humiliating public descent into poverty. In early-twentieth-century small-town California, shaken and scared, Steinbeck sought out secure, successful peers and became their shadow. In high school, when he was a cripplingly shy, bookish teenager, he crept in beside Bill Black, a boy who biographer Jay Parini suggests Steinbeck didn't even like. But association with popular, athletic Bill Black brought kudos.

Although, at least, the young Steinbeck had friendships that he could look back on and rethink later, it seems that the young William Hazlitt couldn't form any sort of friendship with other children. Doomed to a peripatetic

childhood by his fiery father's inability to secure a satis-
factory position as a Unitarian pastor, the young William
was uprooted from Norfolk at the age of five and whisked
off to the United States. His sister Peggy's memoir presents him as a lonely boy, tramping the woods with one of
the Boston neighbours, Captain Abiah Whitman, or following the plough. And back in England, this preference
for adult company became fixed.

'Adults often liked him for his precocious intelligence, and
his sententiousness,' says his biographer A. C. Grayling,
noting that, aged eleven, at home in Wem, Shropshire,
William impressed the widow of a West Indian merchant,
Mrs Tracey, so much that she invited him to Liverpool so
that he could study French with her daughters. But it wasn't
the daughters he became friends with. William's letters home
were about befriending 'a very rich man', a Mr Fisher, and
going to the theatre with one Mr Corbett. As an adult,
Hazlitt returned regularly in his essays to the subject of
friendship, under such titles as 'On the Pleasure of Hating'
and 'On Disagreeable People'.

But even the most settled children can find friendship a
tussle. When Florence Nightingale was young, her wealthy
family spent 'the season' in London and the rest of the year
in their house in the New Forest doing the elaborate social
rounds of christenings and birthday parties with members of
her mother's extended family. There was no big domestic
disaster in her life, as there was for Steinbeck. She wasn't
uprooted to a place where she knew no one, as Hazlitt was.

Biographers present different pictures of her emotional
response to all this enforced socialising. Elspeth Huxley says

Florence hated it, that it distracted from the thing she really loved as a child, learning. With her father as tutor, from the age of twelve, she was reading Italian poets such as Tasso. Intellectual pursuits excited her, whereas the kind of easy social friendships her mother and sister so enjoyed didn't. Mark Bostridge maintains that, actually, Florence set high store by the get-togethers with friends and extended family. But his biography also makes clear that if she valued them, that didn't mean she always took part in them. When she was fifteen, her mother noted in her diary that she was more likely to be found 'sitting by the bedside of someone who was ill, and saying she could not sit down to a grand 7 o'clock dinner'.

'I was afraid of speaking to children because I was sure I should not please them,' Florence said later. Yet this makes her sound timorous. Florence Nightingale went on to get a calling from God and become 'the lady with the lamp', tending soldiers in the Crimea and revolutionising nursing. Huxley's and Bostridge's accounts both suggest that really she wasn't worried about failing to please the other children at all, but rather, she wanted to stand out.

As adults, we have to negotiate the pull of our own narcissism with the fact that our friends have their own desires and needs too. You scratch my back, I'll scratch yours, the saying goes. And this applies emotionally too. You can reasonably expect a friend to lend you a cup of sugar or give up their evening to supply comfort and tissues as you unload a tale of woe if you have already done the same for them or are fully prepared to do so at some point in the future. But sometimes, the process of getting something from someone, then staying in the position of recipient, is just too tempting.

Like Florence Nightingale, the botanical artist Marianne North was exceptional. Throwing aside all the Victorian expectations of what a well-bred young lady should do, she travelled the world to paint plants and flowers. Narcissism can make a person – especially when he or she is not close – charismatic and exciting to be around. And her own charisma helped Marianne enormously. She presented herself as extravagantly independent. Yet she could not have achieved what she did without a wide network of friends.

Marianne North went to remote parts of the exotic lands she visited – from Brazil to India and Japan to Tenerife and South Africa. Her family was well connected and she invariably arrived with letters of introduction. Again and again in her autobiography, *Recollections of a Happy Life*, we hear 'A friend met me', 'I telegraphed a friend, who met me on arriving.' There are so many friends, most of the time they are not even given names. They find her lodgings or put her up themselves; they organise transport and hire servants for her; they construct her itinerary; they accompany her if a destination is even remotely threatening. '[A]s soon as the ship touched the shore at Cape Town, two friends met me, and put me and my boxes into a hansom-cab,' she writes. 'One of them took me all the way out to Wynberg, seven and a half miles, round the western side of the Table Mountain.' Over lunch at Port Elizabeth she tells yet another friend of her dismay that she'd found a good specimen of *Protea cynaroides*, but only of the *plant*. 'He rubbed his head for a moment, then said: "I know where it is!" rushed into a neighbour's house a few doors off, and brought me out a magnificent flower. I almost cried with joy at getting it at last.'

Back in England, she regaled her friends with exotic stories. Single women were usually pitied at the time. Unmarried, her adored father dead, North could by travelling repeatedly show her friends that she was the most interesting of all of them.

She once went to a party that had been thrown for fellow traveller Isabella Bird. And in *Recollections* she presents 'Mrs Bishop née Bird!' as absurd, describing her enthroned in an armchair in the back drawing-room with 'gold-embroidered slippers and a footstool to show them on, a petticoat all over gold and silver Japanese embroidered wheels, and a ribbon and order across her shoulders given her by the King of the Sandwich Islands'. When North was introduced to Mrs Bird, she couldn't get away quickly enough. Another, less famous traveller, Miss Gordon-Cumming, was there too. 'Lady A. joined our three pairs of hands and blessed us – "three globe trotteresses all at once!" It was too much for the two big ones; and we retreated as fast as we could, leaving Miss Bird unruffled and equal to the occasion.' The last thing Marianne North wanted was to befriend women who were equally or more adventurous. A narcissist does not want an equal.

We get an early glimpse of the novelist Edith Wharton's desire to be separate in her short story 'The Valley of Childish Things' (1896). Here, a girl gets bored with 'building mudpies and sailing paper boats in basins'. She becomes irritated by the fact that her young companions stay perfectly happy with such activities. So the protagonist sets off for the elevated 'table-land', which leaves her alone but proud of her maturity and superior knowledge. In her autobiography *A Backward Glance*, published in 1934, Wharton wrote her friends out of her life just as determinedly.

While her family was in Rome in the late 1860s, she spent a great deal of time with a girl called Margaret Terry; they went on to become lifelong friends. Yet, notes Wharton's biographer Hermione Lee, Margaret is only mentioned in *A Backward Glance* as part of the local colour of Italy. The affection of another childhood friend, Emelyn Washburn, is described by Wharton as a mark of 'degeneracy' in a draft of the memoir. 'In the published version, she does not even name her,' says Lee. 'Wharton left these women friends out of her autobiography, partly because she preferred not to talk about her personal friendships, but also because she shapes her life-story as one of solitude, self-education and self-creation.'

It was all about her.

# 7

# Philia and Amicitia

The theories about friendship that Aristotle and Cicero developed both look to a modern reader fantastically, even ridiculously, high-minded. In their eyes, true friends had to be so pure and good that they would *die* for each other. But actually, neither of them was averse to the idea of pragmatic friendships – far from it. For them, a bit of nepotism was fine.

Friends can, indeed should, help each other, they said. It's just that true friendships can't be *solely* about 'utility'. Both parties must be spiritually evolved too. Interestingly, their assertion that practical benefits are fine as long as the friends supplying them are virtuous represented quite a dramatic shift. Compared to their predecessors, Aristotle and Cicero were being remarkably progressive.

It is usual today to translate the Greek *philia* simply as 'friendship'. But there is quite a lot of debate around the meaning of the word. In Aristotle's *Nicomachean Ethics philia* covers a wide variety of friendly relationships, from what we'd call soulmates through to acquaintances.

Aristotle was writing about *philia* in the fourth century BC. In her book *Aristotle's Philosophy of Friendship* Suzanne Stern-Gillet points out that for Herodotus, who was writing in the fifth century BC, and for Homer, three centuries earlier, *philia* was used primarily to denote 'guest-friendship': 'A reciprocal relationship, guest-friendship provided men of substance and high lineage,' she says, 'with a range of private and political benefits which considerably reduced the hazards of travel.' Guest-friendship was cold: it was about each person making his own life easier. Neither liking nor inclination had to play any part.

For Homer, *philia* was simply an agreement that if one high-born Greek was away from home and in a difficult situation, another high-born Greek would offer hospitality and protection. For Herodotus, the word meant something a little warmer, but not much warmer. It referred to the bond that should exist between companions-in-arms. It was effectively a code of honour that encouraged allies to help each other, not just once in a while but possibly even daily.

The Homeric standard makes friendship, as Stern-Gillet puts it, 'a relation of last resort in times of extreme need'.

War was a regular part of Greek life when Homer was alive in the eighth century BC, and during Herodotus's time three hundred years later. Aristotle's teacher, Plato, was born about 428 BC, more than a generation after Herodotus, and he too was familiar with war, growing up in Athens when it was an embattled city. Its defeat by Sparta in the Peloponnesian war in 405 BC was echoed internally by fights for power between democrats and oligarchs. Plato's account of friendship, *Lysis*, is brief and equivocal. He raised questions, but essentially left Homer's and Herodotus's interpretations intact.

By contrast, Aristotle grew up in a settled, powerful Athens. From fighting small wars for plunder, glory and fame, Athens had become a superpower. With shallow steps that were easy for sacrificial animals to climb, rebuilt, the Acropolis, or the 'High City', with its dramatic white columns soared into the sky. As the arena in which Athens was playing grew, Aristotle could see that the ideas of what constituted friendship in politics had wider implications. He started thinking about how friendship relates to justice. He became interested in how friendship could be remoulded to help society.

'If there is to be friendship, the parties must have good will towards each other,' he wrote. True friends must 'wish good things for each other, and be aware of the other's doing so'. 'When people are friends, they have no need of justice, but when they are just, they need friendship in addition.' Furthermore, Aristotle wanted the men who wielded power to embrace a version of friendship that would make them compassionate.

'Aristotelian selfhood,' Stern-Gillet says, 'is an evaluative, commendatory notion.' If one can be worthy of self-love, then to love a friend as another self, as Aristotle suggests, is likely to lead to more good people in society as a whole. In the light of Homer's and Herodotus's definitions of friendship and even Plato's reflections on the subject, Aristotle's struggle to identify and celebrate the elements of friendship that are not merely about self-interest looks brave, even rash. Friendship had been about getting what you wanted – in commerce, in war. Rejecting that notion, Aristotle proposed that it should be ethical.

He was trying to transform friendship into an attachment so strong that the parties would as soon harm themselves as they would the other. At a time when politics was largely about the brutal acquisition of power and land, Aristotle presented the possibility of a new generation of statesmen who would rule with integrity.

In the first century BC, Cicero tried to do something similar. His essay *De Amicitia* has been criticised for being a rewrite of Aristotle's thoughts on friendship. At the time, any attempt to inject into Roman politics the idea that friendship should be moral was radical enough in itself. By the time he was twenty, Cicero had experienced several civil wars. In 63 BC he was the target of an assassination plot. Individuals who were ambitious for power would do anything to get it. There were no rules or codes to stop them. Rich individuals simply hired henchmen to protect their interests and intimidate any rivals.

The Latin word *amicitia* still meant something very much like Herodotus's 'guest-friendship', indicating merely 'mutual indebtedness among equals'. Cicero tried to transform the concept. In 66 BC, when he was forty, he attempted to forge a level, rational *amicitia* with the fêted general Pompey. And he did manage, as the historian Beryl Rawson puts it, to bring Pompey round 'from cold silence about Cicero's consulship to a frame of mind in which he made generous references in the senate to Cicero's services'. But this marked the peak of their relationship. There were clear advantages to be had for both of them, and they tried to be friends for thirteen years, until 48 BC when 'Pompey's death ended the services they might offer each other'.

An inbuilt problem with *amicitia* was that it was meant to be between equals. The reason Cicero wanted a friendship with Pompey in the first place was because he didn't feel very secure in the Senate. Pompey was the stronger partner, and he periodically received better offers. But once a man had forged *amicitia* with a fellow Roman, it was not supposed to be broken. 'For nothing is more discreditable,' declared Cicero in his treatise, 'than to be at war with one with whom you have lived on intimate terms.' For the relationship to work, both parties had to be very sure that they would make significant, lasting gains.

Towards the end of his unsatisfactory attempt to establish a friendship with Pompey, Cicero finessed his approach. In a letter to Appius Claudius, he made the potential rewards more convincing by being honest about his motives: 'What could serve my interests better than association with a man of the highest rank and aristocracy, whose resources, talent, children, and relatives by marriage and blood could offer me great distinction or protection? I sought all these things in cultivating your friendship – not through cunning but rather through a degree of wisdom.' Meanwhile, Cicero managed to establish *amicitia* with Julius Caesar, to the extent that Caesar visited him at his house in the seaside resort of Puteoli with a retinue of two thousand soldiers. Yet in his biography, Anthony Everitt notes that when Caesar was assassinated in 44 BC in the Senate, Cicero was mainly hurt that he had not been included in the plot to stab him.

The idea in Ancient Rome that a cool, pragmatic *amicitia* could bond politicians together and make them behave altruistically as a group didn't work. Everitt says that instead, *amicitia* turned Ancient Rome into 'a hullabaloo of equal and individual competitors who would only guarantee to co-operate for one cause – the elimination of anybody who threatened to step out of line and grab too much power for himself'. Indeed, Beryl Rawson says that the 'ruinous egalitarianism' it generated stopped any real political leadership emerging and so allowed Caesar to establish a dictatorship. *Amicitia*, she argues, killed the Republic. Intended to ensure stability, instead it imperilled the Roman Empire itself.

Cicero could see only too well the problems inherent in the version of *amicitia* that held sway for most of his life. He didn't write *De Amicitia* until 44 BC, when he was in his early sixties. With this treatise, he was trying to change his peers' understanding of the concept. 'Friendship cannot exist but between good men,' he says. A man must 'give proof of loyalty and uprightness, of fairness and generosity'. 'Therefore let this law be established in friendship,' he declared, 'neither ask dishonourable things, nor do them if asked.' Moreover, a man must withdraw immediately from 'friends who are sinning in some important matter of public concern'.

With their writings on friendship, Aristotle and Cicero hoped to entwine friendship and politics so thoroughly that men in power would not face the sort of dilemma the twentieth-century writer E. M. Forster articulated: 'If I had to choose between betraying my country and betraying my friend I hope I should have the guts to betray my country.' They wanted to achieve a revised version of friendship that could make the interests of a man, his friend and their country one and the same.

But Cicero argued only that *amicitia* ought to feature a moral dimension. He didn't say that there should also be warmth. And Cicero was clearly an irrepressibly warm-hearted person.

If you disliked someone in Ancient Rome, it was unwise to be honest about it (assassinations were a regular feature of Roman life). But in his letters to his close friend Atticus, it seems Cicero could rarely restrain himself. Even while he was courting Pompey, he told Atticus that he thought the former 'a quite paltry man interested only in popular favour'. After Caesar's visit to Puteoli, Cicero wrote to Atticus: 'His entourage was lavishly entertained in three other dining rooms. The humbler freedmen and slaves had all they wanted – the smarter ones I entertained in style.' This was straightforward enough. Everitt notes that Cicero couldn't resist concluding: 'In a word, I showed I knew how to do things. But my guest was not the kind of person to whom one says "Do come again when you are next in the neighbourhood." Once is enough.'

When Cicero was courting Appius Claudius, it was with clear relief that he felt able to say at the end of a letter to him: '[the] bonds which, I am delighted to say, bind us closely together are very considerable: the similarity of our interests, the pleasure of each other's company, the pleasure in life and our way of life, the conversations that draw us together and our more profound literary activities.'

It wasn't to one of his more powerful friends that he dedicated *De Amicitia*, but to Atticus, his oldest, most treasured one. Cicero talked to Atticus about their shared interest in buying properties. He talked about his personal life, he shared his grief following the death of his daughter. In January 60, when he was forty-six, he wrote of how empty *amicitia* could leave him feeling:

What I most badly need at the moment is a confidant ...
And you whose talk and advice have so often lightened
my worry and vexation of spirit, the partner in my public
life and intimate of all my private concerns, the sharer of
all my talk and plans, where are you? ... My brilliant
worldly friendships may make a fine show in public, but
in the home they are barren things. My house is crammed
of a morning, I go down to the Forum surrounded by
droves of friends, but in all the crowds I cannot find one
person with whom I can exchange an unguarded joke or
let out a private sigh.

With merely 'useful' friendships, it is often wise to suppress one's real feelings, and to be a bit covert about one's weaknesses too. As Cicero had discovered with Pompey, it is rare that friends can in fact be mutually indebted in an absolutely equal way.

Immanuel Kant observed that the minute one friend is differentiated from the other in terms of wealth or social standing, the relationship is doomed. 'A friend who bears my losses becomes my benefactor and puts me in his debt. I feel shy in his presence and cannot look him boldly in the face. The true relationship is cancelled and friendship ceases.'

Were Aristotle and Cicero just hopeless idealists? Are 'guest-friendship' and the more brutal version of *amicitia* really the best we can hope for?

# 8

# BFF

In 2005, Ali G interviewed Victoria and David Beckham for Comic Relief. The interview came at an interesting point in Victoria Beckham's career.

By 2005, her days as someone known only as a member of The Spice Girls were behind her. She had married one of the world's most famous footballers and launched a solo music career. Half a dozen television documentaries had been made about her. Pictures of her had featured in practically every issue of *Heat*, it seemed, as well as in magazines such as *Vogue*. She had appeared on the London Fashion Week catwalk and designed her own line of clothes. She was a fashion icon. Having been 'Posh Spice' before, when Ali G interviewed her, she was simply 'Posh'.

At one point during the interview, addressing David, Ali G wondered: 'Do you reckon the better the footballer you is, the better the girl you get? You is the best, so you go out with Posh. So does Sporty Spice go out with someone from Scunthorpe United?'

'That is horrible,' said Posh. 'She's my friend and she's lovely.' But she only delivered this spirited defence after she had already laughed at the idea of Sporty Spice as a second-rate prize for someone in a second-rate team.

The Spice Girls made their name advocating 'Girl Power', a slogan that told the girls buying their records they could be sexy *and* strong, as long as they kept tight, loyal friendships. For the band's 1996 debut single 'Wannabe', The Spice Girls' shouted out to any would-be lovers that they had to 'get' with their friends. Because, they concluded, friendship doesn't ever end.

Just two years later, Geri Halliwell left The Spice Girls, reportedly because of 'differences' between the band members. In the aftermath, gossip columns reported avidly on which Spice Girl had invited who to which of their weddings and babies' christenings. Every one of the women launched a solo career, each fighting for chart dominance. In the 1999 official biography *Forever Spice*, though, friendship was still presented as meaning everything. They were sad to see Geri go, they said – stunned, even. But Victoria reminded readers that not long before The Spice Girls first queued for a Brit Award, they'd been together queuing at the dole office. Before they were famous, they shared a house for nearly a year in Maidenhead. In the book's photos they seem to be forever hugging backstage, sprawled on sofas, snuggled round cups of coffee on hotel-room carpets. 'We know each other so well, and we've all seen each other happy, sad, crying, whatever,' said Victoria. 'The great thing is that I can be totally myself with them, all the time.'

Sure enough, Geri came back. For the band's 2007 reunion, they entitled their comeback single 'Headlines (Friendship Never Ends)'.

Part of the narcissism of friendship is that once we have been best friends, we do feel, as Aristotle and Cicero advocated, that we have to stay best friends for ever, or it makes us look bad. If we squabble, it means our judgement was suspect when we chose each other in the first place.

But what does it mean to be best friends forever, 'BFF'?

On the one hand, the fact that the phrase is known by its abbreviation trivialises it. Bryant Oden writes tunes for toddlers. The lyrics of his relentlessly bouncy 'The BFF Song' tell under-fives that being best friends is about being 'here' for each other. Can a toddler even understand the concept of duty that comes with a promise to always be 'here' for someone emotionally? An eight-year-old girl might call 'BFF!' to a friend at morning playtime, have a fight with her at lunchtime and declare someone completely different her BFF just before home time.

On the other hand, we all yearn for a soulmate. We can't help it. And of course, we want someone who completely understands our every need and mood. The abbreviation itself, BFF, is something we associate with girls' friendships. It is hard to imagine two eight-year-old boys after a kick-about with a football calling to each other, 'Best friends forever!' Yet boys can want best friends just as desperately as girls. Characters such as Ron Weasley and Hermione Granger are Harry's best friends in the *Harry Potter* series. His adoptive family is mean. His real family have left him an inheritance of enemies with supernatural powers. But Ron and Hermione are always there for him, to get him out of trouble and stand by him.

We all want a friend like that. What do we have to do to get one?

Like Aristotle, the twelfth-century Cistercian abbot Aelred identified three types of friendship, and, like Aristotle, he dismissed two of them as unworthy. He said 'carnal' friendships spring from 'mutual harmony in vice' and therefore must be denounced, and 'worldly' friendships are 'enkindled by the hope of gain', so these too are bad. But when it came to 'true' friendships, Aelred was much more forgiving than Aristotle. To have a soulmate, a man didn't have to be so morally evolved that he was unimpeachable, as far as Aelred was concerned. A main way of identifying 'true' friendship, he said, is simply *intimacy*: the common-or-garden desire by man and all God's creatures for 'mutual company'. And true, spiritually uplifting friendship is at least theoretically accessible to anyone who is inspired by Christ. However, Christ is a hard figure to live up to.

Aelred also said that a best friend has to consider all his possessions shared. And, like Aristotle and Seneca, he believed that a man has to be prepared to die for that friend. Specifying that to be good, a man must 'live as to give proof of loyalty and uprightness, of fairness and generosity', Cicero concluded, 'Friendship cannot exist but between good men.' For Aelred, Aristotle, Seneca and Cicero alike, the focus is on being righteous and willing to make the ultimate sacrifice. And many people try for this kind of friendship.

In 1775 when Mary Wollstonecraft was sixteen, she met Fanny Blood. Fanny was two years older. They were both eldest daughters who were often put in charge of broods of children; both had improvident fathers and gentle mothers. Fanny looked angelic to Mary, who immediately 'vowed eternal friendship', as William Godwin put it. In her autobiographical novel *Mary*, Wollstonecraft presents her feelings for Fanny as 'a passion'. Even when she and Fanny were both married, her commitment didn't waver. In 1784, Mary learnt that Fanny, weakened by tuberculosis, and pregnant, had fallen dangerously ill. Fanny was in Portugal. Mary had recently set up a school in Stoke Newington, but she didn't hesitate to drop everything and set sail for Lisbon to be by Fanny's side.

Actually, letters suggest that Fanny found Mary's demands for intimacy alarming. From the start, she tried to distance herself. It was just that Mary was never deterred.

Simply deciding that someone will be your best friend, regardless of their thoughts on the matter, is one way of doing it. But even iron determination may leave the question, where should you look for this person? Cicero was clear that the kind of 'good men' you're looking for must come from the upper class. Any intimates from boyhood who were 'devoted to hunting and games of ball', he said, should be discarded. Similarly, 'nurses and slaves who attended us to and from school, will, by right of priority of acquaintance, claim the largest share of our goodwill. I admit that they are not to be neglected, but they are to be regarded in an entirely different way.'

In mid-nineteenth century England, it seems Thomas Hughes agreed. In *Tom Brown's Schooldays*, he suggests that the village boys the protagonist mixes with before he starts at Rugby School may offer fun. But Tom shouldn't set too much store by them. Like Cicero, Hughes acknowledges, that friendships with working-class boys do have value. Young Tom plays 'peg-top' and marbles with them; together they enjoy chasing and catching a Shetland pony. There's warmth and emotion here. Grief-stricken when they learn that he is going away to board, the village lads load Tom with gifts: 'white marbles (called "alley-taws" in the Vale), screws, birds' eggs, whip-cord'. 'Poor Jacob Doodle-calf, in floods of tears, had pressed upon him with spluttering earnestness his lame pet hedgehog.'

The feelings are genuine. Hughes says: '[They] were full as manly and honest, and certainly purer than those in a higher rank; and Tom got more harm from his equals in his first fortnight at a private-school, where he went when he was nine years old, than he had from his village friends.' The village boys provide useful trial runs at friendships that are not meant to last. Tom's 'sorrow was not unmixed with the pride and excitement of making a new step in life'.

On his first day at Rugby, when he's only just arrived in the school grounds, a boy called East runs up beside him. And when Tom tells him his name he responds: 'Ah, I thought so, you know my old aunt, Miss East, she lives somewhere down your way in Berkshire. She wrote to me that you were coming today, and asked me to give you a lift' – a 'lift' being here just a case of jumping on the back of the horse-drawn coach Tom is in and checking that his clothes won't get him ridiculed.

'Only the louts wear caps,' confides East. 'Bless you, if you were to go into the quadrangle with that thing on, I – don't know what'd happen.' And after a quick dive into 'Nixon's the hatter's ... Tom is arrayed, to his utter astonishment, and without paying for it, in a regulation cat-skin at seven-and-sixpence'. And with their families' seal of approval, he and East become best friends for Tom's entire school career.

Women were first admitted to full-time university courses when Emily Davies founded what would later become Girton College at Hitchin in Hertfordshire in 1869. It is striking that one of the things the students most wanted was to meet other women like themselves. As adult daughters in privileged Victorian families, they'd had enough of doing the social round, encountering people who made them feel unnatural, first for being unmarried and second for wanting to engage in intellectual conversation.

When twenty-eight-year-old Louisa Lumsden saw the first prospective advertisement for the college in *Macmillan's Magazine* she wrote: 'My ambition was at once fired with the thought of possibly belonging to such a community of studious women.' Lumsden's student colleague Emily Gibson wrote in her diary during her first term: 'College life is to the full as delightful as I expected. Work, above all, geometry, is most delightful.' And, she said, 'one of the things here that has pleased me is to find that I can enjoy the society of women as much as the society of men'. She didn't want to discuss trousseaux or domestics' wages any more. She wanted to talk about coordinates and classify angles.

But are we going down the wrong path if we look exclusively for friends who are either the same as us or who fit some idea of 'good'? The notion of being prepared to die for a friend is pretty remote to most of us, and we may want to dismiss those aspects of the writings of men like Aristotle

and Seneca. But we still hope for big things from friendship.

Proverbs tells us: 'He that is a friend loves at all times.'
In St Jerome we find the statement, 'A friendship which can
cease to be was never true friendship.'

Mary Wollstonecraft knew she had formed 'romantic
notions of friendship'. She couldn't let those notions go.
Sandra Lynch discusses in her book *Philosophy and
Friendship* the problems that highly idealised treatments of
friendship can lead to. We might not expect a friend to die
for us, but if we say 'Best Friends Forever' to someone, even
if it is only for a split second, we most likely really do hope
that they will stay absolutely loyal and trustworthy and available *for ever*. 'Friendships of excellence' and BFFs alike are,
as Lynch puts it, 'relatively static conceptions which down-
play the significance of friendship as a dynamic relationship
between individuals'. It feels much safer to be able to tick off
a set of attributes on a list, but we should shake off this
desire for some kind of perfect union of minds.

Although, letting go of the idea that there is a perfect
friend out there if only you can find him or her is a high-
risk strategy too. If you can't find the perfect friend, why
bother with a poor substitute? There is a risk that in rejecting the idea that goodness is pivotal, we will end up
throwing the baby out with the bathwater.

The early-eighteenth-century essayist Joseph Addison was
MP for Malmesbury, a prominent member of the Kit-Cat
Club, a contributor to *The Tatler* and co-founder of the
*Spectator*. Addison was quite rabidly sociable himself,

regularly breakfasting with friends, reconvening for lunch at a tavern and again for an afternoon at Button's coffee house in Covent Garden. He seemed to have a whole host of best friends. Yet his essay about friendship 'We Two Are a Multitude' is full of warnings.

At first he appears to be advocating the idea that you should focus on finding a few soulmates. But when we meet up with a group of friends, he says, although we might expect to be rewarded with a 'greater Variety of Thoughts and Subjects', instead 'we find that Conversation is never so much straitened and confined as in numerous Assemblies'. Gossip and trivia – 'the Weather, Fashion, News' – take hold. It is preferable, he argues, to stick with a small 'knot' of friends – then talk 'descends into Particulars and grows more free and communicative'. And best of all, says Addison, is conversation between 'two Persons who are familiar and intimate', when a man 'exposes his whole soul'.

But then he panics about such a concept. When you are getting to know someone, how can you be sure that he will be faithful and 'continue in the Day of thy Affliction'? You may invest time and energy in someone you think of as a best friend, but find that he is fickle. It could even be after as much as 'a Year's conversation; when on a sudden some latent ill humour breaks out upon him'. Then one finds oneself entangled with an individual 'who by these changes and Vicissitudes of Humour is sometimes amiable and sometimes odious'.

For Addison, the biggest danger of all in hoping for a best friend is that he in turn could find *you* 'sometimes odious'. And therefore, he counsels, a best friend is after all someone you keep at a distance: 'It should be one of the greatest Tasks of Wisdom ... never to go out of that which is the agreeable Part of our Character.' If a friend has failed to see your faults, he is quite close enough. Exposing your soul involves exposing your weaknesses and revealing your ill-considered outbursts and tempers. It can mean having to be quite brave, to take people with all their flaws, and to recognise that they might be taking you with yours.

'A model of friendship which emphasises difference, rather than similarity,' says Lynch, 'opens the relationship to possibility, and of course to the vulnerability inherent in possibility, since the relationship may not survive the strain that difference can impose on it.'

Is this a risk worth taking?

In Sue Gee's novel *Reading in Bed*, Dido and Georgia have been friends since university. Marriage, children and living hundreds of miles apart haven't weakened their relationship. They sneak away to literary festivals together. Sitting close with a pot of Assam tea and a Victoria sponge between them is good. And when they haven't talked for a while, just a quick phone conversation is enough to make everything feel right – until Georgia's husband dies.

Georgia has always been self-contained. She doesn't mind being needed. She dislikes intensely feeling needy herself. Each woman considers the other her dearest, oldest friend. But Georgia's visit to Dido in the Lakes becomes a trip she can't wait to bring an end to. Not despite, but because of, the decades they've chalked up, it looks as if their friendship won't last.

It is possible to get *too* close. It can feel claustrophobic.

We may long for a friend who'll do anything for us then find, when we get one, that we don't like it.

In Nicci French's thriller *Complicit* Bonnie Graham, a teacher, forms a band, and loves the intense friendships that come with it. But rivalries come too and she finds herself standing over a dead body, unsure who the killer is but sure that the police could think it's her. Staring down at the bloody corpse of her ex-lover, she feels catastrophically alone.

Can she? She telephones her friend Sonia. The call involves enormous trust. She needs Sonia to believe she didn't do it, agree not to tell the police and then help her dispose of the body as well.

'I'm so sorry.'

'Sorry?'

'That it was you I called.'

As they struggle to sort this mess out, instead of gratitude Bonnie has 'the clutching sense of a friendship coming to an end because what she had done for me was so huge, a favour that overshadowed everything else'. Sonia engages in back-breaking labour for Bonnie (the body's heavy, they wrap it in a rug, cram it in the car boot). She is willing to circumvent the law and even incriminate herself. Her help makes her noble and self-sacrificing, and highlights how stupid Bonnie has been. The power Sonia has is scary.

The philosopher Elizabeth Telfer thinks we should do away with fantasies of irreproachable BFFs. She says in an essay on friendship that came out in 1971, 'We can, I think, reject the notion that we need to think of our friends as good people, as Plato and Aristotle seem to assume.' She points out that in the real world 'it is quite compatible with a friendship for a man to lose concern temporarily for a friend – perhaps as the result of a quarrel'. Absolute honesty isn't necessarily a characteristic of a true, truly valuable friendship either. A friend might consider that they are fulfilling the duties of friendship perfectly well even if they can't bring themselves to tell a 'home truth' – for example, that their friend has body odour. Furthermore, says Telfer, many friendships are intrinsically unfair. If there is a choice between helping a friend paint their flat and helping an OAP who is a stranger, or of giving a bit of spare cash to a friend who is broke as opposed to Oxfam, 'Most people would say that friends had, if not a prior claim, at least a competing claim.' If they favoured the person whose need was less insistent, few people would judge them bad.

Human beings are flawed. Friendships will inevitably be flawed too. But perhaps this is something to be celebrated. Rather than trying to iron out the wrinkles, maybe we should enjoy negotiating them.

In Barbara Pym's novel *Excellent Women*, when the glamorous Mr and Mrs Napier move into her lodging house Mildred suddenly yearns for a picturesque friendship with them. He's a naval officer. She's an anthropologist who's forever giving high-powered lectures. Mildred's old schoolfriend Dora, by contrast, is quite happy to spend her afternoon off trying on dresses in the 'inexpensive department of a large store' and then buying one that's frumpy and doesn't even fit. In her big brown wool dress and with her tendency, when she comes to visit, to festoon Mildred's kitchen with fawn lock-knit knickers, there's no doubt Dora is irritating. However, Dora's may be bigger, but Mildred has fawn lock-knit knickers too. It's Dora Mildred feels comfortable with.

Marvel Comics' creations 'The Fantastic Four' gain super-powers as a result of being exposed to cosmic rays. But they were already friends before that. The relationships between the Invisible Woman, Mr Fantastic, the Human Torch and Thing are so appealing precisely because these superheroes engage in squabbles and hold grudges. Then there are 'The X-Men', who are a tight band because they are all mutants. Outside their haven, Westchester Mansion, they face prejudice. But inside Westchester Mansion, guided and trained by Professor Xavier, characters such as Jean 'Jeannie' Grey, Cyclops, Storm and Wolverine, women and men alike, become part of the 'Brotherhood of Mutants'. They use the 'extra' power they gained when exposed to radiation to help humanity, despite the prejudice that's shown against them. One of the great appeals of these comic-book heroes is that they are allowed to be flawed, but heroes all the same.

In the children's novel *Charlotte's Web*, the protagonist befriends a character who on first assessment looks downright bad.

The runt pig Wilbur just wants to play with the other farm animals, but they have refused. 'Friendless, dejected and hungry, he threw himself down into the manure and sobbed.' Then, a saviour arrives. A voice comes out of the darkness. 'It sounded rather thin, but pleasant. "Do you want a friend, Wilbur?" it said. "I'll be a friend to you. I've watched you all day and I like you."'

Except, this enticing offer is from a spider, Charlotte, who is quite upfront about the fact that she is a 'trapper', telling

Wilbur that she sucks the blood of the flies and bugs that she catches.

"'Don't say that!" groaned Wilbur. "Please don't say things like that!"

"'Why not? It's true, and I have to say what is true. I am not entirely happy about my diet of flies and bugs, but it's the way I'm made.'"

Wilbur thinks to himself, "'Charlotte is fierce, brutal, scheming, bloodthirsty – everything I don't like. How can I learn to like her ...?'" Yet his new best friend proves 'loyal and true to the end'.

"'Well," he thought, "I've got a new friend, all right. But what a gamble friendship is!'"

# 9

# Holiday Romance

While I was at university, I had one impulse-driven holiday that was brilliant. Nothing amazing happened. I went to Barcelona with a handful of people, of whom I only knew two. There could have been terrible personality clashes, or differences of opinion over what we each wanted to do. It turned out we were all happy to see as many Gaudí buildings and sculptures as we could fit in, and drink sangria.

For my next holiday, an impulsive gesture backfired. I went with a woman who had recently 'come out'. She'd been rejected by the woman she had secretly adored for months. I had just finished a particularly stressful run of work. We got the cheapest flight we could find to somewhere in the Mediterranean with a beach. It was out of season, there weren't many tourists there, we didn't bump into many other holidaymakers. On the second day, my friend met a single, gay Australian dentist. They started an affair that was my friend's first since she'd come out and so was particularly exuberant and loud. Having gone away with a friend to escape, I spent the rest of the holiday a gooseberry.

The vacation and the friend became the things I wanted to escape from, back into the real world. But my friend never looked back. From that holiday on, she was out and proud.

In Ridley Scott's film *Thelma and Louise*, Geena Davis's Thelma is a downtrodden housewife and Susan Sarandon's Louise is a frazzled waitress. They set off on a fishing trip in Louise's 66 T-bird convertible.

In a bar, ordering 'Wild Turkey straight up and a Coke back please', when Louise looks dubious Thelma demands: 'What? Tell me somethin', is this my vacation or isn't it?'

And that sets the tone. Whatever happens no one can make them feel bad. A lorry driver leers at them. They give him a piece of their minds. Thelma meets a young Brad Pitt and has phenomenal sex.

On the highway, hats pulled low over their sun-kissed, grinning faces, hair escaping and flying behind as they drive, Louise asks, 'How do you like the vacation so far, honey?' By now they are on the wrong side of the law. The police are chasing them. They laugh.

'We're gonna be drinking margaritas by the sea, honey!'

We go on some of our most exciting holidays with friends. With friends, there is a feeling that we can go anywhere, do anything.

Jack Kerouac found his real-life, drug-fuelled road trip across America with Neal Cassady in the 1950s so stimulating that, calling himself 'Sal' and his friend 'Dean', he turned the experience into a novel, *On the Road*.

Sal and Dean stay up all night; they steal food and petrol. Dean's wife Marylou is with them too. There's a sense that she's shared. 'We didn't know what we were talking about anymore. [Dean] took the wheel and flew the rest of the way across the state of Texas, about five hundred miles, clear to El Paso, arriving at dusk and not stopping except once when he took all his clothes off, near Ozona, and ran yipping and leaping naked in the sage.' The feel of the text is breathless. It's as if Sal doesn't have time to make decisions for himself. His friend has taken over that laborious process for him. Back in the car, Dean says:

> 'Now Sal, now Marylou, I want both of you to do as I'm doing, disemburden yourselves of all that clothes – now what's the sense of clothes?' ... Marylou complied; unfud-dyduddied, so did I. We sat in the front seat, all three. Marylou took out cold cream and applied it to us for kicks. Every now and then a big truck zoomed by; the driver in a high cab caught a glimpse of a golden beauty sitting naked with two naked men: you could see them swerve.

It was Dean's idea, but they all have the power to make trucks swerve.

Journeys are full of possibilities. They can change relationships.

When she was young, Zora Neale Hurston took a job as secretary to the writer and socialite Fannie Hurst, who insisted on being addressed as 'Miss Hurst'. As Hurston tells it, she toyed with Zora, she sent her on fool's errands while they were in New York. But things changed when they went on a work trip one day. Zora describes how her employer suddenly decided to do a purely recreational detour via Niagara Falls. Miss Hurst took her minion 'rolling south by east laughing, eating Royal Anne cherries and spitting seeds'.

It was on trips like these, relaxed and free, that Miss Hurst might suddenly discuss her next book with Zora. And these must have been prized moments for Zora, then an aspiring writer herself. For all her boss's 'impish behaviour' back in New York, out on the road Fannie Hurst was Zora's friend.

Although sometimes you don't even have to travel anywhere. Just being with your friends can give that sense of escape. With them your surroundings can be forgotten.

I meet up with a few different friends regularly for coffee. And just the prospect lifts my mood. As long as the coffee is good, it doesn't even have to be an especially nice café. The decor can be horrible, the smell of chip fat strong. The minute we start talking, the furniture and the pictures on the walls, the café itself, will all be forgotten. My friends know how I take my coffee, I know how they take theirs. If there has been some kind of minor crisis – or major – I don't have to explain the history because they know most of it already, and vice versa. We can launch straight in, get through the things that are bothering us, and start laughing.

The psychologists Reed Larson and Nancy Bradney put it like this: 'With friends our attention becomes focused, distractions lessen, awareness of them disappears: we emerge into a world in which the intimacy and joy shared with others are the fundamental reality, and for a time the world becomes a different place.'

For their 1980s study 'Precious Moments with Family

Members and Friends', they took 174 'research participants' including high school students and workers around Chicago, and prompted them every two hours with an electronic bleeper to write down how they felt. When Larson and Bradney started, they assumed that friends are more important for teenagers, and that family provides most of the 'precious moments' as we grow older. Some of their findings were entirely to be expected. Thirteen- to sixteen-year-olds spend much more time with their friends than do adults of working age. 'Yet through adulthood and old age, friends continue to play the role they did in adolescence as a reliable source of positive experience.'

Larson and Bradney conclude: 'Friends much more than family can affect moods and transform attention. They can make us happy, changing our thoughts from preoccupation with the trivial, mundane, or wearying routines of daily life to attention centred on more meaningful exchanges ... They are partners in the pursuit of liberating experience.'

# 10

# The Time, the Place

We think of friendship as being about choice. If we meet someone and get that spark, we pursue them. We feel we *have* to be friends. Of course, they may not feel the same. But their consent isn't all that counts – we have to contend with other factors. Time and place count too.

The historical context in which we live makes a fundamental difference to how we make friends, and who with. For example, children's friendships through the centuries have encountered some major practical impediments. In Shakespeare's *Romeo and Juliet*, given that her father is planning a marriage of convenience and Juliet is plotting to marry for love, the only real space for friendship in the heroine's life is with her nurse. And although Juliet has reached the age of thirteen, in reality many children were routinely married off younger than that.

Penelope Fitzgerald's novel *The Blue Flower* explores the courtship by the eighteenth-century German Romantic poet and philosopher Fritz von Hardenberg (known as Novalis) of a twelve-year-old girl, Sophie. Fitzgerald shows only too vividly just how much Fritz's love hems her in and prevents her from interacting with friends her own age. Standing at the window, she just wants to go out and play in the snow. But Fritz monopolises her. Fitzgerald evokes with awful poignancy how, after feeling special and elevated for a brief time, Sophie comes to feel reduced. On one of his visits, Fritz sees that right now she would rather get involved with games. Even as two obstreperous children run beside them rolling their hoops, he entices her with talk of fairs and singing and dancing. Day after day, Sophie's journal entries read simply, 'Today once again we were alone and nothing much happened.'

In 1522, the young Michael V Behaim was also deprived of the chance to make friends. He was sent from his home in Germany as apprentice to a merchant in Italy at the age of twelve. The amount of work he was given to do meant that he was left with little if any leisure time. Apprenticeships were defined by competition, and most if not all of the other boys Michael knew were apprentices in the same establishment, all vying for favourable treatment. Friendship was simply not an option. The historian Steve Ozment notes: 'There is scant evidence of his ever having had close friends his own age. Of the two people he describes as friends, one is his second cousin once removed, Paul Behaim, who was nine years his junior and whom he watched over out of gratitude to the boy's father, Michael's own guardian and mentor. The other "friend" was a some-time business associate in Cracow who was slow to repay his debts.'

A lot of the drama in Jane Austen's *Emma* comes from the

fact that wealthy, petulant Emma is so bored by English village life that she does the unthinkable and resorts to what is
referred to in the novel as the 'second set'. She is actually
glad of tea and conversation with two lowly spinsters, Miss
Bates and 'poor' Harriet Smith, an orphan.

And in eighteenth- and nineteenth-century England it
wasn't just that friendships were difficult to establish and
maintain *between* classes. There were snobberies within
classes, too. One of the most tragic elements of Thomas
Hardy's *Tess of the d'Urbervilles* is that once Tess has become
a fallen woman she can't even be friends with the women of
her own community. Only Marian, because she too was dis-
graced early on – caught drinking – remains loyal to her
throughout. A particularly sad scene sees Tess and Marian
in the barren 'starve-acre' landscape of Flintcomb-Ash, hacking turnip roots from the ground, drenched in rain. Her
bonnet flapping 'smartly' in her face, this sparse friendship
with Marian is all Tess has left.

Social mores are not the only obstacles to friendship. The
farmers of the village of Montaillou in thirteenth-century
France were poor and at the bottom of the French feudal
system. Because the land where they lived was so moun-
tainous they couldn't even mix much with the peasants from
the next village. Although there were advantages. Geography
usually helped keep communities close.

Five hundred years later, like the farmers of Montaillou,
many Scottish farmers worked the land together, tilled
together, harvested together, sat on stones or bits of turfs
round peat fires together. In *Change in the Village* George
Sturt describes how in rural Surrey, the regular Saturday

shopping expeditions could turn into homespun festivities for the villagers, who would 'meet their friends in the street, have a chat, wind up with a visit to the public-house, and so homewards at any time between seven and ten o'clock, trooping up the hill happily'. In Thomas Hardy's novels, peasants are often seen taking breaks on hay ricks, stopping for a chat in the dairy, or quaffing drink after a long day at the agricultural fair or market.

But Sturt's *Change in the Village*, first published in 1912, and Hardy's Wessex novels, written in the 1870s and 80s, were laments for a rural life that had already gone. Industrialisation disrupted easy-going comradeship.

In England and Wales between 1851 and 1871, the population increased by five million. People crammed into the cities to work in the new textile, metal, engineering and ship-building industries. Because there were plenty of workers for the employers to choose from, conditions were hard, hours were long. In *The Unquiet Grave* (1944) the writer Cyril Connolly argued, provocatively, that industrialisation 'made an end to friendship'. He said the 'tempo' – of the working days, and of the machines – increased to such a pitch that friendships became impossible.

Human beings will usually find friendship even if they can reserve only the tiniest chinks of time and energy for it. But the 'tempo' that Connolly talks about certainly made it harder. The sheer grimness and grind are evoked vividly in novels such as Dickens's *Hard Times*, in which Coketown, a version of the Preston of the time, is a place of massive machinery and tall chimneys that seems to have arisen out of its own furnaces. Even the canals run black with dye. In the vast piles of buildings, 'the piston of the steam-engine worked monotonously up and down' and 'there was a rattling and a trembling all day long'. The people of Coketown struggle on 'in convulsions', craving 'some physical relief – some relaxation, encouraging good humour and good spirits … some recognized holiday, though it were but for an honest dance to a stirring band of music'.

In Émile Zola's novel *Germinal*, set in a nineteenth-century French mining village, no one has enough food or money. The miners work endlessly but are perpetually in debt. Twists of coffee wrapped in bits of paper, along with snippets of gossip, are swapped fast and joylessly. Zola calls the mine that enslaves its workers *le Voreux*, 'the voracious one'.

Even the number of public spaces where people could relax were reducing. Paris and London, of course, had their pleasure gardens. Kensington Palace's park was opened to the public in the 1860s. Alarmed by the impact of unrestricted industrialisation, three valiant philanthropists founded the National Trust in 1895, with a view to protecting the landscape and its historic buildings for everyone to enjoy.

Nonetheless, the overall picture was bleak. The social historians J. L. and Barbara Hammond point out that through the early part of the nineteenth century, in parliament, bills were still being passed that gave more and more 'common land' round the country into private hands. In 1840, one Mr Lister set about buying up 170 acres of common land near Bradford, including an area called Fairweather Green. J. L. and Barbara Hammond note that he was required to reserve just three acres as 'a Place of Exercise and Recreation for the neighbouring Population'; the population numbered about 120,000. One witness, Mr Joseph Ellison, protested that on Fairweather Green the locals played cricket, as well as 'a game we call spell and nur; they will drive a ball, 10, 11, 12, 13, and 14 score; they cannot play at those games in three acres'.

Today, I could visit my friend in Paris tomorrow. I would only need to book a ticket on Eurostar; or I could jump on a ferry or a plane. I have no constraints; I am free to gather my friends from all sorts of places. Aren't I?

Research by three Dutch sociologists suggests that there are more restrictions than we like to think. In 'Changing Places: The Influence of Meeting Places on Recruiting Friends', Beate Völker and her co-authors say that the places where we recruit our friends have changed dramatically, in ways that can be problematical.

For the villagers of Montaillou and Sturt's Surrey farmers, work, home and social lives were intertwined. There was little chance of finding friends outside, but the locals' immediate environment was rich with friends. Völker argues that, by contrast, nowadays we tend to like to keep our work and social lives separate. We prefer not to make new friends in our domestic environment because that doesn't feel adventurous enough. But work isn't a place where we like to make friends either. The end result is, she says, that many of us travel from home to work and back feeling increasingly alone.

She puts figures to it. Völker and her colleagues analysed one-and-a-half-hour-long interviews with 1007 respondents from 168 different neighbourhoods in the Netherlands. Their research shows that we are eleven times more likely to find friends in an 'achieved context' – that is, in a place where we are engaged in an occupation we like and have aspired to – than in an 'ascribed context'. And they class both the workplace and home as 'ascribed contexts'. They suggest that the home–work split that characterises the twenty-first century has created contexts that are 'highly bundled', to a dangerous degree. Work accounts for a significant proportion of your week. If you feel an aversion to becoming friends with people you spend so much time with, inevitably, as Völker et al. put it, that reduces your 'supply' of 'interaction partners'. And as the recession continues to bite, as companies push more employees into going freelance to economise on deskspace, the number of work hours that individuals put in rises and the energy available for leisure falls. That voluntary work you meant to do, that bridge circle you meant to join, get postponed. Your supply of interaction partners goes down still further.

But Völker's respondents may have had different understandings of what constitutes an 'interaction partner'.

I grew up near a market town in Yorkshire where when you bought something in a shop the assistant was likely to call you 'love' and ask after your well-being: 'All right?' That shop assistant could be an 'interaction partner'. When I moved a couple of hundred miles away to London, after months of using a nearby corner shop every day the assistant and I managed only basic civilities. As I bought my milk and bread in the morning, we remained strangers.

There are differences between towns and cities. There are differences between countries. As Harry Triandis notes in his essay 'Cultural Syndromes and Subjective Well-being', cultural norms can affect not only your chances of friendship happening, but whether or not you describe someone as your friend at all. In parts of Russia, to admit that you are happy is to tempt fate. So in such a climate, says Triandis, most people who are asked about friendship in the context of what makes them happy will give answers characterised by reticence or even deceit.

And then there are the different ways we show our appreciation of friendship.

A fair few Spaniards live in and around our street, and for a while one moved into our house while he did a Ph.D. in astrophysics. He'd come fresh from Bilbao, and was far from fluent in English. Luckily, the Spanish woman who lives opposite us and who has been in Britain for twenty years thought to warn us that Spaniards can appear unfriendly, because of a few cultural differences. 'Please' and 'thank you', she told us, are generally considered superfluous in Spain. And thank goodness she did warn us.

I thought that I was not the kind of person to stand on ceremony, but I was still learning. 'Would you like a glass of wine?' might get a bored-looking shrug from our astrophysicist, and an 'OK'. He had considered the matter. He did want a glass of wine. It was that simple. I realise that, like 'sorry', the way 'please' is used in the UK, it's often only punctuation anyway. But it does grease the wheels of social interaction.

As the months went by, the times we spent chatting at

the kitchen table became longer and more enjoyable. We did become friends – partly because we had both been warned at the start to expand our ideas of what constitutes 'friendly'.

# 11

# Vinous Mist and Hallowed Halls

'Softly, through a vinous mist,/ My college friendships glimmer,' wrote Alfred, Lord Tennyson.

Universities are particularly conducive places for friendship. A lot of our most enduring relationships start on campus. Simply to arrive at university is a sign of having made a choice. You've shown that you're independent.

At home, maybe you were pigeon-holed as the reliable older brother, or the flaky younger sister. It is possible to move away from those pictures of yourself, through friends, in a more thoughtful and meaningful way. Back home, you rebelled through your friends. Perhaps they were picked for their shock value rather than for any individual qualities. You had ulterior motives. At university, inclination and sheer chemistry can come to the fore, and quickly too.

Whether a period at university is funded by parents or grandparents, scholarships, government grants or loans, it is time out from the need to earn a living. The very walls of a university, the removal of the need to go outside for food, drink or company: these things can make students feel that the outside world is superfluous. Everything you could possibly want is supplied on site. And often everyone you would want to meet is supplied too. A lot of sifting has been done already. You are attending the same lectures because you chose the same course. You already have that in common. You share a commitment to the subject. Seminars are not things to skive but rather opportunities to discuss in more detail topics about which you're passionate.

And then there's the extracurricular life. Cambridge University's Footlights dramatics club famously spawned comedy teams made up of friends, including John Cleese and Graham Chapman (*Monty Python*) in the 1960s and Bill Oddie, Graeme Garden and Tim Brooke-Taylor, who went on to form *The Goodies* in the 1970s; the 1981 Edinburgh comedy prize, the Perrier Award, went to a group from Footlights that included Emma Thompson, Hugh Laurie and Stephen Fry.

Damien Hirst organised a show featuring fellow Goldsmiths students Sarah Lucas, Michael Landy and Gary Hume. The show was called *Freeze* and it turned a group of young unknowns into the Young British Artists, who soon dominated the art world, Lucas shocking with a self-portrait featuring fried eggs as breasts, Hirst with a shark pickled in formaldehyde. Such ideas could easily have seemed crazy at the time.

There is always a bar on campus. The bricks and mortar

of the university can help weave a spell – although the original intention was not that the spell should be quite so exciting.

When the two universities, Oxford and Cambridge, were founded in the twelfth and thirteenth centuries, their function was, says historian G. M. Trevelyan, to train up the next generation of clergy. The institutions aimed to be morally and spiritually unassailable environments. Except the college system at first put students four or five to a room, with little supervision. Through the fourteenth and fifteenth centuries, whether the authorities wanted them to or not, Oxford and Cambridge fostered vibrant friendships.

By the mid-1600s, some of the college wardens were beginning to see that such friendships may not be a bad thing. It might help students study if the environment was more genial. Dr John Wilkins, warden of Wadham College, took a fresh look at the physical setting. Oxford had a reputation for being 'sour'. Wilkins worked hard to make the interior of his college more appealing. He created formal gardens, with clipped borders and walkways and elaborate waterworks.

And Wilkins's decision to create a more sociable atmosphere paid dividends. It was in his rooms that the group that was to become the Royal Society had some of their early meetings. The Society's members have since explained to the world at large gravity, evolution, the electron and the double helix. It is now in its fifth century. All this from the starting point of a group of friends who enjoyed the intellectual freedom they found at Wadham.

Music could be heard in the college. Wilkins organised chamber concerts. He even played practical jokes. The gardens featured a statue he had built with a concealed pipe so that, by whispering into a mouthpiece, he could make it appear from a distance that the statue was talking.

In his novel *Brideshead Revisited* (published in 1945) Evelyn Waugh devotes long descriptive passages to the Oxford University that was the backdrop to Charles Ryder and Sebastian Flyte's growing intimacy. '[As] one by one, the lamps were lit in the windows round the quad, the golden lights were diffuse and remote, like those of a foreign village seen from the slopes outside.' In Linda Grant's novel *We Had It So Good* (2010) the main female character Andrea explains that her friend Grace 'made' her when they both arrived at Oxford: 'It's true. We met on my first day. We had rooms in college next door to each other. I was a country hick with hay in my ears in a mouldy crimplene mini skirt from a charity shop in Truro, and Grace showed me how to dress and what films to say I'd seen, even when I hadn't.'

In Donna Tartt's *The Secret History*, when Richard Papen first approaches the elite, geographically remote Hampden College in Vermont, he becomes high just at the sight of 'Commons clock tower; ivied brick; white spire', surrounded by bright meadows 'spellbound in the hazy distance'. A scholarship boy, he has come from a 'silicon village' called Plano where his father runs a gas station. The protagonist targets the most unapproachable group on campus, five Classics students, three of whom are characterised by English tweed, neckties and umbrellas; two have 'epicene faces as clear, as cheerful and grave, as a couple of Flemish angels'. When he's with them, mundanities like gas and silicon might not exist.

While bunches of hippies, beatniks and preppies nurse hang-overs and play bongos outside on a bit of grass, the Classics students discuss for fun how to correctly translate a passage about the Greeks sailing to Carthage: 'It should be accusative,' says Camilla; 'We need a dative,' argues Charles; 'Ablative's the ticket,' pipes up Bunny.

Indeed, the way friendships within university marginalise the world and boost one's sense of self can make it tempting not to leave at all. C. S. Lewis was in many ways out of step with his times, and his tight friendships with Oxford colleagues allowed him to stay that way. A. N. Wilson's biography presents a man who was seen as so bullish by so many that the 'beer and Beowulf Lewis', who smoked and drank excessively and roared out unfashionable views in pubs in 1950s Oxford, had no choice but to cling more and more closely to a group he headed called 'the Inklings'. Members included his brother Warren ('Warnie'), and fellow professors Adam Fox and J. R. R. Tolkien, with whom Lewis bonded especially closely. They both hated most of the fiction that was being published.

'Tollers,' said Lewis, 'there is too little of what we really like in stories. I am afraid we shall have to try and write some ourselves.' The Inklings operated with a rising sense that they were 'embattled against a hostile world', says Wilson; they had a tendency 'not only to see merit where none existed (in the poetry of Fox, for example), but actually to think that belonging to the group ... was in itself a sort of merit. One gets the feeling from Warnie's diary, for example, that it was better to be a good Inkling than a good poet, or even a good man.'

Ivy Compton-Burnett's novel *Pastors and Masters* is a predecessor of the campus novel, and Malcolm Bradbury's *The History Man* is a seminal example of the genre. In both, the main characters cling desperately to the corralled socialising that comes with university. In *Pastors and Masters* the pompous Nicholas Herrick, a man with literary pretensions, runs a prep school. He lives in his old university town and spends all the time he can with old friends who teach at the university, discussing literature as marmalade is spooned on to toast and bacon sits crisping by the fender. For the main character of *The History Man* (set in 1972), the sociology lecturer Howard Kirk, one of his most important achievements is that he has gained a reputation for giving the best parties in the university town where he lives and teaches, Watermouth. He chooses his house because it is a 'perfect social space', he prides himself on having 'a wide intellectual constituency, an expansive acquaintance'. He invites fellow lecturers, students and near-strangers: 'a radical vicar, an Argentinian with obscure guerrilla associations, an actor in moleskin trousers who has touched Glenda Jackson in a Ken Russell film'.

Intellectual stimulation and meetings of minds within closed walls can have powerful effects. Friendships made under such circumstances often feel transformative. In 1770, shortly after leaving Königsberg University, Marcus Herz wrote to his friend and old tutor Immanuel Kant about how different he felt as a result of meeting him. 'It is you alone whom I have to thank ... to whom I am indebted for my entire self.' Newly graduated, inspired, he could see a future for himself as a philosopher now, whereas, 'Without you I would be what I was four years ago, that is to say, I would be nothing.'

The friendships we forge at university are preternaturally vivid, gloriously intoxicating.

# 12
# Gr8 2 C U

When I was a teenager, the process of making social arrangements involved some trauma. Phone calls to fix the place and time to meet had to be made the previous day, either in the kitchen in front of parents or in phone booths that reeked of pee. Then on the night, if your mate was held up on a bus and you'd left the house already, you'd have no clue what had happened to him or her. You'd be left standing on a street corner, wondering. Mobile phones have taken the skulking and uncertainty away. Like air traffic controllers, my friends and I can guide each other into place.

I went for lunch with a friend of mine and her daughter. Afterwards as we walked from the café to the nearby rep theatre where the seventeen-year-old was doing a drama workshop, I was vaguely aware that she'd taken her phone out and was texting as we went. The theatre was two blocks away. Within a couple of moments a male friend had appeared, ready to escort her the distance of not very many paving-stones to the theatre.

Texting is great. I love it. It is like having all your friends in your pocket. It seems you can contact them any time for a quick injection of their warmth or humour. It feels illicit. You can do it while you're waiting at a bus-stop. There is no dead time. Even when your schedule is ridiculously tight and you couldn't possibly arrange to meet up for a drink, or even spend five or ten minutes having a telephone conversation with them, you can grab a moment while you're waiting for your porridge or walking to a meeting to text a quick hello. And a text here and there can keep you in touch with an awful lot of people.

The Mobile Data Association reported in 2008 that Britons sent 1.4 billion text messages every week. That amounts to twenty-three texts per week for every man, woman and child in the country, a figure that was up 30 per cent on 2007; it went up by a further 31 per cent in 2009, when getting on for two billion texts were sent in Britain every week, or 265 million a day. With the advent of smartphones, it's not even possible to work out how much we're texting and Facebooking each other now. But is this all just too much? Of course, some texts and other messages sent while we're on the move are to family members or are work-related. But the vast bulk are to friends. Do all these texts we're sending really have much to do with friendship?

In 2003, email and texting facilitated a sudden trend for 'flashmobbing', whereby hundreds of people would descend on a site to perform apparently random acts simultaneously. Flashmobs that made the papers include a pillow fight in a high street, hundreds of people suddenly turning up in a sofa shop, and a synchronised dance in an Underground station. A flashmob makes the person organising it look amazingly popular, and all those who receive an invitation feel fêted too. Hundreds of people who don't know each other are suddenly, very publicly, inundated with 'friends'.

On Twitter, I can feel I'm bosom buddies with Simon Pegg, who tells me on his way to Chicago that Lake Michigan looks like a seething ripple of ragged grey silk – and he just farted. If I'm bored in the supermarket checkout queue, I can take out my phone and see what the pop star Britney Spears has to confide. It cheers me up if I see that from Japan she's tweeted, 'I think all the tiny cars are so cute!'

Sites such as Friends Reunited give us the impression that all the friends we've ever had are waiting for us in cyberspace. On social networking sites such as Facebook, I can press 'Add a friend' again and again and again. Indeed, once I have joined Facebook, I must. The *London Lite* newspaper featured a cartoon by NAF in which two men appear to be begging, sitting hunched on a pavement. One holds up a sign saying, 'Please help, homeless'. The other holds up a sign saying, 'Please help, only 3 friends on Facebook'. Many teenagers have two or three hundred Facebook friends when they have just started out.

With many of these new technologies, friends can be picked up as easily as handfuls of penny chews from a sweet counter. Only, you don't even have to go as far as the corner shop to get them.

Does the new technology lead us to cast our nets too wide? The cognitive psychologist J. L. La Gaipa points out: 'To maintain an extensive personal network requires engagement, time and attention.' And although La Gaipa is so alarmed by the down sides of the technology that he can barely take a cursory look at the rewards, in his essay "The Negative Effects of Informal Support Systems', he does have a point. Sometimes I value a wait at a bus-stop precisely because it's a pause in my day, and then I feel irritated if my phone beeps or vibrates or blurts its tune and wish I'd switched it off, to stop these constant demands. Conversely, if when I switch it on my phone shows just the screen saver and no missed calls or messages, I can feel a surprising amount of distress. Does no one *like me*?

The notion that we must have hundreds of friends and be in touch with all of them all the time is not realistic. With so many friendships now made possible, a lot of them are inevitably superficial, or even fake.

If rapper MC Hammer tweets to say thank you for love and support following a Super Bowl commercial, it's easy to forget that 'you' refers not to you and you alone but to tens of thousands of twitterers. Britney Spears's tweet about Japan brought a smile to my lips partly because I enjoyed the illusion that she was informing me personally. Sure, the record-breaking cyclist Lance Armstrong's tweets say things like 'About to do a shoot for Parade magazine.' But first he lets me know how things are with his family: 'Got the kids off to school', for example. Everything about his tweets suggests that he only provides the Web link to the *Parade* magazine article because I'm his mate, and mates support each other.

If you're feeling a bit lonely or down, it can be hard to keep things in proportion. A rash of articles, news bulletins and books all warn us that Facebook is addictive. Social networking sites are about acquisition. Just as people become addicted to shopping for clothes, they become addicted to acquiring Facebook friends. If you have a sidebar that scrolls on and on with 'friend' after 'friend', you can feel popular and successful. Except, there's always someone on Facebook who has more, or more impressive, friends than you do.

And if you find making friends difficult, cyberspace offers comfort. For a piece in the *Sunday Times* magazine, Anmar Frangoul spoke to the mother of an eighteen-year-old boy who spent so much time on computer games that he was thrown off all the school sports teams as his weight ballooned to twenty-five stone. She described the computer as the only place where her son felt happy: 'He's got friends there who can't attack him.' Programmes and centres designed to treat children and adults who have become addicted to computer games are springing up quite fast now. There's Broadway Lodge just outside Weston-super-Mare, London's Capio Nightingale Hospital, the Smith and Jones clinic in Amsterdam. And they all say games appeal because they offer escape from the pressures of having to deal with real friendships.

For children who are being bullied or excluded at school, on-line games are a chance for them to fight back, perhaps with machine-guns. And while parents and teachers see them playing in their bedrooms in pitiful isolation, that's not how it feels to the children themselves, particularly when the games are online. With 'massively multiplayer online role-playing games' (MMORPGs) such as *World of Warcraft*, a child can feel as if he has armies of friends. Tens of thousands of people can be playing an MMORPG simultaneously, each with an avatar that other players can admire, align with or defeat. Players feel as if they are getting to know particular avatars and developing relationships with them. Even relatively innocuous sites such as Disney's Club Penguin, which is aimed at primary school children, give the players avatars that all move about on screen together in real time gathering 'fans'.

In 2008 there was an outrage when a social networking site, schooltogethernow.com, launched with the aim of attracting children as young as five. The idea was innocent enough. It was meant to be a version of the school gates – an online space where parents could swap gossip and where children could be 'buddies'. In December 2008, a month after it went live, the site reportedly got 1,000 hits a day, more than half from primary-school-aged children. A newspaper claimed that the site had weak privacy settings, and allowed pupils and interested adults alike to register without verifying their identity. Therefore, the paper warned, it could easily be used by paedophiles.

Except the big dangers are serious dangers in themselves. The extremes are easy to see: total addiction to online friendships; total aversion to real friendship as a result of online games; so much texting that the upshot is repetitive strain injury, job losses and ruined lives.

Advances in technology bring other, subtler losses as well. Precisely because Skype, email, texting and Facebook feel so immediate and real, there's still more room for misunderstanding. If I'm out of range, I may not pick up a text for several hours. On Facebook, the way the technology works, if you click 'Reply all' to something that's been posted on your wall, your message can end up as a message in the email inbox of people who certainly aren't your friends and who may not even like you. With Facebook and email, we may often press the 'Send' button before we've thought our response through. Perhaps we picked the message up in the middle of a particularly stressful day at work when we just wanted to clear the inbox: the conversational ball has been chucked, we are absolved, it is the other person's responsibility now. It is so common, indeed, for people to send short angry emails they immediately regret that the phenomenon has acquired a name, 'flaming'.

Unless an email has to go absolutely this minute, if it's even remotely sensitive I often let it sit in my 'Drafts' folder overnight. One friend told me she grew so alarmed at how abrupt and then abrasive text exchanges can become that she always makes a point now of scrolling back and inserting one warm, friendly comment.

Although of course there's no point just retreating and being fearful of change. My grandma wouldn't use the telephone for years because she was so unnerved by the idea of talking to friends and family who weren't in the same room.

For people who are physically close to each other, does it seem a bit daft if they're constantly emailing, texting and Facebooking friends who live a couple of streets or even houses away? One of my male friends goes on Facebook to play Scrabble with a woman who lives a few doors away and to gossip with someone who lives opposite; I'll confess – now I do too. But for many who are distant geographically, the new technology is not remotely superfluous. It is a lifesaver, allowing you not just to keep in contact but to feel as if your friendship is still being lived in the moment.

The kind of heady exclusivity that used to be the preserve of private school or university is being generated on the Internet. Mobile phones can promote a feeling that friendship is the only thing that matters. Contrary to all the nay-sayers and doom-mongers, technological developments are injecting a new dynamism into friendship.

# PART TWO

# IN THE THICK OF IT

'When my friends are one-eyed, I look at them in profile.'

Joseph Joubert

# 13
# Strength in Numbers

Contestants on the TV quiz show *Who Wants to Be a Millionaire?* can, if they are stumped by a question, 'Phone a Friend'.

But who do you pick? And if we *don't* pick someone as our Phone-a-Friend option, does that mean we don't value them? Our friends fit in all sorts of places in our lives. They serve an odd variety of functions. And it's hard to know sometimes exactly who makes up this loose assembly.

In an episode of *The Simpsons*, Homer is trying to work out, first, who his friends are, and then, where each falls within that general category. The bartender, Mo, suggests that he himself is a 'well-wisher', in the sense that 'I don't wish you any specific harm'. When Peter Corey was looking for a simple definition of 'friend' to use in his self-help book for teenagers, *Coping with Friends*, he found a bewildering assortment. His Collins dictionary and thesaurus gave, amongst other definitions: 'person who acts for one, i.e. as second in a duel' and 'adherent, supporter' – a pairing which led Corey to conclude that, according to dictionary definitions, 'a friend is a cross between a tube of glue and a football hooligan'.

And just how many of these sticky hooligans do you need? Studies suggest that there is an optimum number of friends, and that this optimum can help you live longer. But, what is that number?

'I had three chairs in my house; one for solitude, two for friendship, three for society,' said Thoreau, whose personal optimum number of friends proved perhaps rather low – he lived to the age of forty-five. The poet Alexander Pope took quite a different view, asserting that 'True Friendship's laws are by this rule expressed,/ Welcome the coming, speed the parting guest.' Pope made it to fifty-six. Thoreau's statement must at least have been clear to those who knew him. The occupants of his three chairs would have been able to see a pattern and so deduce the position they occupied in his hierarchy. But Pope probably neglected to mention to 'coming' guests when they arrived that they would soon be forced into 'parting', to make room for new ones.

The feeling of liking someone is hard to define. It shifts about. At times it's intense. At others, we're quietly pleased to see that individual. Defining exactly why you choose someone to be your friend is a tricky business. In her book *Friends and Enemies*, the psychologist Dorothy Rowe addresses the fact that friendship means different things to different people. In the introduction she tells us that she has travelled to Serbia, Lebanon, Northern Ireland, South Africa, Vietnam and Australia to talk about friendship. And her conclusion is this: '"You don't make friends. You recognize them." This is what people told me again and again.' She quotes a series of one-liners: 'A friend should share my sense of humour.' 'We have a similar morality.' The list goes on: 'A friend will have my welfare at heart and is prepared to accept me as I am.' 'I want a friend to hear what I have to say.'

I don't doubt the truth of any of them. But it isn't long before these statements start to sound trite – and no more or less insightful than the observations about friendship in Charles M. Schulz's *I Need All the Friends I Can Get*. In this early book version of the *Peanuts* strip cartoon, a typically gloomy Charlie Brown is challenged by Lucy: 'Define "friend"!' 'A friend is someone who will take the side with the sun in his eyes,' he says, thinking of a tennis game; 'A friend is someone who likes you even when the other guys are around', thinking of Linus smiling at him surrounded by team-mates as they leave the baseball pitch. Charlie Brown conducts a straw poll and is told: 'A friend is someone who understands why you like your strawberry sodas without any strawberries in them.' 'A friend is someone who doesn't think it's crazy to collect old Henry Busse records!'

Furthermore, we don't want to be told who to be friends with, or what to do when we are with them. Friendship charts its own course.

In *Bridget Jones's Diary*, friends are the cavalry when sexual relationships go wrong. In Chaucer's *Canterbury Tales* the shifty Pardoner and the pimply, swindling Summoner are partners in crime. In the novel *Suite Française* by Irène Némirovsky, for those fleeing Paris at the start of the Second World War friends are whoever will share food and comfort. Groucho Marx was quite clear, noting in his *Memoirs of a Mangy Lover* that if he had a friend at all, she was a dog called Zsa Zsa. 'Oh, occasionally she bites me, but when she does I bite her right back.'

The essayist Randolph Bourne (1886–1918) wrote: 'We have as many sides to our character as we have friends to show them to. Quite unconsciously I find myself witty with one friend, large and magnanimous with another, petulant and stingy with another, wise and grave with another, and utterly frivolous with another. I watch with surprise the sudden and startling changes in myself.'

I like this about friendship. The fact that you can have such a range is brilliant. Wherever they fit, they're all good for us.

# 14

# Friends Are Good
# for Our Health

In a supermarket at the pharmacist's counter, I picked up a free booklet entitled *Tackling Stress*. In different wordings it said again and again, Talk to a friend, relax by seeing a friend, spend time with friends.

One study I came across, 'The Effect of Workplace Laughter Groups on Personal Efficacy Beliefs' (2007) by Heidi Beckman, Nathan Regier and Judy L. Young, showed that 'The act of vigorous laughter energizes our physiology in much the same way that aerobic exercise does, increasing heart and respiration rate and activating various group muscles.' Their study was conducted in rather po-faced conditions. Determined that their experimental 'laughter interventions' with staff at a large behavioural and mental health facility in America's Midwest would provide a 'pure, independent variable', in their workshops the researchers allowed only 'laughter without humour'. That is, jokes weren't part of it. The laughter wasn't spontaneous. Staff had to laugh on request. The programme comprised forty-five-minute sessions in the work-place, in which a professional laughter coach led participants through vocalisations of 'Ho-ho-ho, Ha-ha-ha' – the 'laughter interventions'. The participants' morale and resilience were measurably higher after the experiment.

It's with friends that we laugh most readily, most heartily. We experience the increased circulation and stimulation to our muscles, as well as boosts to positive emotions, that the people in this survey who 'laughed without humour' felt. And if you experience laughter *with* humour, you gain more cognitive benefits including, as Beckman, Regier and Young describe it, 'the recognition of some incongruity and perhaps an increase in perceived control'.

Three years earlier, as part of a World Health Organization Cross-National Survey, the Canadian Health Agency's report on its exploration of 'Health Behaviors in School-Aged Children' had concluded: 'Having close friends is associated with positive emotional health and social adjustment. Children with close friends demonstrate better academic performance, lower rates of juvenile delinquency, and lower dropout rates, compared with children who do not have friends as sources of intimacy and social support.' More than ten years in the making, informed by extensive Q&As with young people as well as the work of many researchers, advisers and analysts, the report states: 'The type of peer relationships, number of friends, and extent of involvement in a peer group evolve over adolescence and may influence the degree to which adolescents become involved in health-promoting or health-compromising behaviours.' So whether teenagers go off the rails or stay on them may relate directly to the role of friendship in their lives.

In a paper entitled 'Friendship, Social Support, and Health' two behavioural scientists, Patricia M. Sias and Heidi Bartoo, cite various studies that detail more of the health-promoting aspects of friendship. In one, a group of chronically depressed women were allotted individual 'befrienders' – that is, people who visited each of them, went on outings with them and became their confidants. It would be surprising indeed if this intervention hadn't helped at all, but what Sias and Bartoo in fact report is that 'the first year of befriending yielded the same success rate as traditional medical and psychological interventions (i.e. antidepressants or cognitive therapies)'. They conclude that friendship could, and indeed *should*, be 'conceptualized' as 'a behavioral vaccine'. In their frame, friendship is not just good for you. It serves as preventative medicine.

In a 1991 article in the journal *Psychosomatic Medicine*, using a study of 1409 adults between the ages of twenty and seventy in Buffalo in 1961, authors including Susan Bland and Warren Winkelstein reported on the relationship between social network and blood pressure: 'Higher total social network scores were associated with lower systolic and diastolic blood pressure in both males and females.'

But Sias and Bartoo's statement that friendship helps us live longer, and Bland and Winkelstein's claim concerning blood pressure, are still vague. By how much *precisely*?

The Alameda county study in the US, conducted through the 1970s and 80s, gathered material that allowed the authors of *Health and Ways of Living: The Alameda County Study* to be categorical. Analysing detailed interviews with 6928 people, Lisa Berkman and Lester Breslow looked at factors that affected the risk of death for residents between the ages of seventy and ninety-four and found that the statistic was simple: the men and women who did not have friends were 31 per cent more likely to die.

But what about all those citizens who are under seventy?

Some time later, sitting in the British Library with books banked up all around me, it seemed I'd found the answer. A three-volume 2028-page publication by Ruut Veenhoven, *World Database of Happiness: Correlates of Happiness*, presents 7838 findings from 603 studies in 69 nations 1911–1994.

Between its plain, worn covers I found an equation. Amidst pages full of arid tables – or 'mini-abstracts of the separate findings' – I located one set of letters and numbers that represents the precise health benefits of friendship: 'rs=+.87' – 'rs' stands for 'Spearman's Rank Correlation Coefficient', a method used to analyse the links between sets of data: according to this, '+1.00' is the top possible score, '–1.00' the worst. So '+.87' means friendship brings a very large amount of happiness indeed.

It is a delicious cheat to think that you can go into a coffee shop, think 'high correlate values' and, even with caffeine and cake in the equation, if you are with a friend still come out with a percentage decrease in your risk of death.

But rs = +.87? *'Behavioral vaccine'*? Can such sums and labels really be attached to the kinds of heady pleasures that come with friendship? Perhaps, after all, we're on the wrong track if we keep seeking still more precise calculations.

It's a bit formulaic, but maybe the journalist and novelist Mark Rutherford, writing in the late nineteenth century, had the right idea. He suggested: 'It should be a part of our private

ritual to devote a quarter of an hour every day to the enu-
meration of the good qualities of our friends.' Although, of
course, friends aren't necessarily good for each others' heath
in quite the same ways.

# 15

# Very Convenient

'Batman' and 'Robin' leap to mind as a duo. But Batman is very clearly the dominant partner.

When the cartoon first appeared in May 1939, Batman worked alone. But creator Bob Kane saw that his hero needed an equivalent of Sherlock Holmes's Dr Watson. The masked, caped crusader was a bit severe in his execution of justice. He killed mercilessly; he knew categorically the difference between right and wrong, and so acted without prior discussion or semblance of doubt. To allow the reader to become more engaged, Batman needed someone to bounce his ideas off.

Robin was introduced in September 1940. Sales soared.

Robin is physically smaller, boyish. While Batman wears authoritative black, Robin wears a perky red and yellow outfit. Robin's famous exclamations, such as 'Suffering swordfish!' and 'Holy nightmare, Batman!', are awed and admiring. His job is absolutely not to take the initiative. He is there to show up Batman's brilliance.

In Elizabethan England Francis Bacon, as a young and

ambitious courtier, had a clear-cut view of friendship. He changed his views later, but five of the ten essays in his 1597 collection are about friendship, and they are largely damning. In 'Of Honour and Reputation' he outlines the value of friends who can ask favours on your behalf and talk in a way that will enhance your reputation. 'Of Negotiating' details how to work someone to your own ends 'and so governe him'. 'Of Followers and Friends' analyses the qualities that make the ideal follower: 'costly' followers make your 'traine' longer but your 'wings' shorter, while 'factious' followers gripe about you behind your back. So both should be rejected in favour of 'ordinary' followers, who are both useful and easy to manage. Despite its title, in this last essay only once does a derivative of the word 'friend' figure: 'There is little Friendship in the world, and least of all between equals.'

When the poet, critic and socialite Edith Sitwell reviewed Dylan Thomas's first volume of verse badly in 1934, the vitriol flowed: he described her as 'a poisonous thing of a woman, lying, concealing, flipping, plagiarising'. By 1935 she had changed her mind and was reviewing his work enthusiastically; now he was sending her wheedling overtures.

But even as the twenty-one-year-old poet begged Sitwell for contacts, editorial guidance and help in publishing his new collection, he clearly couldn't bear the fact that she had such power over him. She wasn't a Dame yet, but she was very grand.

'Again, I won't try to thank you, because I couldn't enough, for your advice and help and encouragement,' he wrote in January 1936.

Sitwell agreed to meet him. In September that year he was already having to apologise for failing to turn up: 'I was dreadfully rude, not turning up and everything ... But I hope you aren't cross with me really ... Will you meet me again, in spite of things?' In August 1937 he was apologising again, for being slow with thanks for gifts she'd sent, including cash, which had been with him for some time. His excuses involved elaborate tales of having to spend twelve-hour shifts on trawlers off the coast of Cornwall to scrape a living and being 'awfully bad with letters' (it is worth noting that Paul Ferris's collection of the poet's letters runs to 982 pages). Thomas closes the letter: 'It's impossible for me to tell you how deeply I appreciate your kindness, and value your friendship.'

Clearly, the apologies didn't wash. Ten years later, in March 1946, he was writing again, purportedly to resurrect the friendship. But he spends much of this letter reminding her that he offended her. 'I think that, in some way, I offended you ... And I can't forgive myself that I can't remember what, exactly, the offence was.' His gushing declaration of innocence invites other readings. He must have noticed she'd cut off communication. Whether he knew he'd offended her or not, the letter seems designed to alienate her further.

If he had managed to pull it off, the friendship could have been very good for his career. The trouble was that it was proving very inconvenient for Thomas's ego. When push came to shove, he just couldn't bear what he felt to be grovelling.

Inequality in a relationship can cause surges of bitterness and rage.

For the English painter Walter Sickert, though, periods of grovelling were quite compatible with a vigorous ego. Matthew Sturgis's biography is affectionate. He presents Sickert as charismatic, but pretty hard-nosed when it came to friendship.

While he was at the Slade School of Fine Art in the early 1880s, he made friends with few if any of his fellow students. Instead he sought out the American artist James McNeill Whistler. He admired Whistler's work. Whistler was established. Sickert ran errands for him. He arranged his studio for him when a model was due to come for a sitting. At the drop of a hat, he'd transport 'the Master's' pictures to Paris. In return, he got to go on a Cornish painting tour with him. And here he took every opportunity to watch Whistler at work and learn his techniques.

The minute he became successful himself, Sickert dropped the older man and set his sights on becoming friends with Edgar Degas. While he was on his honeymoon in Dieppe in 1885, he learned that the French Impressionist was staying nearby. Romance went out of the window. His focus turned to Degas. And his determination to impress him paid off. Back in Paris, Degas introduced him to various salons. As a direct result, Sickert made a gratifying number of contacts and sales.

We like to think that this kind of ruthlessness will come back to bite the perpetrator. But it doesn't tend to. Their own mindset keeps them safe.

Towards the end of his life, when Sickert was in financial trouble, some friends including Henry Tonks clubbed together to bail him out. Sickert's response was to confess that he was 'rather surprised not to feel more shame at being caught guilty of some mismanagement'. But he concluded: 'It is evident, however, that the friends whose names I have on your list confirm me in my opinion that they must all be convinced of a measure of approbation of my painting and my teaching.'

The playwright Bertolt Brecht was similarly light-hearted about taking what he could from friends. He too thought that his talent justified his behaviour. Even writers who rise to his defence, such as James K. Lyon in *Bertolt Brecht in America*, can't avoid the way he serially used his friends.

While Brecht was in America during 1941–7, he befriended the actor Peter Lorre. 'In his efforts to use Lorre, Brecht never misused or abused him,' protests Lyon, and goes on to reveal that Brecht largely ignored the actor's own literary ambitions while squeezing him for film-world contacts. Lorre got Brecht three days with the screenwriter Ernest Pascal; he arranged financial backing for him. But because Lorre's soliciting on Brecht's behalf didn't amount to a film, Lyon seems to think this somehow exculpates Brecht. The writer repeatedly borrowed money from Lorre; he got Lorre to cover the cost of flying his pregnant mistress over so that the baby could be delivered in the States. The playwright wanted Lorre to go back to Germany with him, as a high-profile draw for Brecht's new ensemble. By 1950, Lorre would have nothing to do with him.

Describing the screenwriter Ferdinand Reyher as 'perhaps one of the best male friends in [Brecht's] lifetime', Lyon tells how their attempt at a collaborative adaptation of Brecht's

*Galileo* faltered to the extent that Reyher was writing in his diary: 'Something demoralizing in this ... A cheap view of one; a subconscious wish to make my work on *Galileo* unimportant, even unnecessary ... Never or rarely credits a line ... Too bad; I can be had so cheaply.' Lyon's take on this is: 'Because he possessed a stronger personality, a greater conviction of his own genius, and a surer sense of purpose than Reyher, Brecht's actions occasionally hurt this sensitive American.'

But while Lorre and Reyher may have been genuinely drawn to Brecht, they were trying to use him too. It's just that they weren't such effective manipulators. Nor had it been only Sickert who benefited from his relationship with Whistler. It boosted Whistler's image to have a disciple who happily called him 'Master'. When Sickert moved on, Whistler had to find a new minion to do those boring chores for free.

Some ulterior motives are harder to condone than others, certainly. But everyone has their reasons when they seek someone out as their friend. Maybe you are feeling depressed, and the person you target seems always to be smiling. Maybe your new neighbour has had builders in redoing her kitchen and you have been thinking about redoing yours, so as her builders are finishing you invite yourself in for a cup of tea. It doesn't necessarily undermine the whole friendship if there is a degree of convenience. Apart from anything else, a friendship can start with one feel to it, then change.

At first glance, the writer Wilkie Collins's friendship with Charles Dickens looks *too* convenient. The younger novelist stood to gain so much from Dickens. He was relaxed about taking his help from the outset.

Dickens counselled Collins on publication arrangements; he 'listened to Collins' stories', says Dickens's biographer Peter Ackroyd, 'and then endeavoured to correct or advise the younger man'. But Collins was relaxed about the help he was receiving only as long as it stayed private – he didn't want other people to know. '"Keep all this a secret," he wrote to his mother, "... for if my good-natured friends knew that I had been reading my idea to Dickens – they would be sure to say when the book was published, that I got all the good things in it from him."'

For years, Collins gained from the unequal friendship. Dickens didn't only give him advice and editing suggestions, he gave him paid work as a contributor of articles and short stories to his periodicals *All the Year Round* and *Household Words*. And the novel that made Collins' name, *The Woman in White*, was first serialised in *Household Words*.

Their relationship altered after the success of *The Woman in White*. In 1868, a story Dickens and Collins had collaborated on, 'No Thoroughfare', was dramatised, and the production at the Adelphi Theatre was reviewed in words that put Dickens and Collins on a par. A critic wrote in *The Mask*: 'Charles Dickens and Wilkie Collins have made their dramatic hit at last!' Dickens had not managed a 'hit' on his own. His collaboration with Collins had '"money" draw', as *The Mask* put it. It ran for more than 150 performances. Collins subsequently turned down a request from Dickens to come back to work on *All the Year Round*. It was clearly good for him to flex his muscles like this. And the men remained friends. But the relationship was on a new footing: each now stood to benefit from the other.

For the American poets Elizabeth Bishop and Marianne Moore, as David Kalstone shows in *Becoming a Poet*, it was a bit more complicated. Their influence on each other was evident in their published work. Critics were always commenting on it, pointing to this or that textual proof of their symbiotic relationship. It was worse for the younger poet, Bishop (born in 1911), who was inevitably treated as having arrived on Moore's coat-tails. What is striking is that this aspect of their relationship remained a subject of discussion between the two women. Once, when their names had been paired yet again, this time in a French magazine, Bishop wrote to Moore defensively that, yes, while she was at college Moore's poetry had 'opened up my eyes to the possibility of the subject-matter I could use', but really that was all: 'Can't they *see* how different [my poetry] is? But they can't, apparently.'

Bishop maintained a courteous, even complaisant tone with Moore while expressing her irritation. Moore managed to respond with amusement and tact. 'I can't see that I could have "opened your eyes" to subject matter, ever, or anything else,' she wrote. 'I roam about in carnivorous protest at the very thought of unimaginative analyses.'

Moore insisted that they call each other 'Miss' for the first two years of their friendship. Bishop entitled her memoir of Moore, equivocally, *Efforts of Affection*. One of Bishop's New York friends thought that her poem 'Invitation to Miss Marianne Moore' was simply 'mean'. 'Mean' does seem a bit excessive. The 'invitation' is to someone with a broad black hat who has a 'slight censorious frown'. And there's nothing in the poem much worse than that. Moore liked the poem. It triggered a memory for her of the women's first meeting in 1934, when Bishop turned up at Vassar as an undergraduate, with a 'seal-enriched jacket and white gloves and pearl earrings' and a list of questions interesting enough to keep their friendship going until Bishop's death in 1979.

Maybe a friendship of convenience can have more than the obvious rewards, after all.

# 16

# Bullies

Everyone's had one (hopefully in their distant past): the 'friend' who bullies. They loom large and terrifying, especially when we're young.

One summer holiday when I was quite small, I was signed up for a play scheme in Reading. Only about twenty children attended. The wire fence around the playground was high. From her seat in a tree behind a piece of play equipment, Marie ruled. It felt as though every minute of the day centred on what cruelties she would force on whom. We waited in awe, because the only reason for the torture was that she desired it.

There was no point telling. Marie used to have a hole in her heart. She was older than us but all the adults around her treated her delicately because the condition and then the operation to fix it had been life-threatening. She had a scar that was so long you could see the top of it at her shirt neckline. As far as the staff were concerned, she was not capable of bullying.

Marie never did the dirty work herself. When other children

forged friendships, it was the new friends she'd manage to pitch against each other: perhaps she'd instruct a pair of friends to take turns punching each other in the stomach; or she might force one to pour another's crisps on the tarmac, stamp on them, then make the owner eat them.

But sometimes, there's no need for someone like Marie to call the shots. It is perfectly possible for friends to bully each other of their own volition. It can become the dynamic that drives the relationship.

In *The Simpsons*, Milhouse is Bart's best friend, and his stooge. Milhouse wears glasses and has allergies. Bart tells him to do stupid, dangerous things just so he can laugh at him. In episode after episode, Milhouse gets hit on Bart's behalf and has doors slammed in his face. But then in one, Bart makes a Faustian pact and sells his soul to Milhouse. He thinks Milhouse is the fool for giving him $5 in return for a bit of paper with 'BART SIMPSON'S SOUL' scrawled on it. But later, Bart's dog won't play with him, automatic doors refuse to open for him, and when he breathes on cold windows no condensation forms. Bart panics. That panic excites Milhouse. He will only sell Bart's soul back to him for $50.

Milhouse has always been the sap in their relationship. Now, with his friend's soul in his possession, he is transformed. Bart has to watch from the edge of the garden while Milhouse in his sandpit laughs maniacally as he makes his toy soldiers rip and trash Bart's soul.

One of the things that makes this episode so gripping is that we can't quite believe Milhouse is acting out of character like this. Bart will get his soul back, we know that. And then

Milhouse will have to return to being the one who's pushed around. His parents seem perpetually to be breaking up. Even his ancient grandma terrorises him. Milhouse needs Bart, desperately.

In Margaret Atwood's novel *Cat's Eye*, set in Toronto in the 1960s, the nine-year-old narrator Elaine has to wait outside her friend Cordelia's bedroom while Cordelia, Grace and Carol talk. 'They're having a meeting. The meeting is about me. I am just not measuring up, although they are giving me every chance. I will have to do better. But better at what?'

Elaine does everything they tell her. At one point Cordelia digs a hole in her garden. They dress Elaine as Mary Queen of Scots and put her in the hole, which 'smells like toad burrows'. Boards are laid on top. 'The daylight air disappears, and there's the sound of dirt hitting the boards, shovelful after shovelful ... When I was put into the hole I knew it was a game; now I know it is not one. I feel sadness, a sense of betrayal. Then I feel darkness pressing down on me; then terror.'

They let her out eventually. But even after she's been buried alive by the other three, still Elaine does anything they say. Furthermore, there are so many gaps in her knowledge. She doesn't know what a 'cold-wave' is, she has never seen a 'coat-tree'. Her father has an eccentric job (he is an entomologist). 'If a man who catches fish is a fisher, what's a man who catches bugs?' asks Cordelia. 'A bugger.'

They make Elaine feel so bad about herself that at night she peels skin off her feet until they hurt so much it is hard to walk. She chews the ends of her hair, she gnaws her cuticles until they are 'oozing flesh' and later 'harden into rinds and scale off'. Because 'Cordelia is my friend. She likes me, she wants to help me, they all do. They are my friends, my girlfriends, my best friends. I have never had any before and I am terrified of losing them.'

But it is not only Elaine's lack of self-esteem that makes her easy prey: she admires Cordelia, just as Milhouse admires Bart. Milhouse is accomplished – he can speak Italian – but Bart can do tricks on his skateboard.

At that summer play scheme, I admired Marie. I knew that what she was doing was wrong, and that I was wrong for failing to stand up to her. Yet I found her power, and the coolness with which she wielded it, captivating. Sometimes she chose me as her ally. If I'd been asked to name my friends, as morally dubious as this may be, I would have put Marie on my list, probably quite near the top.

In *Tom Brown's Schooldays*, the Rugby School code says only sixth-formers can command new boys to fag for them. Flashman is a *fifth*-former. Tom and his friends rebel when they're asked to fag for him. '"Fa-a-a-ag," sounded along the passage from Flashman's study.' It is hard, it takes enormous willpower, but Tom and his friends stand firm. Behind their big oak door, 'They held their breaths, and heard whispering, of which they only made out Flashman's words, "I know the young brutes are in."'

Flashman and 'his party' begin to break the door down. It is strong, the bolts are good. 'Then came attacks on particular panels, one of which at last gave way to the repeated kicks; but it broke inwards, and the broken piece got jammed across, the door being lined with green-baize.' A sofa is rammed against the door as added reinforcement. 'Flashman & Co. retired, vowing vengeance in no mild terms.'

In fact, another fifth-former supports the youngsters. Flashman's behaviour is judged out of line by him too. Tom and his friends win this battle. The author's message to the reader is that as long as you and your mates stick together, bullies like Flashman *will* be defeated. Flashman is such a potent figure, though, that the poster for the 1951 film *Tom Brown's Schooldays* was dominated not by the eponymous hero but by Flashman, grim hatred on his face, hands round young Tom's neck.

But it is not often that children feel strong enough to stand up to bullies. Bullies divide and rule, they create their own laws. It's not unusual to be enthralled by their determination. The poet William Cowper wrote in 1785:

> I would not enter on my list of friends
> (Though graced with polished manners and fine sense,
> Yet wanting sensibility) the man
> Who needlessly sets foot upon a worm.

Yet it is often precisely those who will 'needlessly set foot upon a worm' who attract us.

# 17

# With Friends Like These

Kant was adamant: 'Place no weapon in the hands of a hot-headed friend who might be capable of sending us to the gallows in a moment of passion.'

In the film *My Best Friend's Wedding* (1997), Julia Roberts plays Julianne, a tough, beautiful restaurant critic. The plot turns on the main male character Michael's decision to marry someone other than her. Suddenly Julianne doesn't want to be his best friend any more, she wants to be the one wearing his engagement ring. And she decides the way to make this happen is to become bosom pals with his fiancée, Cameron Diaz's character Kimmy.

Julianne orchestrates intimate chats. Bubbly, naive Kimmy unwittingly hands over more and more ammunition. She admits that she's a terrible singer, for instance. Julianne grasps her opportunity: she forces her to go up on stage and do karaoke in front of Michael and a whole barful of strangers. Kimmy's voice is worse than Julianne could have hoped. Even she winces as Kimmy starts to destroy a Dusty Springfield tune, 'I Just Don't Know What to Do with

Myself'. With Kimmy, every note's a bum note. It's a slow, intense song. Kimmy continues to massacre it, each note dragging, transmogrifying into a cacophony of clashing bum notes. Michael and the other people in the bar are appalled, embarrassed – and suddenly rooting for her. Kimmy carries on so gamely that by the end of the scene she has won the hearts of everyone in the bar, and it is Julianne who feels ousted.

But not everyone is as lucky as Kimmy. The film depicts what might well become a new friendship. The bride-to-be is naive, certainly. But she harbours just enough suspicion. She sees in the nick of time what her maid-of-honour is up to.

In Malcolm Bradbury's novel *The History Man*, set in the claustrophobic campus university of Watermouth, sociology lecturer Howard Kirk is out for what he can get.

In bed with his lover Flora one night, engaged in post-coital departmental gossip Howard says: "'I'm quite attached to Henry. I've known him for ages. We were research students at Leeds together."

"'I've noticed your hostility towards him," says Flora, "I ought to have guessed you were friends.'"

Everyone's a cynic at Watermouth, except Henry Beamish, who determinedly thinks of Howard as his best mate. If you have known someone for a long time, you have probably grown to trust them. It seems the very blindness of Henry's trust provokes Howard. He can't believe Henry continues to invite him amiably to his local pub. Close, adored, Howard is better placed than any foe to destroy him. Howard sleeps with Henry's wife. He makes a fool of him at a departmental meeting. And he turns a blind eye when it looks as if Henry has attempted suicide. 'Most friendship is feigning,' wrote Shakespeare. And there are countless examples in fiction and real life to back this statement up.

Ernest Hemingway's stories about his friends are notoriously unreliable. It is not wise to be too credulous about any of them. Hemingway's resentment would grow particularly intense if a friend ventured to help him, as Scott Fitzgerald did, for example, when he stepped in to do some critical editing on Hemingway's novel *The Sun Also Rises*. But whether or not anything he says about Scott Fitzgerald is true, the place he gives Fitzgerald in his autobiography is interesting.

One chapter, entitled simply 'Scott Fitzgerald', starts as if it's going to be a eulogy. But soon Fitzgerald is portrayed as effeminate and embarrassing, gushing about Hemingway's greatness to the extent that Hemingway says even he can't listen any more. Yet this ridiculous drunk, with his worryingly 'delicate long-lipped Irish mouth', goes on to dominate yet another chapter, 'A Matter of Measurements', a phrase which refers to a single incident.

As Hemingway tells it, Fitzgerald asked if they could meet for lunch at Michaud's, the fashionable Paris restaurant. He was too nervous to say what was on his mind initially. Then at the end of the meal, with the cherry tart and a last carafe of wine, he announced: 'Zelda said that the way I was built I could never make any woman happy.' Then, Hemingway says, he led his friend out to 'the office', *le water*, where at his request Fitzgerald took out his penis to show him. Having judged that it looked fine, Hemingway nevertheless kept the conversation going: 'You look at yourself from above and you look foreshortened' – perhaps that was the problem. He advised Fitzgerald to go to the Louvre and look at statues there, then later to look at himself sideways on in the mirror at home.

Since Fitzgerald appeared unconvinced, Hemingway continued to advise: 'It is not basically a question of the size in repose,' he said. 'It is the size that it becomes. It is also a question of angle.' And he went on to make recommendations, including that Fitzgerald could use pillows, and to wonder about Zelda's motivation for making the statement that provoked the lunch with him in the first place, suggesting that she was trying to put Fitzgerald 'out of business'.

The story is outrageous, and horribly plausible. When someone is desperate, they are vulnerable, and if they mistakenly believe they are confiding in a person who is honourable, chances are, the person in a state of need is doomed. You tell intimate details to a therapist or analyst in the knowledge that confidentiality is part of their code of practice. With a friend, you may assume it is obvious that a confidence is private, whereas he or she may just think you have made a foolish revelation. Or your friend may promise to keep something secret and fully intend to do so, but in anger or in a moment of drunkenness simply fail. These are dramatic examples, though. I don't think many people would get as far as exposing themselves in *le water* before they realised something was awry.

But friends can put you down in subtle ways as well. Indeed, if the put-downs stay subtle, the perpetrator can keep on delivering them for longer.

In her autobiography Zora Neale Hurston has a chapter called 'Two Women in Particular'. The first woman is Hurston's bullying early employer, Fannie Hurst. The second is Ethel Waters, a singer Hurston developed a friendship with later on. Hurston says with pointed ambiguity that she chose Hurst and Waters from all her friends for this chapter because they 'force me to keep them well in mind'.

On first glance her relationship with Waters looks like a friendship between equals. But she opens with this strange statement: 'I am due to have this friendship with Ethel Waters, because I have worked for it.' It comes after Hurston's description of the indignities she suffered under Fannie Hurst, which included being sent scurrying through the snow to fetch Hurst's galoshes while all along Hurst was back at home, 'stretched out on the divan, all draped in a gorgeous American Beauty rose housecoat ... and eating candy'. Hurston seems to be suggesting that she was due her friendship with Waters because she'd done her time as the inferior 'friend' – now it was her turn on top.

She makes much of an exchange at a society dinner. When Waters revealed that she wanted to sing spirituals at Carnegie Hall, an Italian soprano seated nearby advised her not to, suggesting that she would only be unfavourably compared to Paul Robeson. 'I saw the hurt in Ethel's face and jumped in,' says Hurston. 'I objected that Ethel was not going to do any concertized version of spirituals. She had never rubbed any hair off of her head against any college walls and was not going to sing that way. She was going to sing those spirituals just the way her humble mother had sung them to her.'

Hurston's loud protest in defence of her friend came with

inbuilt put-downs: Waters was uneducated, she had a humble mother. As the chapter unfolds, Hurston draws attention again and again to Waters' lack of education. Details that she includes ostensibly to prove her love suggest instead that she rates Waters somewhere between quaint and ridiculous.

For instance, if Hurston was deep in thought Waters might say: 'What are you doing, Zora? Pasturing in your mind?' 'The similes and metaphors,' notes Hurston, 'just drip off her lips.'

As the saying goes, with friends like these, who needs enemies?

# 18

# My Best Frenemy

The more intense a friendship, the more badly it can go wrong.

Speculation was rife in 2009 when Gwyneth Paltrow wrote on her website about how a one-time friend had become her 'frenemy': 'venomous, dangerous and hell-bent on taking me down'. Who was this 'venomous' ex? Most newspapers settled on Winona Ryder.

When Paltrow and Ryder were first starting out, they shared a flat. Then in 1999, Paltrow won an Oscar for the part she played in *Shakespeare in Love*, a role Ryder was reportedly offered first. Paltrow said that at first she tried to rise above her friend's jealousy. But then, she admitted, when 'I heard that something unfortunate and humiliating had happened to this person' – journalists suggested she was referring to the time when Ryder was arrested for shoplifting – '... my reaction was deep relief and happiness'.

One of the reasons Paltrow's outburst got such wide coverage is that many people do feel this kind of grim delight at an ex- or even current friend's fall from grace, but few like to admit to it. It was scary and exciting to see this feeling – often referred to as 'Schadenfreude' – aired publicly. The *Shorter Oxford Dictionary* defines Schadenfreude as 'malicious joy in the misfortune of others'. Paltrow's relief and happiness surfaced specifically because someone she had liked and felt betrayed by had been humiliated.

Friendships are complicated. We would prefer to feel straightforwardly benevolent. We like to think of a good friend as someone who jogs along beside us. But that jogging may only feel good if you harbour a conviction that you could, if you wanted, sprint ahead. If that is your fellow jogger's secretly held conviction too, you might find they have suddenly run ahead and grabbed a piece of fortune while you weren't looking. And if they trip and hurt themselves in the process, you may well feel glad. They somehow cheated by doing well without your consent. It is right and proper that they should fall.

And if they don't fall, you might just get the urge to push them.

Nietzsche may be well known as a proponent of nihilism, but the political philosopher Ruth Abbey notes that he could be quite effusive about friendship. In 1872 he dedicated his first book, *The Birth of Tragedy*, to his friend the composer Richard Wagner. Ten years later, in *The Gay Science*, he described Wagner as 'Schopenhauerian' and his music as characterised by 'mystic pomp' and 'peculiar airs'. He concluded: 'Let us be loyal to Wagner in that which is true and original in him, and especially in this point, that we, his disciples, remain loyal to ourselves in that which is true and original in us. Let us allow him his intellectual humours and spasms, let us in fairness rather consider what strange nutriments and necessaries an art like his is entitled to, in order to be able to live and grow!'

Then, in 1888, he 'declared war' on Wagner, as he put it. In his essay *Nietzsche contra Wagner* and in the book *The Wagner Case* he explained why he thought the composer's music decadent and the man himself deplorable: 'The greatest event of my life took the form of a *recovery*. Wagner belongs only to my diseases.' He calls him

> the most *impolite* genius in the world ... Ah this old sorcerer! how he took us in! The first thing his art proffers us is a magnifying glass: one looks into it, one doesn't believe one's eyes – everything becomes big, *even Wagner becomes big* ... what a cunning rattlesnake! Its whole life long it rattled to us of 'devotion', of 'loyalty', of 'purity', with a commendation of chastity it withdrew from the *depraved* world! – And we believed it all.

The composer Georges Bizet is *far* superior, he says, and asks: 'Is Wagner a human being at all? Is he not rather a sickness? Everything he touches he makes sick – *he has made music sick*.' And speaking of 'the instability which he disguised as principles', Nietzsche declares that Wagner has sold out to the masses.

One of his main complaints was that Wagner was popular. The complex philosophical language aside, *Nietzsche contra Wagner* and *The Wagner Case* look like expressions of pique. But since the two men operated in very different fields, they could have a flagrant break-up and it didn't matter. They could just not see each other any more.

Jean Rhys's novels were deeply ambivalent about friendship. In *Good Morning, Midnight*, the protagonist Sasha Jensen feels herself a victim in need of protection in a cruel world. She describes the kind of friendship she experiences like this: 'These people fling themselves at me. Because I am uneasy and sad they all fling themselves at me larger than life. But I can put my arm up to avoid the impact and they slide gently to the ground.' Sometimes we may become frenemies but feel we have to carry on pretending otherwise. Rhys didn't like being emotionally close. Her relationship with the socialite Peggy Kirkaldy was particularly turbulent.

Kirkaldy was in a position to help Rhys. Everyone who was anyone in the literary world attended her parties. And this may have been a significant part of the problem. She befriended Rhys when her novel *After Leaving Mr Mackenzie* was published in 1930. Jean's letters were soon to 'My dear Peggy'. And within months they'd had their first argument. 'My dear Peggy,' Rhys wrote after one of them, 'You must try to forgive me. Spiteful was the wrong word – I didn't mean spiteful ... I meant there's a lot of Touché – En garde – Touché – En garde – about one's intercourse with most human beings.'

But there was more. Rhys's biographer Carole Angier says:

How could she not have quarrelled with Peggy Kirkaldy? For Peggy was like her too, but in all the wrong ways. She was highly strung, brittle, very volatile; if she could be overwhelmingly kind she could also be cuttingly cruel. She too had had a preferred sister, a critical mother, a failed marriage; she was socially more adept, but secretly just as insecure. Underneath Jean's shyness lay a great need to be the centre of attention: and underneath Peggy's cultivation of her *salon* lay the same need. 'When she came into a crowded room the lights went up like obedient servants,' says one of her closest friends. Jean would want the lights to go up for *her*, or the room to remain in restful darkness.

The close and complex relationship of Charles and Mary Lamb has been well documented. Brother and sister, and staunch friends too, their life together was nonetheless fraught with difficulties. They both suffered bouts of mental ill-health periodically. When in the early 1800s they began to throw weekly parties for friends on the London scene, things did not always run smoothly. The leading writers and actors of the day who they invited were flamboyant. Egos clashed regularly. But the inevitable flare-ups didn't stop people attending their salons. Indeed, they may well have been part of the appeal. In her biography of Mary, Kathy Watson points out that the siblings' lodgings at Mitre Court then at the Inner Temple were always ramshackle. But few if any people coming for their soirees were put off. Their friends had to 'scramble up several flights of stairs ... Henry Crabbe Robinson noticed the books, "the finest collection of shabby books I ever saw".' Hazlitt was a regular. 'Wit and good fellowship was the motto inscribed over the door,' he said.

Yet, the hosts' 'good fellowship' came with a sardonic edge. Mary Lamb noted after one Thursday evening, 'Kenny has one more child and a successful farce. Martin Burney is going to write a successful tragedy. Godwin has just published a new book, I wish it may be successful but I am sure it is very dull.' Charles Lamb summed up one of their evenings like this: 'Swipes exactly at nine, punch to commence at ten, with argument; difference of opinion expected to take place at about eleven; perfect unanimity with some haziness and dimness before 12.'

Part of friendship – the enjoyable part for some – is often, as Jean Rhys puts it, the En garde! Touché! element.

# 19

# I Want to Be Alone!

Friendship can make you feel smothered, controlled and obliged to conform.

Indeed, in his essay 'The Negative Effects of Informal Support Systems' (1990), the cognitive psychologist J. L. La Gaipa comes to the conclusion that overall, when you weigh up the pros and cons, friendship is best avoided completely. He argues that it is bad for you.

If someone suddenly becomes seriously ill, he says, a friend might arrive trying to help and actually cause distress by being 'strained and clumsy', handing out poorly conceived advice and judgements, talking *at* the invalid and failing to understand that he just wants to be listened to. And most of us have had this experience, when our own misfortune triggers, instead of sympathy, unstoppable tales of others' woe. With friends, it's possible to feel that our independence has been eroded. And this is the nub of it for La Gaipa. His big problem with friendship is that 'social ties' come at the expense of autonomy. In different ways, he says it again and again. 'Maintaining a reliable resource system often comes at a high price of jeopardy to personal integrity.'

It is indeed hard, sometimes, to see the benefits of friendship. But we do know that its absence can be devastating.

If children are socially isolated, they may never recover. In their paper 'The Development of Subjective Group Dynamics', Dominic Abrams and Adam Rutland show that developing a talent for friendship is critical during middle childhood (from about six to twelve). For, if a child can't ensure his or her social inclusion, he or she faces exclusion, which 'is known to have multiple negative effects including anger, depression, withdrawal, self-handicapping, lowered self-esteem, and impaired cognitive capacity'.

The man who is often referred to as the 'father of sociology', Émile Durkheim, famously said: 'A nation can be maintained if, between the state and the individual, there is interposed a whole series of secondary groups near enough to the individuals to attract them strongly in their sphere of action and drag them, in this way, into the general torrent of social life.' The social psychologist Erich Fromm wrote: 'Human beings are more afraid of being outcasts than even of dying.' He argued that union and solidarity with others is 'crucial to every society': the urge 'to share, to give, to sacrifice ... owes its strength to the specific conditions of human existence and the inherent need to overcome one's isolation by oneness with others'. It is in societies with the lowest social cohesion, Durkheim famously showed, that the suicide rates are highest.

But perhaps the most eloquent exploration of the despair that comes with friendlessness is to be found in Daniel Defoe's *Robinson Crusoe*.

Shipwrecked on a desert island, Crusoe lists the 'evils' of his situation, which total six. At the top of the list: 'I am cast upon a horrible desolate island.' Then, evils two and three: 'I am singl'd out and separated' and 'I am divided from Mankind, a Solitaire.' He positions these above the fact that he has neither clothes nor 'Means to resist any Violence of Man or Beast' – evils that are tempered in any case by the fact that he has seen no wild beasts or evidence of human habitation. But solitude as an evil won't go away. It appears again, in the sixth and final item on the list: 'I have no Soul to speak to, or relieve me.' Crusoe tries to find a 'good' to nullify it. He tells himself: 'But God wonderfully sent the Ship in near enough to the Shore, that I have gotten out so many necessary things as will either supply my Wants, or enable me to supply my self even as long as I live.' The novel poses the question: Is that enough?

For nearly two and a half decades Crusoe does survive, roasting turtles' eggs in the ashes of the fire, setting himself the challenge of making a chair and a table. Then in his twenty-fourth year of habitation, he sees a ship in distress – a ship that he assumes carries people like him. He has no physical wants, he has lived quite well. But when no survivor appears, he is overcome:

> I cannot explain by any possible Energy of Words, what a strange longing or hankering of Desires I felt in my Soul upon this Sight; breaking out sometimes thus: O that there had been but one or two; nay, or but one Soul sav'd out of this Ship, to have escap'd to me, that I might but have had one Companion, one Fellow-Creature to have

spoken to me, and to have convers'd with! In all the Time
of my solitary Life, I never felt so earnest, so strong a
Desire after the Society of my Fellow-Creatures or so
deep a Regret at the want of it.

He has been stripped of almost everything – and his deepest desire is for a companion.

'Such were these earnest Wishings, That but one Man had
been sav'd! *O that it had been but One!* I believe I repeated the
Words, *O that it had been but One!* A thousand Times'; and
Crusoe's need is so overwhelming that it becomes physical:
'and the Desires were so mov'd by it, that when I spoke the
Words, my Hands would clinch together, and my Fingers
press the Palms of my Hands, that if I had had any soft
Thing in my Hand, it wou'd have crusht it involuntarily; and
my Teeth in my Head wou'd strike together, and set against
one another so strong, that for some time I cou'd not part
them again.'

Crusoe risks his life to get out to the wreck, only to find
his feelings of loneliness intensified. He starts to fantasise
about how fate might bring someone to him. And his wish
is granted. Cannibals come to his island, and one of their
prisoners escapes, in Crusoe's direction! In the thick of the
action, the author gives his protagonist a pause for thought.
When Crusoe is watching someone running for his life, he
suddenly stops and questions the precise nature of his own
needs. He notes that he is 'call'd plainly by Providence to
save this poor Creature's Life'. But does he want a 'Servant',
a 'Companion', or an 'Assistant'?

Once saved, the 'Creature', Crusoe sees, is clearly in a

desperate, vulnerable state. Crusoe could easily take advantage. The fellow is so grateful that he kneels before him and puts Crusoe's foot upon his head. But even though he can't understand a word, Crusoe is moved just by hearing the man speak, 'for they were the first sound of a Man's Voice, that I had heard, *my own excepted*, for above Twenty Five Years'.

The escapee makes it clear he *wants* to serve Crusoe. And Crusoe does teach him to say 'Master', and sets out to 'civilise' him. But within three pages he is tired of the master–servant relationship and is calling him 'Man Friday', 'my New Companion'. They work together on the land; it is the 'pleasantest Year of all the Life I led in this Place'. Within another ten pages, he is calling him 'Friend'.

What had at first been cited as the primary evil – 'I am cast upon a horrible desolate island' – seems to have dropped off the list. The idea of escaping the island is nearly forgotten. Indeed, Crusoe becomes so content that the three years he and Man Friday spend together before they are rescued are so different in his mind from his preceding isolation that they should be 'left out of the Account' altogether, he says.

And here is perhaps a key issue. Unless we are out climbing on a spectacular mountain or it's a particularly brilliant autumn morning, we wouldn't sit around discussing the benefits of breathing the air. And so it is with friendship. Its absence is terrible, but after the initial thrill of its arrival we can sometimes take it for granted.

On 31 August 1998, the prime minister of Norway, Kjell Magne Bondevik, was diagnosed as suffering from a severe 'depressive reaction', and he published a press release announcing that he needed time off to recover. He and his doctors were clear that it was not the pressure of the job that had caused his breakdown. After a three-and-a-half-week break, he returned to office and governed till March 2000; he was re-elected in 2001, and continued to serve as prime minister until he stepped down in 2005. Bondevik's doctors concluded that the episode was due to strong feelings of loss and grief. Speaking on the radio, Bondevik was disarmingly frank about the trigger: 'Over a three-year period, three of my best friends, all of them, died of brain cancer, and grief is according to experts in the field very exhausting, more than I was aware of.' They weren't flesh and blood. Bondevik didn't expect to feel so much grief, and hadn't allowed for it.

Friendship is confusing.

Open the *Shorter Oxford English Dictionary*, and you'll find under 'friend': '1. One joined to another in mutual benevolence and intimacy'. Then, applied loosely, 'an acquaintance', 'a stranger whom one comes across or has occasion to mention again'. The entry goes on to say that the word 'friend' is not ordinarily used of lovers or relatives but can apply to 'a kinsman or near relation'. The *OED*'s list of options for the definition of 'friend' continues for another four inches. The word covers such a wide variety of relationships in our lives.

But we need them all.

La Gaipa seems irritated to have to admit, fleetingly, at the end of his essay: 'Autonomy is not the absence of dependency. Moreover, autonomy is not necessarily a positive state of being.' Even the Lone Ranger needs a friend.

The Lone Ranger's back-story differs slightly if you look at the early 1930s radio series as compared to the subsequent television series or the spin-off comics and novels. But the main myth is always the same. On the pioneer trail, decent people are terrified of cattle thieves and outlaws. One man rises to the challenge: the Lone Ranger. He wears a mask, uses silver bullets, and cries 'Hi-yo Silver! Away!' as he gallops off on his white stallion to do more good deeds. But actually he's not 'lone' at all. He is always accompanied by Tonto, his 'faithful companion'. Tonto is capable enough. He met the Lone Ranger in the first instance when he nursed him back to health after bandits had left him for dead. Tonto can even manage the odd rescue himself. But he doesn't say much. In a typical exchange, the Lone Ranger might explain to him some wrongdoings that have taken place, then spot more potential victims and declare: 'Come on Tonto, we'd better warn them!' Most likely, Tonto will just nod earnestly, then together they'll ride purposefully out of shot.

He is always at the Lone Ranger's side. The Lone Ranger can't function without him. And Tonto addresses the Lone Ranger as 'Ke-mo sah-be' ('Trusty friend').

One thing that struck me about La Gaipa's description of the ill person being visited by a 'strained and clumsy' friend is that few of us would prefer to have no one visit at all when we're ill. With or without clumsiness, a friend arrives with intent to help. And that intent is welcome. Furthermore, if they go on too much about themselves, you can try a tactful reminder that you're a bit tired, and if that doesn't work you can always just ask them to stop. If they're visiting during a period of recuperation yet appear to expect you to make a cup of tea, you can point them to the kettle. A good friend won't mind – indeed, he or she may well be glad that you have been straightforward.

I didn't put down La Gaipa's essay feeling too bogged down by all the negatives, but rather that actually he hadn't managed to find so many, and certainly none that a bit of straight talking couldn't resolve.

When Abbot Aelred was writing about why friendship was so important to him, in the end he simply quoted Genesis: 'It is not good for man to be alone.'

# 20

# Pen Pals

Email correspondence has largely replaced letter-writing, which in many ways is sad, because writing a letter to a friend is a very different form of communication. Letters involve forethought. They take a bit of time.

Pressing 'Send' on an angry email before you quite mean to, is all too easy. 'Flaming' doesn't happen with a letter. It can be screwed up and written again, or never sent at all, as we come to realise that catharsis has been achieved in the writing of it.

In a letter to Neal Cassady dated 26 August 1947, Jack Kerouac opens with a description of the appeal of letter-writing: 'But see this – the first time at a typewriter for weeks, and you being an old typist, and you know the feeling you get, just writing anything that comes to your head, "scribblings-away", etc. You just like to see the words come out on the page, small and neat and all in straight lines, and whatever you say almost doesn't matter.'

Although letters are not fault-free, by any means. Letter-writing can be very narcissistic, for instance. When you're young, it is often about finding a sense of yourself. The friend who is being addressed can fade from mind. You may grow more aware of the image of yourself you are portraying – what kind of light do the activities and emotions I'm describing shed on *me*? And some fervent letter-writers keep more than half an eye on posterity.

Jack Kerouac wrote obsessively to other Beat generation writers. His life was his material, so letters were a sound investment. Large tracts of *On the Road* came practically verbatim from letters he'd written to friends. And even as he worked so hard to generate a reputation for himself as wild, he filed the letters he received back with incredible care. 'In June 1949, for example,' says Ann Charters in the introduction to a collection of his letters, 'when John Clellon Holmes asked him for information about Allen Ginsberg, whom Holmes wanted to make the central character in his novel-in-progress *Go*, Kerouac replied that he would "prepare a special brief on A.G. ... One thing I have is several score letters from him full of information at various points in his life."'

If someone writes lots of drafts, it's not necessarily posterity they're worried about. The playwright Tennessee Williams was close friends with the Russian émigrée, actress and socialite Maria St Just for more than three decades. Yet St Just's collection of his letters to her shows that even after they had been corresponding for twelve years, he still wrote drafts first. She found some in his house while she was helping sort through his things after his death. And it is sometimes sad to compare the drafts with the versions that he posted – in some instances the drafts were clearer indicators of how he really felt.

One is dated 'Xmas day, 1960'. In it Williams said: 'I have over-played my hand lately and it wound up with the month of bleeding and then an attack of pneumonia which put me in Miami hospital, what sounded like the terminal ward, with groans, coughs, gasping, nuns saying prayers at dark hours and the Reaper whisking someone out on a rolling table.' In another draft of the same letter, he tried to make the news more upbeat, opening: 'On top of the internal bleeding, I now have a touch [of] pneumonia! A witchdoctor just shot me full of Demerol to which I am allergic, it nearly drives me wild. He didn't tell me what it was till after the injection. Tomorrow I go to Mercy Hospital. Oh, mercy!' But it seems even this draft revealed too much. Maria didn't receive a final version at all.

Maria St Just was the model for Maggie in *Cat on a Hot Tin Roof*, played so memorably by Elizabeth Taylor in the 1958 film version as vain, over-sexed and greedy. Maria's own editorial notes in *Five o'Clock Angel: Letters of Tennessee Williams to Maria St Just* don't paint her as a particularly compassionate person. Perhaps Williams felt that if he revealed too much torment, she would just have dropped him. In his 10 August 1960 letter, one that he posted, his closing comment is: 'Write me another of your wildly amusing letters.' Maria took him out of himself. Perhaps it was precisely the distance that letter-writing affords that enabled him to keep what he valued most about their friendship. Maria cheered him up.

Many women were cheered enormously by the formation of the Cooperative Correspondence Club (the CCC) in the 1930s. In her book *Can Any Mother Help Me?*, Jenna Bailey describes how in the Britain of that time, women habitually moved to new places for their husband's work when they married, and often, in those days before the Pill, fell pregnant by accident. Caught out, removed from friends and extended family, they could feel desperate.

'I get so down and depressed after the children are in bed and I am alone in the house,' wrote a mother who called herself 'Ubique' in the letter to *Nursery World*'s letters page in 1935 that started it all. 'I sew, read and write stories galore, but in spite of good resolutions, and the engaging company of cat and dog, I do brood, and "dig the dead".' A woman who called herself 'Sympathiser' sent this reply to the magazine: 'I am indeed sorry for "Ubique" . . . I wonder if "Ubique" would care to correspond with readers. I should be very pleased to exchange letters with her, and this would give her fresh thoughts and would, I should think, cheer her up. Perhaps she will tell me if she cares for this idea.'

Ubique did care for the idea. Soon, she and Sympathiser and a growing number of other women were writing directly to one other. Membership of their CCC snowballed. Hundreds of strangers who felt they were in the same boat were suddenly in contact with each other, exchanging tips and confidences. 'Mother of Three' noted briskly: 'Letters are a wonderful help when one is lonely.'

Letters give friendship a chance to grow. They involve a more leisurely, intimate revealing of oneself. If the recipient likes what is revealed, the friendship deepens. Letters offer opportunities for fine-tuning, for carving out a space for your personality. And if you are shy in company, letters can be liberating. Susan Chitty says in her biography of Gwen John that the artist found relationships difficult. 'I don't pretend to know anybody well,' John wrote. 'People are like shadows to me and I am like a shadow.' Letters for her are 'the only chance I have, for in talking, shyness and timidity distort the meaning of my words in people's ears'.

Kerouac clearly felt pretty intimidated by Neal Cassady and Allen Ginsberg, in the flesh. With letters he could assert himself – give his opinions, relax. As he wrote to Cassady in 1947, 'The person you're talking to in the letter is like a person sitting right nearby to whom you make all kinds of silly little remarks and noises.'

In *Testament of Friendship* Vera Brittain shows that letters were more than a poor second when she and her friend Winifred Holtby were apart. They added a whole new dimension. Brittain describes Holtby as 'a gay, grateful, infinitely responsive letter-writer, whose correspondence suggested a long, vivid, unbroken conversation. "Why is it I always have to sit down and answer your letters at once?" I asked her that summer. "Is it because of that irresistible conversational quality, or because I have so much to say to you that five minutes after I have written I could always sit down and write another letter, just as long?"'

Even if some people who sit down to write a letter do have an eye on posterity, is that so bad?

The Italian Abbé Galiani wrote playfully to the fashionable blue-stocking Louise d'Épinay on 5 June 1773:

You must well know, *ma belle dame,* that after we're both dead, our correspondence will be printed. What a pleasure for us! How diverting! For this reason I'm working as hard as possible to make my letters predominate over yours, and begin to flatter myself that I'm succeeding. Readers will notice, in yours, a somewhat monotonous emphasis on friendship. Always tender, always affectionate, always caressing, ever applauding. Mine, on the contrary, will display a charming diversity: at times abusive, at times sarcastic; I can be in a wretched humour, and I may even begin in one tone and end in another, and I'm invariably in good health ... certainly, your four most recent letters – what a pitiful, lamentable impression they will make in the collection! So: admire my adroitness even in my occasional scoldings; and keep well, if only for the success of our future anthology.

In her reply, dated 26 June 1773, she says: 'You are unbearable, reminding me that our correspondence will be published after we've gone. I was aware of that, but had forgotten ... Besides, my dear abbé, you know that rests [in music] are one of the rules of beauty; and since my letters will be alternated with yours, the whole will make a sublime collection.' Thoughts of others' responses to their relationship reminded her of its value. 'Everything that comes from you is precious to me, you may be sure of that,' she wrote. 'History will doubtless speak of our friendship, since it speaks of men's misfortunes: is there any greater misfortune than being separated from those one loves?'

Indeed, letters can offer more consolation than do face-to-face meetings.

Jane Carlyle and her husband the essayist Thomas Carlyle led a busy social life, so when her mother died she had plenty of people around her to offer support. Her friend the novelist Geraldine Jewsbury saw that Jane was in such a state of grief that she could not absorb any of the sympathy friends offered. In a letter of condolence in May 1842 she said plainly that she knew she couldn't make her feel better, but she too had lost a parent and had been devastated. 'I know full well what it is to cease to see the necessity of struggling,' she wrote. 'Why, indeed, must we go on struggling, rising up early and late and taking rest? ... it is not well that you feel this so constantly that it swallows up all other feelings ... There is a strength in life to make us endure it ... I am astonished sometimes to find that I am glad to be alive. And this is a feeling that will spring up in your heart after a while, crushed and dead as it seems now.'

As a compassionate friend, Geraldine was hoping that Jane would come back to her letter and be able to gain some peace of mind from it later.

# 21

# Hot Gossip

Soap operas appeal because they are instalments of gossip about characters you get to know so well they feel like your own neighbours. There were three episodes of *Brookside* a week in the 1990s, four of *EastEnders* in 2001. There are omnibuses, Christmas specials. Viewers become embedded in the characters' lives.

Soap operas are very different from feature films. One of the key appeals of most mainstream movies is that the characters get into trouble, and then out again. There is resolution. In soap operas you know things will only keep getting worse, and you rub your hands at the prospect. Soap operas are the morally acceptable face of Schadenfreude. The characters are our friends, but not close friends. They provide glorious sagas that we can salaciously dissect and ponder on.

Christine Geraghty notes in *Women and Soap Opera* that soaps are also striking for the way they celebrate community. 'As Albert Tatlock puts it in a 1961 episode of

*Coronation Street*: "more sharing and less grabbing ... that's what happens when you bring folks together" or as Arthur Fowler remarked, over twenty years later, in *EastEnders*, "we haven't got much round here but we try and help each other out".'

But the kind of gossip that soaps thrive on has a bad image. It's not nice if you catch yourself being pleased to hear something awful about real people who you really like. Significantly, there are some fairly ugly synonyms for 'gossip' – 'chinwag', 'scuttlebutt'. Moreover, gossip is traditionally thought of as the preserve of women. Curlers held tight in her headscarf and a cigarette hanging out of the side of her mouth, *Coronation Street*'s Hilda Ogden is a classic picture of a gossip. Bet Lynch is another. If barmaid Bet's arms are not folded under her bosom it's only because they are propped on the bar as she shares or absorbs a fresh piece of jaw-dropping news.

Yet the idea that there is a gender gap when it comes to gossip does not bear scrutiny.

In 1769 Abbé Galiani was sacked as representative of the Neapolitan embassy in Paris and sent back home for – amongst other misdemeanours – indulging in gossip. From his exile in Italy he chose Mme d'Épinay as one of his Paris correspondents because she was a distinguished member of the intellectual society he had left behind and because she shared with him a love of gossip. In her first letter, on 9 September that year, she said: 'Tell me in general what direction you would like our correspondence to take, and you will be served with all the zeal that affectionate friendship can display.' The next year, he was keen for news of how his new book *Dialogues on the Grain Trade* was being received in the French capital. And he was particularly interested in receiving anecdotes that were at least slightly naughty. D'Épinay wrote back, describing daily life in her household, 'our fat little curé walking about farting, having overeaten'.

On 25 April 1771, she sent him news of their mutual acquaintance the Marquis de Croismare, who

> had a severe onset of haemorrhoids last week, and was ordered to bathe his behind in milk. If you could have seen the trouble he had getting into the milk! There was never anything like it. First he filled the biggest earthenware crock he could find, and settled himself therein. He was wearing an elegant new redingote. Suddenly the crock broke, and the marquis was inundated. He didn't give up. He took his barber's basin and filled that with milk; but he miscalculated the space needed to accommodate his behind; the milk flew up, splashing everything, including his face and his nightcap – everything except his rear.

Evelyn Waugh maintained a close friendship for fifteen years with Ann Fleming, who was married to the writer Ian Fleming. Waugh was an inveterate gossip. He filled his letters to Ann with largely delightful guff, gas, yakketyyak and causerie that only just stayed the right side of calumny.

By 1957 Waugh had settled into the habit of using his ear trumpet to intimidate people, showing them just how dull they were simply by putting it down while they were talking. 'The end of the ear-trumpet came,' says Waugh's biographer Christopher Sykes, 'when Evelyn attempted to use it as an offensive weapon at a lunch-party in Ann's house. One of the guests asked Evelyn a question. Evelyn turned his ear-trumpet to Ann saying: "Would you repeat what has just been said?" For reply Ann gave the ear-trumpet a bang with a spoon.'

Moving in the same circles, she and Waugh both knew Cyril Connolly. On 7 April 1953 Waugh wrote:

At present I gather [Connolly] is under the illusion that he is the reincarnation of Coleridge. I heard a good old story of him last week. Someone met him about six months ago and he, Cyril, said: 'People think I have no sense of loyalty & honour. I admit that now and then poverty has obliged me to do things I regret. But I have some standards of decency. I was offered a large sum of money by a Sunday newspaper to write personal revelations of two friends who had become notorious. One with a wife & children in this country. Of course I refused with disgust. That at least I could not sink to.'

'This', noted Waugh, 'was a fortnight before the appearance of the Burgess–Maclean articles' – the revelatory pieces that Connolly did in fact publish in the *Sunday Times* on the Cambridge spy ring.

The philosopher and statesman Cicero was a terrible gossip. With his old friend Atticus, whom he had met when he was a teenager and to whom he remained close all his life, he couldn't help himself.

When a man in female attire managed to sneak into a strictly women-only sacred festival being held at the official residence of Julius Caesar, only to be found out when, lost in the corridors, he asked for directions in a ringing bass voice, Cicero wrote to Atticus: 'I imagine you have heard that P. Clodius, the son of Appius, was caught dressed up as a woman in C. Caesar's house at the national sacrifice and that he owed his escape alive to the hands of a servant girl – a spectacular scandal. I am sure you will be deeply distressed!' 'It was, in fact,' says Cicero's biographer Anthony Everitt, 'as Cicero knew, a serious business. Religious ritual accompanied almost every public event. It was an accepted condition of public life and to breach it was unforgivable. Clodius would almost certainly face grave charges.'

Clodius had put himself in serious danger. By reporting the incident to Atticus, Cicero had put himself in danger too. It bordered on reckless to indulge in gossip in Ancient Rome, where ambitious 'respectable' men could hire assassins and not be judged particularly harshly by their peers for doing so.

Life is a scary business. Gossip helps us cope.

To the end of his life, Waugh maintained his gossipy tone with Ann Fleming. 'They all say that Sir Anthony [Eden] is dying. Clarissa will be left penniless and friendless in the Antipodes,' he wrote in January 1957. 'Also said to be dying is Ronnie Knox. I went to visit him at a hospital in the City Road, E.C.1, which had without compromise painted across the front in enormous letters *St Mark's Hospital for Diseases of the Rectum.*'

When malicious gossip becomes the driving force of a relationship, that is the time to walk away. But I wouldn't forgo 'juicy' gossip, or even hot gossip, for anything.

# 22

# Friends with Balls

Four of us had been having coffee most Saturdays, for three years. We had done things like dinner together, movies. During a rounders game one bank holiday, which went on over an afternoon with a break for a picnic, demon hits sparked reminiscences of school sports triumphs. Friends we had in common came to light. We learned surprising new facts about each other's childhoods, careers, politics, shopping habits. All because of a rubber ball.

Lots of activities with friends centre on balls.

For rounders you just need a bat, a ball, a bit of space and some people. You can chuck a racket and squash ball in your kitbag and dash up to the sports centre for a fun, invigorating hour with a mate. Or maybe you'll grab your tennis balls and racket and pop up to the park for a quick run-around. A ball as a starting point is beautifully simple.

Although there *is* a ball hierarchy.

Out on the links, as golfers in twos and threes wheel their putters and long irons past bunkers towards the green, they can have long, intimate conversations. Friends can pursue business deals. In the seventeenth century, it took a day for an artisan to make just three or four golf balls, all of which could be lost in thickets in a matter of minutes during play. In most places where golf developed, the sheer expense of the balls kept the game, and the friendships that came with it, elitist for two hundred years.

Previously, the discovery in the fifteenth century that the wood of the hornbeam tree was unusually resistant to hard knocks, and was cheap, had made many new ball games widely available. With hornbeam and a sharp blade, good strong skittles were possible too. Bowling evolved and friends everywhere could play it. Today, bars and clubs in rich and poor districts alike have pool tables. You just have to put a couple of coins in the slot. There is usually a jukebox so you can choose your atmosphere too. Yet, for a long time, only the wealthy played billiards, because although the balls could be made quite economically from hornbeam, the game also required long, fine cues and hefty tables lined with felt.

Clearly, though, the amount of fun friends can have with a ball doesn't necessarily go up incrementally with the acquisition of expensive equipment. Of all the games that we've laid on for my children's birthdays, one called 'snowballs' has worked the best. You wrap as many scrunched-up bits of newspaper in white tissue as you can bear, securing each with Sellotape. Put them in two boxes at either end of the room. And then, ten minutes before home time you yell: 'Snowballs!'

'But what are the *rules*?' I'd asked when my friend first told me about the game.

'None.'

Kids chuck wildly. Allegiances shift. It's girls against boys one minute, children against adults the next. The sofa's safe haven – then nowhere is. Adults and children alike are ducking, yelling, aiming, stockpiling, scrabbling about on the floor, behind chairs, under tables for more snowballs.

Football is the same. It's rowdily inclusive. On pretty much any village green or campsite field, in the scruffiest park, you only need to throw down a few coats and bags and you've got goalposts. It takes just a few sliding tackles and free kicks for strangers to become friends.

And balls do seem to hold a particularly important place in men's friendships. My partner belongs to a cricket team that every year does a tour round the tip of Cornwall. Since these games with a handful of local teams, spread over six days, are played on idyllic grounds with views of the sea and include cricket teas featuring six-egg Victoria sponges and scones with clotted cream, many of the players' families go too. With increasing regularity, as my son has grown older and joined the team, I've trotted along to the sidelines to watch.

It's sometimes jokingly said that sport gives men an excuse to hug, but it does appear to be the case. A spectacular wicket can send half a dozen otherwise diffident men into each other's arms remarkably quickly. And a ball game gives the time and excuse for blustery reserve to dissolve. It even gives them a subject to start them off.

Tennis proved an important part of one of Abraham Verghese's friendships. He describes his experience in his book *The Tennis Partner: The Story of a Friendship*. When Verghese, a doctor, relocated to a hospital in El Paso in Texas in the 1980s, he instinctively liked the young intern he met there, David Smith. But their friendship only really got going when it emerged that Verghese liked tennis and Smith was very good at it. With Smith sometimes coaching him, they began to play regularly. Smith was a recovering cocaine addict, and Verghese's marriage was in trouble: tennis allowed the two men to get close and help each other. Towards the end of the book, Verghese remembers his friend: 'I hear the squeak of his sneakers, and watch him plant his front foot at just the right distance from the oncoming ball. I see the grace of that pose, just before he leans into the ball, the racket held high and laid back, his arm straight, his lips slightly parted, his left hand gently cupping the throat of the racket.'

Such intimate thoughts are safe if they come to the surface while two men are playing a ball game.

# 23

# Bromance

Blokes, chaps and gentlemen have friendships involving cool distance and action. Whether they are actually playing cricket, squash, golf or football, or going to watch professional games of baseball, rugby, ice hockey, male friends do hearty slaps on the back, beefy hugs and bawdy jokes. That's in the cliché.

And the cliché has given rise to some great entertainment. Eric Morecambe and Ernie Wise worked as a comedy duo for forty years. The basic premise of their television series *The Morecambe and Wise Show*, which ran from 1961 to 1983, is that Eric and Ernie are long-standing, extremely close friends, who share not only a flat but even a bed. There is not the remotest suggestion that they are gay. Indeed, in their striped or paisley pyjamas, Ernie reading a book, Eric eating wine gums or smoking his pipe, the fact that they sleep in a double bed is only a sign of how close, platonically, they are. In the show, as they perform sketches and talk to guests, they rarely touch, unless it is for Ernie to slap Eric's shoulders or cheeks. A vast proportion of the humour stems from the fact that Eric ribs Ernie all the time. He is constantly referring to Ernie's 'short, fat, hairy legs', accusing him of being mean with money and commenting on his friend's alleged toupee in amazement – 'You can't see the join!'

Theirs is not by any means the only fictional male friendship to be characterised by a semblance of disregard. Sir Arthur Conan Doyle's detective Sherlock Holmes is also serially rude to his sidekick, Dr Watson. Yet it's accepted that their friendship, which goes back years, is inextricably close. When they were younger, they too shared a bachelor pad – although it was not neat and spare, like Eric and Ernie's. In the short story 'The Musgrave Ritual', Conan Doyle presents another aspect of the cliché of male friendships.

When they lived together, says Watson, Holmes kept 'his cigars in the coal-scuttle, his tobacco in the toe end of a Persian slipper, and his unanswered correspondence transfixed by a jack-knife into the very centre of his wooden mantelpiece'. And Watson found this messiness infuriating. 'I have always held ... that pistol practice should distinctly be an open-air pastime; and when Holmes in one of his queer humours would sit in an armchair, with his hair-trigger and a hundred Boxer cartridges, and proceed to adorn the opposite wall with a patriotic V.R. done in bullet-pocks, I felt strongly that neither the atmosphere nor the appearance of our room was improved by it.'

But what infuriates Watson most of all is that it is unmanly of him to mind. He is desperate to assure the reader that he himself is of 'a natural Bohemianism of disposition'. It's just that Holmes takes his Bohemianism too far. When Watson finally screws up the courage to confront his friend about 'his personal habits', Holmes says that he will either clear up, or tell him about one of his early cases – which would Watson prefer? And of course, faced with this choice, Watson, being Holmes's self-elected chronicler, chooses to hear the story.

Their flat stays in a state of macho disarray.

In these kinds of friendships, the idea that a man should pay much, if any, attention to possessions and their upkeep is also scorned.

In Alexandre Dumas's *The Three Musketeers*, Athos confesses to d'Artagnan that while drunk the previous night he gambled away his own horse, d'Artagnan's horse, all the horses' tack, and d'Artagnan's diamond ring too. The worst d'Artagnan can muster is 'Zounds!' And that's only because he can't imagine how they can carry on with their mission to save the queen without horses. Mainly, d'Artagnan is impressed and amused by his friend's antics. It's clear: no amount of lost mounts, tack or diamond rings can damage the swashbuckling friendship of Athos, Aramis, Porthos and d'Artagnan that takes them duelling and drinking their way around France, their devotion to each other regularly expressed in their 'All for one, and one for all!'

And that's another facet of these depictions of male friendships: unerring loyalty.

In P. G. Wodehouse's 1934 novel *Right Ho, Jeeves*, the amiably foolish upper-class Bertie Wooster doesn't even like his old schoolfriend Gussie Fink-Nottle, who is alarmingly fond of collecting newts ('those little sort of lizard things that charge about in ponds') and then, 'against all the ruling of the form book', falls in love. Most perplexing of all, he comes to Bertie for help. 'I couldn't see what had made him pick on me,' Bertie muses. 'It wasn't as if he and I were in any way bosom.' But the fact remains: 'I was exercised about the poor fish, as I am about all my pals, close or distant, who find themselves treading upon Life's banana skins.' And moreover, 'this man and I had once thrown inked darts at each other'. But of course Bertie helps Gussie get the girl.

In so many ways, Bertie is absurd. Yet the reader comes away pleased that he did right by his friend.

In Evelyn Waugh's Second World War novel *Men at Arms*, the emotional distance that can characterise men's friendships is used to comic effect. And it is poignant, too.

Guy Crouchback, reeling after a failed marriage, seeks honour and heroism in the army. Instead, training in the Royal Corps of Halberdiers at an old prep school near Southsand, he experiences a sense of alienation from the younger soldiers. He wants friendship. Apthorpe, an eccentric trainee officer of a similar age, seems the most likely candidate. But he remains elusive. Camaraderie does spring up, though, quite suddenly – because Apthorpe is so utterly committed to retaining sole use of his precious portable porcelain latrine, his 'thunder-box', which Brigadier Ben Ritchie-Hook has commandeered. Apthorpe needs Guy's help to get it back. The episode becomes more and more farcical, the two men puffing and panting as they heave it in the dead of night to ever more obscure locations.

At one point, realising just how much danger Guy has put himself in, Apthorpe says: 'Look here, old man, if you'd care to use the thunder-box, too, it's all right with me.' Soon, things have become so perilous that Apthorpe wears a tin hat on his trips to the thunder-box, and so survives a 'bloody great flower-pot, full of earth and a dead geranium' balanced as a booby trap on top of the potting-shed door. But they are repeatedly outwitted by the Brigadier, who finally decides that if he, a First World War veteran, can't use it, then the rightful owner will not either. So he blows the thunder-box up.

After the explosion, Guy finds Apthorpe 'standing, leaning against the elm, wearing his steel helmet, fumbling with his trouser buttons and gazing with dazed horror on the wreckage which lay all around'. 'Guy was at a loss for condolence,' says Waugh, and the moment contains real sadness. The only way the men could act out their version of camaraderie was over the thunder-box. And the thunder-box is gone.

Fictional pairings such as Apthorpe and Guy, Bertie and Gussie, make for great comedy. But they're funny because they ring so true.

Women's friendships are often portrayed as being as much about family and community as they are about the individuals involved. Whitney Otto's novel *How to Make an American Quilt* is entirely structured around weekly quilting-circle meetings, when a group of friends in small-town California gather to piece together scraps of their families' old clothes to make a bedspread. The friends meticulously salvage bits of their home lives, as the months pass, to create one huge emblem of domesticity. In novels by Barbara Pym, in sagas by Maeve Binchy and Joanna Trollope, women friends come together in their kitchens to laboriously bake cakes or assemble items they've brought from home to give to the village jumble sale or church fête. Fictional characters such as d'Artagnan, Holmes and Apthorpe might look down on such activities. But what if men's attempts to hold on to bluff, macho friendships bring quite serious losses?

In *The Sportswriter*, the novelist Richard Ford suggests that the approved template for friendship that men have inherited can leave them feeling desperate. The narrator, Frank Bascombe, is struggling to come to terms with his divorce and the death of his son. He understands that he needs company, that he needs to *talk*. But he can't work out how.

His ex-wife once told him he had too few 'superficial' friends in his life. So he joins a local suburban Divorced Men's Club, made up of five men who meet in the bar periodically and go on a fishing trip once a year. But none of them have the courage of their convictions. They can't at any point actually ask for advice or share their feelings. 'To start with, none of us is that kind of confessional, soulful type. We are all educated.'

Then Walter Luckett joins the group. He wants to work through his emotions, and he fixes on Frank as the best person to do it with. Frank's a writer. He must understand. But Frank resists Walter's attempts to explain to him how it was that his wife ran off to Bimini with a water-skiing instructor. At times he's plain rude. When Walter attempts to kiss him goodbye he pushes him away.

It is one of the pivotal ironies of the book that Frank Bascombe does end up with a 'best friend', but only because Walter names him as such in his suicide note.

At one point, the protagonist of *The Sportswriter* describes a casual friendship he has with a fellow writer he sometimes bumps into on the train into New York, called Bert Brisker. An attempt at a relaxed evening together ends with Bert 'downing several vodkas' and consequently 'threatening to throw me through the wall'. Frank suspects that is 'the essence of a modern friendship'. *The Sportswriter* was published in 1986. In the twenty-first century men can expect more, emotionally, from their friendships with other men.

Off screen, Matt Damon and Ben Affleck are famous for being childhood friends who dreamed of Hollywood success together. In 2010, at a glitzy ceremony, it was Affleck who presented Damon with his American Cinematheque award. As the camera bulbs flashed, with humour and pride Damon described Affleck as his 'hetero-lifemate'. David Beckham and Tom Cruise, too, are renowned for their 'bromance'. Journalists poke fun at the idea they share an agent; they draw giggly attention to the fact that when the Beckhams moved to LA, they moved on to Tom Cruise's street. The men hug in public. They don't appear remotely embarrassed about showing their affection for each other.

Abraham Verghese is reticent about the depth of his feelings at first. At the end of *The Tennis Partner* he describes a moment with his friend David Smith; he grows lyrical, he sounds positively romantic when he says, 'as our pupils adjusted to the night, and as we looked heavenward, it was as if one by one, then by the tens and hundreds, the stars appeared, a private showing for just the two of us'.

# 24

# Men and Women

Can men and women be friends?

Aristotle's extensive treatment of friendship in his *Nicomachean Ethics* evokes pictures of friendship in which men play dice, do gymnastics, drink and hunt together. As far as he and much of the classical world were concerned, men favoured friendships with men because women, like slaves and children, were considered inferior.

In his *Summa contra Gentiles*, written in the early 1260s, Thomas Aquinas argued that a man should at least try to be a friend to his wife. Of course, he emphasised, 'a wife is naturally subject to her husband as governor'. But within that natural order of things, a man could feel morally elevated if he stuck with a woman after her youth, beauty and fecundity were gone. Aquinas said there were practical reasons for doing so, too. If a wife believed the relationship would last, she was more likely to be careful with their household possessions; there would be fewer breakages, so there would be indirect financial benefits. And, Aquinas said, a man in a happy marriage would help make society more stable. He would benefit his fellow men if he could be friends with his wife.

Yet, bedecked as it was with qualifiers, this suggestion was dismissed by the French writer Michel de Montaigne. In his essay 'On Friendship', first published in 1580, he describes marriage as 'a bargain to which only the entrance is free', and argues that the 'extraneous complications' such as children and domestic possessions 'break the thread and disturb the course of a lively affection'. 'The ancients' were right, Montaigne concludes: women simply aren't spiritually evolved enough for friendship; 'Their souls do not seem firm enough to bear the strain of so hard and lasting a tie.'

Six centuries after Aquinas and more than two millennia after Aristotle, it was still radical of the philosopher and social reformer John Stuart Mill to suggest that, if he made emotional connections with no other women, a man should certainly befriend his wife. At the time when his essay *The Subjection of Women* came out in 1869, a woman's entire wealth – cash, possessions and property – passed to her husband the moment she married, and any money she inherited during their marriage did as well. A man could file for divorce if his wife committed adultery, but the same was not true for her.

The Slave Trade Act had been passed in 1807, the Slavery Abolition Act in 1833. But, said Mill, 'no slave is a slave to the same lengths, and in so full a sense of the word as a wife is.' He admits that he can see the appeal of choosing a wife who is malleable ('a nullity'). But he warns that a man who does so may well be making a fool of himself, as 'dullness and want of spirit are not always a guarantee of the submission which is so confidently expected from [women]'. He argues that it is wrong for a man to treat his wife as a slave. 'The true virtue of human beings is a fitness to live together as equals; claiming nothing for themselves but what they freely concede to everyone else; regarding command of any kind as an exceptional necessity, and in all cases a temporary one.' In *Subjection*, he hoped to shame men into agreeing with him.

There were exceptions of course. A century earlier the Abbé Galiani and Mme d'Épinay remained close because, socially, they had nothing more to lose: Galiani had been very publicly sacked as representative of the Neapolitan embassy; Louise had a broken marriage behind her and was living openly as the lover of a German journalist and critic, Friedrich Melchior Grimm. Furthermore, in 1769 she was forty-three. 'A woman of my age can discuss subjects of every kind,' she told Galiani. 'I don't mind what people say: I shall be writing to my friend, and as long as I am satisfied with what I write, and he is too, all will be well.' Their friendship lasted their whole lives.

John Stuart Mill and Harriet Taylor were friends for two decades before they married, in 1851. The chapter of Mill's autobiography that covers the years 1830–40, entitled 'Commencement of the most valuable Friendship of my Life', opens with a description of Harriet as 'the honour and chief blessing of my existence'. She didn't have a man's education, he relates, but she was as stimulating and intelligent a friend as any man. 'Her unselfishness was not that of a taught system of duties, but of a heart which thoroughly identified itself with the feelings of others, and often went to excess in consideration for them ... To be admitted into any degree of mental intercourse with a being of these qualities, could not but have a most beneficial influence on my development.'

Mill credited Harriet as joint author of *The Subjection of Women*: 'When two persons have their thoughts and speculations completely in common; when all subjects of intellectual or moral interest are discussed between them in daily life ... it is of little consequence in respect to the question of originality, which of them holds the pen.'

Things were changing. Mill wasn't the only man who wanted to be free to count women as friends. In America in 1836, the New England philosopher and poet Ralph Waldo Emerson was introduced to a flamboyant group that included the poet Caroline Sturgis and the New Orleans socialite Anna Barker. These young writers and artists enjoyed challenging stiff New England ideas about friendship. They prized frank, intense exchanges, and they didn't care about the gender of the people they were having them with.

Emerson had only recently married Lydia Jackson. From an old Plymouth family and orphaned quite young, sadness was the 'ground colour' of her life, her daughter said later. Emerson admired Lydia. Sturgis and Barker excited him. And they were keen to embrace Emerson as their friend.

On first meeting Anna Barker he wrote, 'The moment she fastens her eyes on you, her unique gentleness unbars all doors, and with such easy and frolic sway she advances and advances and advances on you.' When he found that she was engaged to be married, he wrote to Caroline Sturgis that the news had 'offended' him 'with a certain terror'. And that terror made him step back from Caroline too: 'I dare not engage my peace so far as to make you necessary to me, when the first news I may hear is that you have found in some heaven foreign to me your mate, and my beautiful castle is exploded to shivers.'

It was all very well deciding to break with convention. Doing it was another matter.

Emerson's most consuming friendship was with Margaret Fuller. Margaret was ferociously intelligent. Educated by her father with the same rigour as if she were a boy, by sixteen she was reading Mme de Staël, Milton and Racine, and by twenty-six she'd translated Goethe's *Torquato Tasso*. She'd heard Emerson speak and realised that his ideal of 'self-reliance' fitted her desire for equality for women. He'd read her translation of Goethe. From the day they met in 1836, says his biographer Robert D. Richardson Jr, 'they were in close and almost continuous contact with each other' for the next ten years until her death.

Thinking about her effect on him, Emerson wrote in his journal:

> She came to me
> And turned on me those azure orbs
> And steeped me in their lavish light …
> I think I could spend the longest day
> In unfolding all that was folded in that ray.

He thought her 'more variously gifted, wise, sportive, eloquent … magnificent, prophetic, reading my life at her will'.

They had their fights. Emerson disliked the way she gathered people like 'a necklace of diamonds about her neck'. In

his opinion, she gossiped too much and her 'rather moun-
tainous ME' led her to patronise almost everyone. She in
turn accused him of an 'inhospitality of soul'. He discussed
all his work with her. If they weren't actually with each other
(she was a regular house-guest) they were exchanging letters.
But she wanted more. 'You would have me love you. What
shall I love? Your body? The supposition disgusts you,'
wrote Emerson despairingly in his journal. 'Your courage,
your enterprise, your budding affection, your opening
thought, your prayer, I can love, but what else?'

Really, did he just want a sexual relationship with her?
In the end, it seems it all became too much for Emerson,
his desire so intense he tried to deny it. His 1839 essay
'Friendship' was inspired by his friendships with women.
Yet in it he only says evasively that friendship is available
to all. It 'cancels the thick walls of individual character,
relation, age, sex, circumstance', and 'makes many one'. He
speaks of the effect new friends can have on us: 'When a
much commended stranger arrives, we talk better than we
are wont. We have the nimblest fancy, a richer memory,
and our dumb devil has taken leave for the time. For long
hours we can continue a series of sincere, graceful, rich
communications, drawn from the oldest, secretest experience so that they who sit by, of our own kinfolk and
acquaintance, shall feel a lively surprize at our unusual
powers.' He effuses about new friends, but without specifying that he is talking primarily about women. New
friends induce 'cordial exhilaration' and 'jets of affection'
and 'carry out the world for me to new and noble depths,
and enlarge the meaning of all my thoughts'. 'A new

person is to me a great event and hinders me from sleep.'

He presents such friendships as of central importance, but concludes that, once a 'sacred relation' has inspired a person to start becoming his or her best self, to finish that process he or she must continue on their own: 'The soul environs itself with friends that it may enter into a grander self-acquaintance or solitude.'

Emerson's biographer Laurence Buell notes of his marriage to Lydia that 'the combination of consistent loyalty versus intervals of discord, mutual disappointment versus mutual admiration, probably had much to do with provoking Emerson's periodic complaints about the artificiality of monogamous marriage and ... his "platonic" view of love and friendship'. Because Emerson found his relationships with women such as Fuller, Sturgis and Barker so unbearably tantalising, in the end he sidelined all friendship completely.

The young journalist Marian Evans, later known as George Eliot, arrived in London in 1851. She wanted to publish books like men did, and have friendships with men, too. In intellectual circles in the metropolis it was possible, just, for men and women to be seen out and about as friends.

Eliot became a bit too emotionally attached to the publisher John Chapman, with whose family she lodged for a while, and alienated both his wife and his mistress. But impressed by her reviewing, Chapman made Eliot assistant editor of the *Westminster Review*, which he had bought that same year. And through her work there she met the political theorist Herbert Spencer, then also an assistant editor, on the *Economist* (founded in 1843), a weekly commercial journal that advocated in particular free trade and the repeal of the corn laws. 'They were the same age, both from the Midlands,' notes Jenny Uglow in her biography. Eliot believed they were of the same mindset. Spencer argued in his book *Social Statics* that men and women were essentially equal. 'Using his free reviewer's tickets to indulge another common bond, a love of the theatre and music, from early 1852,' says Uglow, 'they were constantly together.'

Being seen together was OK. But, *constantly*? That did raise eyebrows. Both felt a need to explain the situation. In April 1852, Eliot wrote to a friend: 'We have agreed that we are not in love with each other, and that there is no reason why we should not have as much of each other's society as we like.'

It seems, though, that neither was being entirely honest with themselves, let alone with each other or with mutual acquaintances. Eliot's biographer Kathryn Hughes suggests that even as he described their relationship as friendship, Spencer worked hard to encourage suspicions of romance. In April, he was also writing to his friend Edward Lott to explain why he was publicly spending so much time with Eliot, 'whom you have heard me mention as the translatress of Strauss and as the most admirable woman, mentally, I ever met. We have been for some time past on very intimate terms. I am frequently at Chapman's, and the greatness of her intellect conjoined with her womanly qualities and manner, generally keep me at her side most of the evening.' It is a teasing letter, juxtaposing words such as 'admirable' and 'intellect' with 'intimate' and 'womanly'.

And he was giving Eliot mixed messages too. Even if she believed initially that the relationship could be platonic, she didn't manage to keep it up. By July she was writing him letters full of heated demands. 'I want to know if you can assure me that you will not forsake me, that you will always be with me as much as you can and share your thoughts and feelings with me. If you become attached to some one else, then I must die.' 'If only,' says Hughes, 'Marian had realised that Spencer was never going to marry anyone – he died a bachelor at eighty-three – she would have been spared a summer of humiliation and despair.'

In fact, the 'humiliation and despair' don't appear to have damaged her too badly. In August 1852 her 'friendship' with Spencer ended. By April 1853, she was spending a lot of time with one of his closest friends, G. H. Lewes, with whom she went on to live, unmarried, for two and a half decades, until his death.

In 1918 in Britain, women of property over the age of thirty got the vote; in 1928, that right was extended to all women over twenty-one. Broadly, men and women were perceived in law to be equal. Surely now they could be friends? Yet still in 1989, with the romantic comedy *When Harry Met Sally* starring Billy Crystal as Harry and Meg Ryan as Sally, the question 'Can men and women be friends?' is presented as rhetorical.

Harry and Sally meet when they graduate from university in Chicago and she gives him a lift to New York. They almost immediately start debating the question that is the basis of the story. Harry tells Sally that he thinks men and women can never be friends because 'the sex part always gets in the way'. The desire for friendship, he says, only happens in the first place if there is a desire for sex, and even if that desire is not acted on, the desire makes real friendship impossible. Sally disagrees. And the film charts their attempt to stay just friends.

The dramatic tension centres not on whether or not they will give in to their sexual desires, but how and when. We know as the opening credits roll that Harry and Sally will end up in bed together.

From *It Happened One Night* and *Bringing Up Baby* in the 1930s to *Jerry Maguire* (1996) and *The Proposal* (1999), countless films have been made on the premise that, really, sexual attraction drives any friendship between a man and a woman.

The main characters may have been thrown together by an unexpected predicament or by work. In *It Happened One Night*, the Clark Gable character is a struggling journalist who just wants his story, and the heiress he meets (Claudette Colbert) merely wants his help to get back to her husband – at first. In *Bringing up Baby*, Cary Grant's earnest zoologist at first only wants the wealthy Katharine Hepburn character to help him secure a charitable donation so he can complete his project assembling a brontosaurus skeleton. Alternatively in such romcoms one of the two might be suppressing their passion for fear of ruining the relationship. In *Jerry Maguire* Tom Cruise is a sports agent who hopes he can stay just friends with his dedicated, hard-working secretary, played by Renée Zellweger, because she's a fantastic business asset and he doesn't want to spoil that.

The pair might even actively dislike each other at first. In *The Proposal*, a New York publisher played by Sandra Bullock is so hard-nosed she is known as 'the witch', and her assistant (Ryan Reynolds), who is helping her get a visa to guarantee his own promotion, hardly dares see that she might have a soft side. But whatever the reason, they're forced to rub along with each other; and in these movies, the transition from hate to love is often swift. Friendship is only ever a lie, or a tantalising interlude. The feel-good part comes when the two individuals admit that they couldn't possibly just be friends. Only sex will do.

In the mid-1990s, rather different portrayals of friendship were starting to appear in the media. The television series *Friends*, which ran from 1994 to 2004, won fistfuls of awards and is still repeated regularly. The show rests on the assumption that three attractive young men, Joey, Chandler and Ross, and three attractive young women, Monica, Rachel and Phoebe, can be friends. In and out of each other's apartments, frequently getting together at the Central Perk café, these sexy, sexually active Manhattanites remain just friends to the last, even when Chandler and Monica get engaged and Ross and Rachel have had a baby and repeatedly broken up.

Byron famously said: 'Friendship may, and often does, grow into love, but love never subsides into friendship.' But is that true today? Love often *has* to become friendship – if, for example, when couples split up, they want to remain on good terms for the children's sake. This is something much tougher to achieve, and nobler, than any subsiding. And it is not only a handful of brave divorcees who manage to forge amicable relationships. Circumstances nowadays bring the sexes together from nursery age. Boys and girls are educated together; in offices and call centres, factories and shops, men and women work together every day, have lunch together, go for drinks.

But the balance between love and friendship is ever teetering. Does it give male–female friendships an exciting, precarious edge? In Winifred Holtby's novel *South Riding*, the stalwart Alderman Mrs Beddows has always had a crush on Councillor Robert Carne of Maythorpe Hall. Whatever her hopes may once have been, she has found that with 'wave after wave of misfortune breaking over him', she has more power over him as a friend than she ever could have had as a lover. Carne's wife is mad and in an institution. Mrs Beddows can remain a part of his life by looking after his daughter whenever he asks. The author's description makes her house feel like a lair – the fact that Mrs Beddows is happily married is part of the trap. Sitting by her fire in an armchair, he is 'at her mercy', 'smiling at her, accepting her reproof, submitting to her advice' – which gives her a 'satisfaction too profound for words ... She loved him so much that to scold him was a sensuous pleasure to her.'

The main female character in Penelope Fitzgerald's novel *The Blue Flower*, set in eighteenth-century Germany, suffers a pain that resonates today.

Karoline loves Hardenberg, who is a poet and philosopher. She is clever and articulate, but leads a hard domestic life and so has few opportunities. Hardenberg enjoys following her around posing intellectual problems and asking for her opinion on drafts of his verse.

When he describes her as 'the thesis, tranquil, pale, finite, self-contained' and himself as 'the antithesis, uneasy, contradictory, passionate, reaching out beyond myself', is he saying that the two of them, as the 'synthesis', could make a life together? Karoline's hopes are raised. He continues to confide in her. Back from a trip, he rushes straight to her, declaring: 'Your friendship – I cannot tell you – even when I am away I have such a clear remembrance of you that I feel as though you are still near me – we are like two watches set to the same time, and when we see one another again there has been no interval – we still strike together.' Karoline's hopes soar. Her focus is so intently on suppressing them that she is completely unprepared for what he has come to tell her: 'I have fallen in love' – with someone else. After a dismayed outburst, she has seconds to grab back their friendship, and she manages. But their relationship is torturous for her for the rest of the novel. She had nurtured their friendship initially because she thought his attentions meant he loved her too. She pays a high price for this misreading.

In any friendship, when emotions run high, it's far from simple.

# 25

# Better than Sex

'I love you!' a friend shouted recently across a pub table. There were three of us; we were having a girls' night out. She reached over the beer and peanuts to squeeze our hands. 'I know you're not supposed to say it, but I do, I love you!' Of course, I was pleased. I love her too. But actually my first response was embarrassment. The pub was busy, the night was hot and sweaty. How long did I have to leave my hand in hers to show that I shared her strength of feeling?

Friends today can hug. They can kiss each other hello, on the cheeks. But at what distance is the kiss too close to the mouth? Unless a hand wanders, a side-on hug is almost certainly innocent. But a hearty face-to-face hug might bring pressure on breasts, on genitals. If one friend is gay, though, and the other straight, physical contact and outrageously flirtatious talk are fine.

An Asian man I know who arrived in this country recently told me he has had to change his body language dramatically. He is married and wears a wedding ring, but if he responds to men here the way he would in Asia, he is treated with distrust. He misses feeling able to throw his arms round people simply because he is enjoying their company.

But what if his desire to embrace people and my friend's urges to shout out her love do have a sexual edge to them? There are friends from childhood who make us feel cosy. There are work friends who are useful. Then there are new friends who, even if our list of friends is already quite long, we pursue because they excite us. Lord Byron may have said 'Friendship is Love without wings', but many of the closest friendships start with a sexual frisson.

In the 1980s in the gay community, sexual partners were referred to as 'friends'. In classical Greece it was considered acceptable for high-born male friends to have sex with each other. Biographers argue over whether or not the young Evelyn Waugh had two or three full-blown affairs with men while he was at Oxford – there is little doubt that he had a 'homosexual phase' during that time. 'I know of these romantic friendships of the English and the Germans,' says Cara, Lord Marchmain's mistress in *Brideshead Revisited*, of the homoerotic relationship between Sebastian Flyte and Charles Ryder. 'I think they are very good if they do not go on too long.' It was OK for lines to be crossed, as long as everyone was clear that there *were* lines and that at some point the individual who had stepped over them would step back again. In the *Brideshead* scheme of things, homosexual friendships stopped after marriage.

Does having a wife mean you can't have women friends, though?

For some men, marriage is just the excuse they need.

After Evelyn Waugh married, he had some very close friendships with women. As mentioned earlier, he remained on
easy terms with Ann Fleming for nearly fifteen years, and
with Nancy Mitford for over thirty. He was still writing
frank, affectionate letters to them both in the last months of
his life. And it is striking that, for both friendships, he got
tacit spousal approval first. He met Nancy Mitford through
his first wife (also called Evelyn); Ann Fleming was a friend
of his second wife and also her cousin. One way he kept
these friendships feeling safe for the duration was via regular mentions of his wife in his correspondence with the two
women. Indeed, he mentioned his second wife Laura so
often that at times the repetition becomes comic.

In a letter to Ann in 1953, a page and a half of giggles
and intimacy are sanctified with an oblique reference to her
husband at the start – 'Welcome home to both of you' – and
a perfunctory 'Laura joins me in love for you' at the end.
The reader gets the feeling that it is her husband Ian he is
placating. Ann had her own relationship with Laura – she
didn't need reminders that Waugh was not sexually available. But it would perhaps have been more seemly for him
to keep in regular contact with Ann's husband. As Waugh's
biographer Christopher Sykes notes, 'The surviving letters
between [the men] are few and concerned with printing
business or Ian's learned bibliographical hobbies.' By contrast, in another letter to Ann in 1953, Waugh says: 'I long
to see you.'

Whereas he tended to start his letters to Ann with
'Dear . . .', when he wrote to Mitford he generally addressed
her as 'Darling Nancy'. His entire correspondence with her

was distinctly flirtatious. Laura's presence in these letters feels very different.

His friendship with Nancy had an inauspicious start. In 1929 his first wife Evelyn announced that she had been unfaithful. Nancy sided with Waugh, which one might think would have brought them close. But there was then a long break, and it wasn't until his first marriage had been annulled and he was safely married again that, in the early 1940s, his friendship with Nancy started up again. Although, when it did, particularly once some distance had been put between them by Nancy's move to Paris in 1946, it seems he let their relationship take him back to something resembling his bachelor days.

In his letters to Nancy, the regular reminders that he is married are still there. In April 1946 he wrote: 'All my children are here for the holidays – merry, affectionate, madly boring ... Laura has bought a minute tractor, like a doll's pram, and has ploughed every available rood up to the windows in order to grow kale and mangolds. I run behind collecting bulbs in full flower as she turns them up.'

By June, Mitford's writing career was really taking off; he wrote:

I long to hear about your American public. Are you greatly troubled by admirers? Do you want any money? I owe you I don't know how much for Debo's hat. Would you like all my francs? ... Can you get rubber corsets in Paris? Laura asks. It is very important to have them after having a baby. If they are procurable do send her a pair by the next chap coming over.

He was hurt in October that year when Nancy failed while back in England to fit in a visit to the Waughs. He drafted his wife in plaintively then, speaking of 'we' and 'us' instead of 'I'. 'It was indeed a bitter disappointment to us both to learn that we shall not see you'. But once he'd used Laura to emphasise his pique, he soon warmed up: 'I am tempted to come to Paris after Christmas. Is it easy?'

The idiosyncratic Baroness Karen von Blixen, who wrote under the name Isak Dinesen, introduced her own particular hazards when pursuing relationships with members of the opposite sex. She was not 'allowed to make love', as she put it, because she had contracted syphilis as a young woman from her husband. Blixen maintained that because she had been abandoned by God, to get compensatory fame as a novelist she'd made a pact with the Devil. She then spent much of her life trying to persuade male friends to agree similar pacts with her.

In the 1930s, when she was in her fifties, the young Danish writer Thorkild Bjørnvig wrote her an admiring letter. Bjørnvig was careful to mention his wife. But, as he says in his own account of the relationship that would soon unfold, his introductory letter also declared: 'I have always sought for someone to serve', and ended with 'Your servant who knows how clumsy he is, and who fails in all things, except one: his ardent devotion'.

Blixen wrote back immediately to say that she was happy to embark on a friendship in which she was served. She was careful to absolve herself, in advance, of responsibility not just for anything *he* might subsequently do, but for her own actions too. At the meeting during which they agreed what she considered an indissoluble contract that gave her powers of witchcraft over him, she instructed Bjørnvig: '... since you understand Nietzsche so well, you must also be able to tell me, if you see, if you have seen, any sign of the same kind of megalomania in me. And if you do, you must warn me immediately – you truly owe that to me, for it is part of our pact: you shall protect my honour.'

She told him what to read. She scattered freesias in his hair. She told him to accept a fellowship in Paris and move there with his family so that he could study French and become more refined. She told him to have an affair with her assistant, Clara. And when he did that too, he seemed genuinely surprised – indeed, enraged – to discover that Blixen couldn't control either his wife's response or her own. His wife attempted suicide; Blixen responded with jealousy. Bjørnvig said he was ending the pact. On the contrary, they must seal it in blood, she told him. He balked at this. She retorted: 'You with your stupid spite and cowardice, you who don't dare to mix your blood with mine, simply because you are afraid.' Recriminations, reconciliations, so the drama went on. He composed a sonnet for her seventieth birthday. She wrote back describing the poem as 'an homage to a friendship ... struck down by a curse', and in the same letter invited him to tea.

'The fool did what I asked him to do,' she complained, referring to Bjørnvig's passivity, to their mutual friend Ole Wivel. 'It made me look ridiculous.' Blixen's biographer Judith Thurman argues that actually she didn't want these complicated male friendships. She longed for one of them to defy her, even simply laugh. 'If only,' she once complained, 'people would treat me like a lunatic. It would be such a relief.' Having thought that by writing down in ink, blood or both the details of what was acceptable in a friendship she could insure against the possibility of any emotional response, she was furious to find that this was not the case.

The American socialite and writer Jane Bowles (1917–73) took the view that she could just keep rewriting her 'pacts' as she went along. The rewriting itself was exciting. She found it almost impossible to decide whether women she liked should be friends or lovers. The agreement she had with her husband, Paul Bowles, meant she didn't have to.

'She would go to bed with almost anyone,' said one woman friend who, like a number of Jane's other friends, asked to remain anonymous in Millicent Dillon's biography *A Little Original Sin: The Life and Work of Jane Bowles.* Paul was fine with an open marriage. If it wasn't a moral issue, why draw the line at talking, why not sleep with someone you find stimulating? And because Jane had no good reason for refraining from sex, she often left it up to the other party. Another woman friend she pursued in New York in the 1940s said, 'When I first met her, she seemed to take a terrific attachment to me. It was unnerving. I admired her, but she would sit and gape at me.' Bowles wasn't offended that this friend refused to have sex with her, or put off. 'She wanted me to return affection to her, but she didn't press me physically. She was aggressive in saying, "You must say you'll see me. Oh, forget what you were going to do," she'd insist, and I'd give in.'

'Sex is all in the mind,' she told Paul. And it seems it was just as exciting for her whether it stayed in the mind or not.

One friend, Pamela Stevenson, moved into their building because, Paul recounted, 'she had a fixation on Jane, not a sexual fixation, but it couldn't have been stronger if it had been. She had to see Jane all the time and confess to her.' Pam had fallen in love with a Spaniard and wanted Jane to tell her how to get him. 'She lay in her bed for nine days, living on canned spaghetti, wearing black lingerie that she had bought especially for the occasion, waiting for the Spaniard to come and ring her bell. "You're not interested in him," Jane said to her. "All you're interested in is your black underwear. You wouldn't mind who came in as long as he saw you in your black underwear."'

She clearly liked the way sex could keep the stakes high.

In the 1950s, Jane lived in Algiers with an Arabic woman called Cherifa, who became her lover. The account of an American friend, Roberta Bobba, who visited her there, suggests that Jane enjoyed causing ructions. She had long conversations with Roberta in English, knowing that Cherifa didn't speak it; she made Cherifa eat at a separate table with the servants. She flaunted the fact that Roberta was gay, and insisted on telling her sexual details of her relationship with Cherifa that Roberta didn't want to know. 'That relationship embarrassed me – and I'm not one to be easily embarrassed,' she said later. 'I believe that Jane was not homosexual by instinct or nature ... [but] she had a great ability to laugh and play. Part of what she enjoyed in the Arab women was that they were so playful. All those endless discussions, whether to have turnips or beets – and she, Jane, playing too.'

Was Jane Bowles gay? Was she horribly manipulative? Did she think it was all just a laugh?

One thing is sure. The kind of confusion she generated in Pamela Stevenson and Roberta Bobba meant that her relationships with them were intense. Pamela wrote to Jane: 'I am writing to you because your image has taken up housekeeping in my head, like a disgusted god ... I am sure you are groaning, which bears out my feeling that you are there unwillingly; however, you are not so unwilling as not to be there. I enjoy your company intensely, although at times it is damned uncomfortable to have another person living inside one's skull.' Even if Jane couldn't persuade her friends to engage with her physically, she could entangle them mentally.

There is one thing that's particularly odd about Bowles's friendships. Although she liked pushing the boundaries and keeping her friends confused, in many ways her ideas of what constituted friendship fitted very well the stereotype of women's friendships. She liked them close and confessional. They involved succour – she would go to some lengths to find a friend the best hotel, the best doctor. They were almost always structured around long talks, secrets, meals, drinks.

Tennessee Williams wrote:

What impressed me most about Jane, the person, was her concern for others, for their comfort and their entertainment. The important little things, especially such as providing meals, acquainting you with the right doctors in foreign places, conducting you through markets, introducing you to the interesting people, and somehow, in the midst of confusion, finding precisely the right words to reassure you in your own confusion – these were her particular gifts.

Wendell Wilcox, a professor at the University of North Carolina, said of the time he met her in Paris in 1950: 'She was the very easiest person to be with that I have ever known. We went to lunch together ... and then again nearly every day after. I can't even remember that we made arrangements. She would call me and come by or else I would go for her to the Hôtel de l'Université where she was staying ... Jane and I would wander around and eat and drink here and there, talking about nothing in particular.'

With her female friends, she was alarming and enticing. She flouted convention. But at the same time she was traditional in ways that many men found reassuring.

# 26

# Dos and Don'ts

The idea that universal dos and don'ts of friendship exist is an appealing one. There is a yearning for rules. Some philosophers have suggested guidelines that are helpful, if rather broad. 'There is little Friendship in the world, and least of all between equals,' said Francis Bacon in 1597. Harsh, but clear. Except, as Bacon's own circumstances altered, his guidelines did too. In 1621, accused of corruption, he was fined, sentenced to prison and banished from parliament and court. He must have wanted friends then. His essay 'Of Friendship' four years later reveals a change of perception: 'Without true Friends the world is but a wilderness.'

Bacon was a keen promoter of the new sciences, and this lends a down-to-earth clarity to his views on friendship, which, he says in this later essay, should do you good like medicine does. It should bring 'peace in affections': 'You may take Sarza to open the liver, steel to open the spleen, flowers of sulphur for the lungs, castoreum for the brain; but no receipt openeth the heart but a true friend ...

communicating of a man's self to his friend works two contrary effects, for it redoubleth joys and cutteth grief in half.' They're not quite rules, but they are certainly useful pointers. If after talking to someone our joys have doubled and/or our sorrows have been halved, then that's friendship. In talking to a friend, he says, a man 'waxeth wiser than himself; and that more by an hour's discourse than by a day's meditation'. Friendship 'maketh daylight in the understanding out of darkness and confusion of thought'.

Ralph Waldo Emerson in his essay 'Friendship' (1841) argued that real friendship can be reduced to just two key elements: 'One is Truth. A friend is a person with whom I may be sincere. Before him I may think aloud ... The other element of friendship is tenderness.'

This at least looks straightforward. *Do* be honest. *Do* be tender. Although Emerson was criticised for being icy with his closest friends. And he concluded that a need for friendship shows weakness. We should all aim to do without it: 'We walk alone in the world. Friends such as we desire are dreams and fables.' But even if we can't have 'friends such as we desire', perhaps that in itself is helpful to know. Abandon that hope, and we can concentrate on setting out what is acceptable in the friends we must make do with.

William Hazlitt did this with seductive conviction. In his essay 'On the Spirit of Obligations', first published in 1824, he said: 'Few things tend more to alienate friendship than a want of punctuality in our engagements.' So that's easily sorted. To keep a friend, all you have to do is to make sure you have set your watch correctly and left plenty of time to get to appointments. Then, 'In estimating the value of an

acquaintance or even a friend, we give a preference to intellectual or convivial over moral qualities,' he says in his essay
'Characteristics'. 'The truth is, that in our habitual intercourse with others, we much oftener require to be amused
than assisted.' So if you need help moving a bit of furniture,
hire someone. With your friends, make sure your focus is on
having fun. Keep it superficial then – that's the answer.

Yet Hazlitt also describes feeling unsurpassable joy on
arriving at the house of a friend who convinces him for a
moment that 'the husk, the shell of humanity is left at the
door, and the spirit, mellowed by time, resides within!' This
doesn't sound superficial at all.

These individual reflections on friendship seem to raise as
many questions as they answer. It must be possible to come
up with a solid framework. If we're looking for rules, we
might do worse than start with Dale Carnegie, who gives us
all the instructions we need in his book *How to Win Friends
and Influence People*, which since publication in 1936 has sold
over ten million copies worldwide. It must work.

Carnegie's chapter titles suggest you can gain control in
this business of making friends: 'Six Ways to Make People
Like You', 'Twelve Ways to Win People to Your Way of
Thinking', 'Nine Ways to Change People without Giving
Offense or Arousing Resentment'. As he presents it, the
scary, unpredictable world can be forced not just to like
you but to think the way you do as well. He defines friendship as a tool, one that is delicate and requires careful
handling but can nevertheless be utilised by anyone with
the right training. He took on board John D. Rockefeller's
conviction, Carnegie says – that 'the ability to deal with people

is as purchasable a commodity as sugar or coffee.' He also quotes Rockefeller as saying that for the ability to deal with people he would pay more 'than for any other under the sun'. Yet Carnegie will *give* it to the reader, for just the price of his book.

When I went to New York in the eighties for work, I was told that a way of remembering someone's name was to repeat it three times as you shake their hand. At work functions and parties, I had my hand shaken again and again by strangers with enormous flat grins saying, 'Josie, good to meet you, Josie, a real pleasure, Josie!' Despite having been forewarned that it was merely a stratagem, I found it disarming – the massive smiles, the close attention – until only minutes later they'd introduce me to someone as 'Tracy'. If it hadn't been for the fact that 'Josie' was a tricky name for those New Yorkers, I would have come away from the events, drinks, meetings with the feeling that I'd made dozens of new friends in just a few working days.

Yet, even though I'd experienced a key flaw in the trick, that didn't stop me trying to make use of it. I never did manage to repeat anyone's name three times in quick succession while shaking their hand without making them frown suspiciously. But I kept on giving it a go for a good few months.

Social theorists Liz Spencer and Ray Pahl come up with some friendship directives that look pretty comprehensive. The research for their 2006 book *Rethinking Friendship: Hidden Solidarities Today* is reassuringly thorough. Using a 'qualitative approach', they interviewed sixty men and women 'of different ages, at different stages in the life-course, from different socioeconomic and ethnic backgrounds and living in different parts of Britain'. In amongst the eye-catching terminology there are some sound insights. For example, we learn that friendship ranges from 'simple' to 'complex'. We are told that within that spectrum it features 'associate', 'useful contact', 'favour friend', 'fun friend', 'helpmate', 'comforter', 'confidant' and 'soulmate'.

Most people could probably divide their address books accordingly – well aware that if they came up with 150 soul-mates they might have to rethink their definitions. The authors also offer us four friendship modes to further sub-divide our social network into. 'Bounded' friendships are settled ones – for example, those that have lasted from school. People who have 'serial' friendships acquire new sets of friends as their life changes. Those with 'evolving' friend-ships have elements of 'bounded' and 'serial'. And a person whose friendship mode is 'ruptured' has, following a life crisis, changed all his or her friends more or less completely.

I know I'd like to think I'm 'evolving' and have only a few 'ruptured' friendships, the rest being a good mix of 'bounded' and 'serial'. And in that sense, too, Spencer and Pahl's attempt to create social psychology's equivalent of the periodic table is quite helpful. They show that some order can be made out of what was coming to seem like a morass of relationships ranging, indeed, from the dictionary's definition of 'friend' as 'one joined to another in mutual benevolence and inti-macy' to 'a stranger whom one comes across or has occasion to mention again'.

Yet even as Spencer and Pahl's welcome grid gives some framework to the concept, the realities of friendship mutate and shift, refusing to fit neat patterns. Bounded friendships can incorporate all sorts of poisonous behaviour, and continue simply because 'we've known each other since school'. Then, a sudden rupture might be just what's needed if an individual has always gravitated towards relationships in which they are used. Their mental health may well improve dramatically if they can throw off such friendships and start again. Alternatively, a mere 'associate' might leapfrog several categories to become a 'confidant' if, during an apparently by-the-by conversation over the kettle in the office kitchen, it emerges that you both went to the same party in June two years ago and both still know Tom Dixon.

In 1981, the French philosopher Michel Foucault had a rethink about the way the word 'friend' had come to be used in the gay community to denote 'sexual partner'. He concluded that the term needed to be expanded again, and not just for the sake of the gay community but for all of us, 'individuals of different age, status and social activity'. In an interview for the magazine *Gai Pied*, Foucault suggested that the gay community had allowed itself to become defined by single, rushed acts of sex. He argued that gay men should work instead at creating a 'homosexual mode of life' with friendship at its heart. It would be difficult, it was 'still improbable'. But he felt able to name the main components: this new mode of life would mix 'affection, tenderness, friendship, fidelity, camaraderie and companionship'.

Couples who marry sign a contract that is enforceable by law. Couldn't friends do that too – make a list of rules and sign on the dotted line? It sounds ridiculous. A main point of friendship is that you can flit about between a whole bunch of different people according to your circumstances and needs – isn't it? Surely the notion of drawing up some kind of legally binding document is at odds with the very *spirit* of friendship.

In fact, such contracts are not unprecedented. The residents of the parish of Swallowfield in Berkshire signed one during Elizabeth I's reign. The historian Naomi Tadmor notes in her essay 'Friends and Neighbours in Early Modern England' that the villagers got together and wrote a set of articles to guide them in living 'in good love and lykinge one another'. They promised that 'non of us shall disdayne one another, nor seek to hynder one another nether by wordes or deedes', and to instead be 'helpers, assisters and councellors of one another'.

It is easy to dismiss this as an archaic quirk. But in early modern England people more often than not lived and died in one small area, rarely travelling more than a few miles, so the stakes were high – friendship *had* to be worked at. And Swallowfield is not an isolated example. In his *Mutual Aid: A Factor of Evolution* Peter Kropotkin reports that in 1188 Philip, Count of Flanders, gave a charter to the burgesses of Aire saying: 'All those who belong to the friendship of the town have promised and confirmed by faith and oath that they will aid each other as brethren in whatever is useful and honest.' And any transgressor was to be cast out, 'excluded from the friendship as a wicked man and a perjuror'.

The leaders of the French Revolution too wanted to give friendship legal safeguards. 'Liberté! Égalité! Fraternité!' they cried. And in a bid to guarantee *fraternité*, notes Robert

Darnton in *The Kiss of Lamourette*, on 14 November 1793 the Tarn department in south-west France declared the formal *vous* ('you') when used in the singular banished from the 'language of the free French'. Every citizen now had to address another by the familiar – and friendly – *tu*.

In her paper 'Friendship' Elizabeth Telfer argues that, actually, *every* friendship involves a contract. And, she says, choice isn't as central to the matter as we like to think; we can't summon at will the passion that is an essential component. And of course, we cannot choose that the other person will reciprocate. The defining characteristic, Telfer says, is acknowledgement by both parties that the relationship *is* a friendship: 'This acknowledgement involves, not so much the formation of a policy, as endorsement of or consent to a policy which is by then enshrined in practice ... friendship is seen as giving rise to duties and corresponding rights', which are agreed to and policed by the parties involved. These duties and rights may not even appear to make much sense: 'our reaction, like a reaction to a picture, is to a whole personality as a unified thing'. We come to like the way a person 'hangs together', she says. We might enjoy the contrasts offered by the disparate traits that constitute a particular friend.

One of my favourite depictions of the kind of natural evolution of mutually agreed rules that Telfer celebrates is to be found in Kenneth Grahame's *The Wind in the Willows*.

The opening is gentle. Mole, fed up with spring-cleaning, runs to the river bank, where he meets Rat. And here we get a lovely true picture of the awkwardness anyone can feel if they think they might just have met a potential friend.

The two animals stood and regarded each other cautiously.

'Hullo, Mole!' said the Water Rat.

'Hullo, Rat!' said the Mole.

'Would you like to come over?' inquired the rat presently.

'Oh, it's all very well to *talk*,' said the Mole, rather pettishly, he being new to a river and riverside life and its ways.

The Rat said nothing, but stooped and unfastened a rope and hauled on it; then lightly stepped into a little boat ... Mole's whole heart went out to it at once, even though he did not yet fully understand its uses.

After this rush of emotion, as well as introducing Mole to boating, Rat shares his picnic of 'coldtonguecoldhamcoldbeefpickledgherkinssaladfrenchrollscressandwichespottedmeat gingerbeerlemonadesodawater,' which puts his new friend 'in ecstasies'. But this feeling can be left to subside, for now. Mole 'trailed a paw in the water and dreamed long waking dreams. The Water Rat, like the good little fellow he was, sculled steadily on and forbore to disturb him.'

Mole and Rat find they share a passion; yet they can give each other space while, at the same time, their relationship is developing. Then, with Toad in the equation, the friends squabble and a whole new set of negotiations begin. Rat is perpetually telling Toad how appallingly he has behaved. 'On your own admission you have been handcuffed, imprisoned, starved, chased and terrified out of your life, insulted, jeered at, and ignominiously flung into the water – by a woman too! ... When are you going to be sensible, and think of your friends, and try and be a credit to them?'

Toad feels huge regret, then immediately gets into trouble again. Again Rat forgives him, not because he's a saint but because he can't help enjoying Toad's flaws. And perhaps Rat, Mole, Badger and Toad's rule is the one to aspire to: Keep it flexible. Perhaps the biggest don't of all is *Don't come up with rigid rules.*

The maxim-writer Joseph Joubert (1754–1824) was extremely good at friendship. His friend and fellow writer Chateaubriand tells us that Joubert always 'forgot' himself completely, immersing himself in concern for his friends. In his *Pensées* (*Thoughts*) Joubert said: 'The only way to have friends is to throw everything out the window, to keep your door unlocked, and never to know where you will be sleeping at night.'

Joubert lived through the French Revolution. He saw the best and worst of humanity. He also said: 'When my friends are one-eyed, I look at them in profile.'

# PART THREE

# ONWARDS AND UPWARDS

'When we have fallen through story after story of our vanity and aspirations, and sit ruefully among the ruins, then it is that we begin to measure the stature of our friends; how they stand between us and our contempt, believing in our best.'

Robert Louis Stevenson

# 27

# Serial Secessions

C. S. Lewis said, 'Every real Friendship is a sort of secession, even a rebellion.' He was thinking about 'why Authority frowns on Friendship'.

When friends get together, he suggested, 'it may be a rebellion of serious thinkers against accepted clap-trap or of faddists against accepted good sense; of real artists against popular ugliness or of charlatans against civilised taste, of good men against the badness of society or of bad men against its goodness. Whichever it is, it will be unwelcome to Top People.' His point is that with friends, we are fortified in our defiance.

Friendship helps you 'secede' through your whole life. Going back to the beginning, right at the start it helps you secede from home when you are a child. On the first day at playgroup, a two-year-old is likely to keep tight hold of her mother, initially. But the sight of other two-year-olds playing with paint pots and Stickle Bricks soon becomes too appealing. When I was strapping my daughter into her booster seat in the car after her second or third day at playgroup, I remember the look she gave me. It was almost indignant, as if to say, *Why didn't you tell me that there were all these other people who are my size?*

The process thickens at nursery in the 'home corner', or in the playground over the monkey bars. Connections are made. If a shared passion for sandpits is discovered, suddenly two five-year-olds who were strangers a minute ago can go running out into the garden united.

Later, as a teenager, when you rush out of the house yelling over your shoulder that you're going out with friends but refusing to say where to or what your plans are, friendship is helping you escape feelings of dependency on your parents then as well. Although not many of us keep all those teenage friends.

Seneca says in his *Epistolae Morales* that it is important to be slow in choosing your friends – because once you have chosen, you should never let them go or it will reflect badly on you. Cicero agrees that you should avoid breaking with friends if at all possible, writing in *De Amicitia*: 'For nothing is more discreditable than to be at war with one with whom you have lived on intimate terms.'

Is this realistic, though? We can convince ourselves that it's OK to shed childhood and university friendships because we were immature then. But growing up doesn't finish when we reach twenty-one. If every friendship is a secession, with each new friendship we are, rather than embracing someone else, rejecting something of ourselves. There can be no state of stasis. After each friendship is made, there will be a fresh urge to move on.

In Kerouac's autobiographical *On the Road*, the narrator

Sal Paradise talks of how intoxicated he was by his university friendships while he was there. But then he left and wanted to become a writer. He met Dean Moriarty, whose dirty work clothes, he says, clung to him gracefully. The son of a wino, Dean had spent time in a reformatory for stealing cars.

> All my other current friends were 'intellectuals' – Chad the Nietzschean anthropologist, Carlo Marx and his nutty surrealist low-voiced serious staring talk, Old Bull Lee and his critical anti-everything drawl – or else they were slinking criminals like Elmer Hassel, with that hip sneer; Jane Lee the same, sprawled on the Oriental cover of her couch, sniffing at the *New Yorker*. But Dean's intelligence was every bit as formal and shining and complete, without the tedious intellectualness.

'My life hanging around the campus had reached the completion of its cycle and was stultified,' Sal says. That was why he accepted Dean's invitation to take off in an old Cadillac 'across the state of Texas, about five hundred miles, clear to El Paso'. He'd got fed up with Chad and Carlo Marx and Old Bull Lee with their cool routines. Sal's aunt had warned him to stay away from Dean. But more to the point, so had Carlo Marx and Old Bull Lee (who are based on the writers Allen Ginsberg and William Burroughs). They said Dean was too crazy.

The road trip that dominates the novel is dizzying and as the two do crazy thing after increasingly crazy thing on their drugged-up journey across America, Dean is Sal's hero. But it's clear that Dean makes Sal feel inadequate in just the same way that Carlo Marx and Old Bull Lee did before him. Sal is full of admiration when he happens to walk in on Dean having sex with two women at once, one of whom he's about to divorce. But he's daunted too. Having used the son of a wino to reject his college friends, Sal spends the rest of the novel building himself up to reject Dean.

After nearly three hundred pages of drugs, sex and revelry, Sal's life in the closing scene has turned comfortable. He's sitting in a Cadillac again, but this time with his well fed, well heeled friend Remi Boncoeur, on the way to New York's Metropolitan Opera. And Dean is outside, desperate for a lift. 'Want to be with you as much as possible, m'boy,' he whispers to Sal, 'an' besides it's so durned cold in this here New Yawk.'

Sal's attempt to persuade Remi to take Dean in is half-hearted. From the warmth of the car, he watches the friend he has outgrown. 'Dean, ragged in a motheaten overcoat he brought specially for the freezing temperatures of the East, walked off alone, and the last I saw of him he rounded the corner of Seventh Avenue, eyes on the street ahead, and bent to it again.' The narrator may feel sad, but he is also relieved.

And perhaps it is only sensible to keep refreshing your list of friends. Samuel Johnson took that view. Apart from anything else, you are bound to get bored once you know someone, he suggests in a gloomy piece for *The Idler* entitled 'The Decay of Friendship', published in 1758.

The most fatal disease of friendship is gradual decay, our dislike hourly encreased by causes too slender for complaint, and too numerous for removal. Those who are angry may be reconciled; those who have been injured may receive a recompence; but when the desire of pleasing and willingness to be pleased is silently diminished, the renovation of friendship is hopeless; as, when the vital powers sink into languor, there is no longer any use of the physician.

So he says, one must repeatedly move on. 'If a man does not make new acquaintance as he advances through life,' Johnson declared, 'he will soon find himself alone. A man, Sir, should keep his friendship *in constant repair*.'

In 1764 Johnson founded what later became known as the Literary Club with friends including Joshua Reynolds, Edmund Burke and Oliver Goldsmith. Apart from providing a congenial meeting-place for an intellectual elite, did this also seem like the ultimate solution to the problem of making and keeping friends? It was an exclusive club that started with just nine members. Any new member had to be proposed by an existing one; a single objection and the candidate was turned down. Nevertheless, membership had reached twenty-one by 1775. Dinners were held regularly. Any London members who failed to attend were fined. In fact, Johnson became life-long friends with some members, including James Boswell who, in writing a *Life* of Johnson, turned him into a legendary figure. But initially, it seems that a key point of the club for Johnson was to guarantee himself a stream of 'new acquaintances'.

If you don't secede from a friend, he or she gradually comes to know more and more about you. And, if you feel you have rather a lot of faults or foibles, that can be a problem.

Unless of course you have a habit of seceding so fast that they don't have a chance to use any of the information they've gleaned against you.

The American suffragist, entrepreneur and spiritualist Victoria Woodhull did just that with aplomb. She was always making new friends. Just as the Leonard Zelig character in Woody Allen's mockumentary *Zelig* (1983) is a human chameleon, she was able – indeed, felt compelled – to blend in with each new set she fell in with. But whereas in Allen's film Zelig's motivation is a desire to be liked, Woodhull was fuelled by a desire for power. She frankly confessed that she wanted 'to be President next time and thus *ruler of the whole world*'. She did run for President, and was the first woman to do so. She also served as Commodore Vanderbilt's spiritual adviser, all that despite an Ohio childhood characterised by, as she put it, 'squalor'. She started a stockbrokerage firm and founded a newspaper, *Woodhull and Claflin's Weekly*. Each time her ambition changed, she changed who she mixed with too – yet seemed adept at convincing new friends that her attachments to them were genuine.

When she arrived on Capitol Hill on 11 January 1871, she was campaigning for the vote. A delegation of suffragettes who were also in Washington at that time realised that their aims coincided, but while they failed to get a hearing in Congress, Woodhull succeeded. To Elizabeth Cady Stanton and Susan Anthony, two leaders of the movement, it was clear that such a beautiful and charismatic woman would be invaluable to their cause. So they recruited Woodhull as leader, and she re-packaged herself in their image. Her biographer Barbara Goldsmith says that she quickly became 'an amalgam of her suffragette friends. Her views of enfranchisement, marriage, divorce, and the relations between the sexes were largely Elizabeth Cady Stanton's. She wore the same stylish black velvet dress and Alpine hat as Anna Dickinson. She pulled her hair back in a bun like Lucy Stone.'

Isabella Beecher Hooker, who brought money and gravitas to the suffragist movement, was entranced. Woodhull was soon one of her most treasured friends. She judged her 'Heaven sent for the rescue of women from the pit of subjection.' She taught her about deportment and how to write a decorous letter. And the attention wasn't all one way. Indeed, Woodhull's counsel proved life-changing for her. By inviting Hooker to call on spiritual powers despite the fact that she was a Christian, Woodhull seems to have given her the psychological resources she needed to overcome her shyness, and on 16 February Hooker gave 'The finest address I ever delivered ... it flowed out of my inner consciousness as if it were part of my very being.' How can someone help so much and not be driven by real affection? As damaging stories from Woodhull's many-faceted and colourful past began to emerge, suffragette friends began to fall away. But Hooker stood firm beside her. Woodhull added a new dimension to her persona for Hooker's benefit. She let her friend know that she had stitched the second verse of Psalm 120 – 'Deliver me, O Lord, from lying lips, from a deceitful tongue' – into the sleeves of her dresses, pleading: 'My Dear, dear friend, I am often compelled to do things from which my sensitive soul shrinks and for which I endure the censure of most of my friends. But I obey a

Power which knows better than they or I can know and which has never left me stranded and without hope.'

Isabella was being assailed from all sides. Her family strongly disapproved of Woodhull and tried to persuade her to drop her. Her friend Anne Savery begged her to. She had been touched too deeply. Hooker wrote back that Woodhull had appeared to her as 'a prophetess full of visions and messages to the people'. She remained committed to her difficult friend.

In 1877 Woodhull sailed to England and reinvented herself again, six years later conjuring up a bloodline that could be traced back to James I of England so that she could marry an eminent British banker. But still Hooker couldn't forget her. Two decades after they had first met, she wrote to Woodhull asking her, in her persona of medium, to contact her dead mother. But Woodhull's quest for respectability now meant rejecting the suffragettes. She replied that she had spoken to Hooker's dead mother, who had told her that she and Isabella should no longer see each other on earth but would meet again 'on the other side'.

Hooker still adored Woodhull, but she was just someone Woodhull had wanted to learn from, and now put behind her. Sometimes the more dizzying a friendship, the more certain it is to end.

Tennyson's poem 'In Memoriam A.H.H' was inspired by and dedicated to his friend Arthur Henry Hallam, whose life was cut short at the age of twenty-two. When they met at Cambridge University in May 1829, almost immediately their lives became entwined. Hallam wrote many letters promoting

Tennyson's work; he became engaged to Tennyson's sister. When, on 1 October 1833, Tennyson received a letter from Hallam's uncle saying that Hallam had died at Vienna of apoplexy, he fell into a state of such deep mourning that it took him seventeen years to write a tribute to his friend that he considered worthy of him. 'In Memoriam' is now regarded as not only one of his best works but one of the nineteenth century's greatest English poems of its kind.

Yet even Tennyson and Hallam's friendship may have been waning when Hallam died. In *Tennyson* Christopher Ricks notes that by early 1833, when 'Hallam had settled to the slow business of earning a legal living', the relationship was already less intense. The friends can be 'glimpsed' in March, he says, sightseeing in London, in the Zoological Gardens. Four months later, Hallam wrote to Tennyson, then in Scotland: 'I feel to-night what I own has been too uncommon with me of late, a strong desire to write to you. I do own I feel the want of you at some times more than others; a sort of yearning for dear old Alfred comes upon me, and that without any particularly apparent reason.' In the summer of 1833 there is still tenderness. But just four years after they first met, Hallam's yearning is occasional, the desire to communicate is rare.

Perhaps it was simply that the feeling of youthful rebellion had worn off. Tennyson had escaped his domineering father and become a poet. Hallam was going to marry Tennyson's sister. The men's relationship was tinged with domesticity. It could also be that Hallam felt some resentment. He too had wanted to be a poet, but his self-confidence was shaky. While at university, to some extent he suppressed his own ambitions in order to advance Tennyson's. Perhaps his urge to distance himself came about because he felt Tennyson's career had benefited from their friendship, while his hadn't.

It is often said that Tennyson was drawn to Hallam because they were different, that Hallam's cheery disposition helped Tennyson through his bleaker moods. Ricks argues that, actually, the potency of the friendship sprang from the fact that they were very alike, both struggling to escape depression. Within months of starting at Cambridge, Hallam had had to leave for a period of convalescence. His father noted that from time to time he suffered 'a considerable depression of spirits'. In August 1832 Hallam wrote to another Cambridge friend of a bout of 'severe anxiety' that had left him 'much worn in spirit'.

'Tennyson's melancholia (with its relationship to what he had seen of his father's melancholia) found in Hallam the deeper reassurance not of serenity but of similar suffering, doubts and morbidities which yet were not ignoble,' says Ricks. 'Such morbidity could thus be seen as something other than a uniquely personal weakness or shame; moreover it could be alleviated and humanized by friendship.' He points out that in a draft of 'Merlin and the Gleam', Tennyson describes Hallam as 'The friend who loved me,/ And heard my counsel'. Ricks suggests that whereas the despondency of Tennyson's father had 'been inaccessible to anything his son might try to do for him, the despondency of Hallam could be soothed and might even be healed by their deep friendship – and likewise Tennyson's despondency in the loving mutuality'.

*

If in your haste to make a new friend you are running not from just bits of yourself but from your whole being, there will almost certainly be disappointment. For it is unlikely that the friend will work as a salve, an emotional boost or a Prozac substitute for long. You may feel anger then. And if you realise your motives for befriending him or her in the first place were suspect, you may find the sight of this person who has highlighted your delusion unbearable. If you feel self-doubt, or even self-hatred, it can only be worrying that your friend seems to have missed your glaring faults.

Nietzsche wrote in his book *Human, All Too Human*: 'Yes, there are friends, but it is error and deception regarding yourself that led them to you; and they must have learned how to keep silent in order to remain your friend.' Similarly, Kant spoke of how in friendship we have to 'withold something, concealing our weaknesses to escape contempt'. We must control our desire to 'unburden our heart to another'. We can't really tell our friend everything, he says, 'for the sake of decency, lest humanity be outraged'.

Yet the desire to connect can sometimes urge us on to quite extreme revelations and confessions – because when we do feel that we have achieved 'complete union', as Kant puts it, that feeling is fantastic.

# 28

# Transcending Reality

In Frances Hodgson Burnett's novel *A Little Princess*, the main character Sara is sent away to boarding school, and at first the headmistress, Miss Minchin, treats her like a princess. Sara's life is wonderful. However, when the news arrives that her formerly rich father is dead and Sara is penniless, Miss Minchin sends her up to live in the cold attic, which echoes with the sound of 'sharp-toed', scurrying mice.

Thinking she has been abandoned by all the other girls out of snobbery, Sara nearly despairs. She weeps bitterly. Her clothes become ragged and, banned from receiving lessons herself, she is forced to teach the younger children. But then from the luxurious downstairs rooms comes one of the pupils – chubby, shy Ermengarde. She is determined to be her friend despite Sara's reduced circumstances. Even though she might get into trouble Ermengarde sneaks up to the attic, where she and Sara sit on the hard floor together hugging their knees and wrapped in Ermengarde's red shawl.

'Other people have lived in worse places,' says Sara, slightly cheered already. 'Think of the Count of Monte

Cristo in the dungeons of the Château d'If. And think of the people in the Bastille.'

With a friend beside her, the chill reality of her circumstances fades. She and Ermengarde can escape into storytelling. Although *A Little Princess* is tinged with tragedy, Sara's friend brings a rather solemn variety of comfort. She is there to help her maintain her stoic heroism.

In the surreal Italian caper *The Adventures of Pinocchio* (1883) by Carlo Collodi, too, friends have transformative powers. But whereas Sara had bravely resigned herself to her fate when Ermengarde turned up, Pinocchio is a very different character. For a start, of course, he is a puppet. And he is an eternal optimist. Yet even he is surprised at the extent to which friendship can change how he feels about his situation.

Indeed, the way friends make him forget his day-to-day obligations is often his undoing. Each friend brings Pinocchio worse disasters. They persuade him to miss school. They trick him and steal his money. Pinocchio wants to become a boy, and to do so he must forget his friends and listen to his conscience and the Blue Fairy and take care of his father, Gepetto, the poor craftsman who carved him out of wood. But when Lampwick, a boy from the village, starts telling him about a wonderful place called Playland and suggests the puppet go with him, Pinocchio can't resist.

And in Playland he finds children everywhere. 'Some were playing skittles, some quoits, cycling or ball, some were riding on wooden horses; others were playing blind-man's buff.' Pinocchio has already been hung, imprisoned and left for dead because he listened to supposed friends. But he feels only excitement at the sight of so many potential new ones: 'There was laughing, and shouting, and hand-clapping; some were whistling ... Who could be happier, or more contented than they?'

In fact, Collodi reveals, the owner of Playland is a villain – he intends to sell the boys as work animals. The children start turning into donkeys, and Pinocchio starts turning into one too. He determines to punish Lampwick for luring him into this dastardly place. But then he sees that Lampwick is sprouting furry ears as well.

'And then something happened that sounds unbelievable, yet it was true,' writes Collodi. 'When Pinocchio and Lampwick saw that the same misfortune had befallen them both, instead of being ashamed and despairing, they tried to wag their long ears, and finished by laughing at each other.' It looks as if, because he let his friend lead him off the straight path, Pinocchio will lose not only his father but also his dream of becoming a real boy. Friendship got him into this awful situation in the first place. Even so, together, Pinocchio and Lampwick 'laughed and laughed, until they nearly exploded'. Collodi's book presents friendship as not only enormous fun but capable of bringing solace in dire circumstances.

Similarly, in *The Adventures of Tom Sawyer*, by the time Tom, Huck and Joe Harper arrive on Jackson's Island, they are in a major pickle. Their friends in the town of St Petersburg believe they have drowned in the Mississippi. They must forage for whatever food they can. Tom and Huck have witnessed a murder and think that the killer is after them. The three of them have had to steal a log raft to

get away. Yet the minute they drag the raft on to the sand, the
town and the people they have escaped from, even the murder,
all recede into the back of their minds. As the boys gather turtles' eggs on the beach we see their comradeship in Glorious
Technicolor:

> They went about poking sticks into the sand, and when
> they found a soft place they went down on their knees and
> dug with their hands. Sometimes they would take fifty or
> sixty eggs out of one hole ... They had a famous fried-
> egg feast that night, and another on Friday morning. After
> breakfast they went whooping and prancing out on the
> bar, and chased each other round and round, shedding
> clothes as they went, until they were naked, and then con-
> tinued the frolic far away up the shoal water of the bar,
> against the stiff current, which latter tripped their legs
> from under them from time to time, and greatly increased
> the fun. And now and then they stood in a group and
> splashed water in each other's faces with their palms,
> gradually approaching each other with averted faces, to
> avoid the straggling sprays, and finally gripping and strug-
> gling till the best man ducked his neighbour, and then
> they all went under in a tangle of white legs and arms and
> came up blowing, spluttering, laughing, and gasping for
> breath, at one and the same time.

They play games with marbles – 'knucks' and 'ring-taw' and
'keeps'. They turn a ring of sand into a circus ring and
pretend to be clowns. Their friendship – the affinity between
the boys – is now all that matters.

What will they do when the townsfolk find they're not dead? What will they do when they grow up, even? It is not only that close relationships with friends distract from daily life and current worries – they can make the future seem not to matter.

Golding's *Lord of the Flies* is most remembered – by me, certainly – for its atmosphere of intensifying horror. When the boys first arrive on the island, they know they are in trouble. Their plane has crash-landed; the pilot is dead. But as they set off to explore the place they are stranded in, thoughts of rescue quickly fade. The kinds of things that count are the fact that Jack is not just a choirboy, but the head choirboy; he can sing C sharp. And Ralph is instinctively drawn to him. As Ralph, Jack and Simon start to reconnoitre the island and assess its dangers, hacking through the undergrowth they begin to feel elated.

> The cause of their pleasure was not obvious. All three were hot, dirty and exhausted. Ralph was badly scratched. The creepers were as thick as their thighs and left little but tunnels for further penetration. Ralph shouted experimentally and they listened to the muted echoes.
>
> 'This is real exploring,' said Jack. 'I bet nobody's been here before.'
>
> . . .
>
> Again came the solemn communion of shining eyes in the gloom.
> 'Wacco.'
> 'Wizard.'
> There was no place for standing on one's head.

So instead, the boys knock each other down, 'and soon they were a happy, heaving pile in the under-dusk ... Once more, amid the breeze, the shouting, the slanting sunlight on the high mountain, was shed that glamour, that strange invisible light of friendship'.

It's by accident that Ralph slips into the escapism that friendship can bring. He doesn't mean to. He knows it's dangerous. But Ralph is like the rest of us – we so enjoy the way friendship helps us suspend disbelief that at times we take refuge in it, only too happy to be deceived.

In the tradition of direct address, novelists from Henry Fielding to Thomas Hardy talk to 'the reader', introducing the sense that this will be a frank one-to-one exchange. A work that many cite as the first novel (c. 1688), Aphra Behn's *Oroonoko, or the History of the Royal Slave*, takes as its background the author's supposed real-life experiences in Surinam, which she visited in 1663. The story is narrated in both the first and the third person. How much is true observation and how much of it is fiction isn't possible to tell. But Behn uses the idea that the friendship is real to coax us in. 'I was my self an Eye-Witness to a great part, of what you will find here set down; and what I cou'd not be a Witness of, I receiv'd from the Mouth of the chief Actor in this History, the *Hero* himself,' says the author-narrator at the start, taking pains throughout the work to add lavish details of her friendship with Oroonoko. She reads him 'the Lives of the Romans'; they discuss at length the strangeness of electric eels.

Italo Calvino extends the tradition of addressing the reader directly, devoting the opening page of *If on a Winter's Night a Traveller* (1979) to settling him or her. 'Relax. Concentrate,' he insists in his lengthy, intimate negotiation. 'Find the most comfortable position ... Stretch your legs, go ahead and put your feet up on a cushion.'

While the 'strange invisible light of friendship' proves hazardous in *The Lord of the Flies*, in *The Little Princess* it saves Sara. Friendship can comfort and protect in real life too.

In 1898, fresh from studying art at the Slade, Gwen John and her friends Gwen Salmond and Ida Nettleship went to Paris intending to break into the art world there. This was a big step for three young women at the time. They took an apartment on the first floor of 12 Rue Froidevaux. They had hardly any money, but it seems everything about the experience was exciting. Earning their way as artists' models, they started each day sociably with readings from *King John* or *King Lear*. In the evenings they made dresses and ate marmalade cake. Ida wrote to her mother: 'The Gwens are painting me and we are all three painting Gwen John.'

Later, in 1903, Gwen John even travelled to Bordeaux with her friend Dorothy McNeil (who everyone called Dorelia). Their friendship fired their ambition. From Bordeaux they set out to walk all the way to Rome. In a letter to another friend, Ursula Tyrwhitt, Gwen described how she and Dorelia earned their living in cafés by drawing customers' portraits for two francs a time, enough to buy them a meal. They slept under the stars, wrapped in each other's arms, portfolios laid on top of them to keep warm.

In 1922, Vera Brittain and Winifred Holtby, recent Oxford graduates, took a flat in London together. Alone, it could have been awful:

> In Doughty Street we had few comforts and no luxuries except a tortoise called Adolphus ... Rents in Bloomsbury were then so high that the bed-sitting-room standards of college were beyond our means; even the garrets in the house to which our chilly habitation was attached fetched 32s. 6d. a week without food. Winifred's letters to Jean [McWilliam] refer enthusiastically to this partitioned 'studio' with its cold skylights and miniature penny-in-the-slot gas fires; they describe the pleasant trivialities of our daily routine with its strenuous arguments over mop and duster, its egg and cheese suppers cooked on a gas ring, its adornment by coloured bowls of bluebells or wallflowers picked up cheap from a pavement flower-seller.

Brittain and Holtby were both full of self-doubt. They felt young and inexperienced – they *were* young and inexperienced. They had moved to London, and to a male-dominated literary world. Singly they would have found it difficult to pursue their desire to make their mark. They steeled each other. And the way in which with friendship you can transcend reality helps in much more serious situations too.

When during the Second World War the child analyst D. W. Winnicott gave a series of broadcasts on the BBC about how adults should deal with the effects of evacuation on children, his main piece of advice was that they should leave them to work it out with their peers. It was important, he said, for children's mental well-being that they should feel included, whatever the circumstances they found themselves in. If an evacuated child suddenly adopted the local accent, for example, their foster parents should suppress any irritation and instead encourage the child to do whatever it took to fit in. And if children didn't voice fears about the war – about evacuation, bereavements or air raids – that was because they were dealing with them through their friendships and through play.

In his talk 'Children in the War', aimed at teachers in 1940, Winnicott observed that children between five and eleven appeared to be only indirectly affected by the Blitz, even sleeping through gunfire. Yet their games were filled with war. Instead of castles and gallant knights, play would now feature aeroplanes and fighter pilots. Adults were likely to find it impossible to get them to talk about the war because they were too busy making sense of it with their contemporaries. Talk was scary because it was about real destruction, real death. Through their friends, children could process what was happening around them, and still feel safe.

On streets that had been reduced to rubble, they could mix with whoever they pleased and use any old debris that was lying around for their games: bits of banister might be turned into goal posts; an area that had once been a living-room could suddenly serve for hopscotch. And, said Winnicott again, this was fine. Parents had to stand back and let this anarchy happen.

By taking us out of ourselves for a while, friendship helps us through difficult transitions.

This ditty that Winifred Holtby scribbled for fun after graduation shows clearly how friendship helped her to see past all obstacles:

> We mean to run this show.
> We are not shy.
> We'll make the whole world go –
> My friends and I!

# 29

# The 'F' Word

Friendship has plenty of detractors – people who distrust it, people who resent the time it takes to nurture it, people who believe it is of no use at all.

I was struck by an address book in the window of a fancy stationery shop in London's Crouch End. The cover read: 'Liars, Cheats, Thieves, Riff-raff, Phonies and Friends', in that order, the words decreasing in size from a massive 'Liars' to a tiny 'Friends'.

The idea of friendship can make some people very jumpy indeed. 'To say that a man is your Friend means commonly no more than this, that he is not your enemy,' said the writer Henry Thoreau in 1849. La Rochefoucauld wrote in his *Maxims* (1665) that 'What men term friendship is merely a partnership with a collection of reciprocal interests, and an exchange of favours – in fact it is but a trade in which self love always expects to gain something.' Nearly two hundred years later Schopenhauer said: 'true friendship belongs to that class of things – the sea serpent, for instance – with regard to which no one knows whether they are fabulous or really exist.' But surely, you only have to glance through the numbers on your mobile phone to know that friendship *exists*.

Even as we rush to meet old friends or to make new ones, we often feel guilt, however fleetingly. Fixing up a social event can seem indulgent, somehow – even wasteful. We could instead be out, for instance, furthering our careers. Or there's the family to see to, a new car, fridge or loft extension to be saved up for. Friendship is so hard to pin down anyway. Even if you feel you have known someone for ever, you can rarely be sure that they won't suddenly turn. The artist John Singer Sargent liked to joke: 'Every time I paint a portrait, I lose a friend.' 'Only reflect to yourself how various are the feelings, how divided the opinions, even among your closest acquaintances,' wrote Friedrich Nietzsche, 'how manifold are the occasions for misunderstanding, for hostility and rupture. After reflecting on all this you must tell yourself: how uncertain is the ground upon which all our alliances and friendships rest, how close at hand are icy downpours or stormy weather.'

We can feel irritated by friends' demands. For his book *Friendship: An Exposé* (published in 2006), the American writer Joseph Epstein kept a 'friendship diary', and this is how it opens: 'Wrote a (lying) e-mail to LF, telling him I could not meet him ... I like him but not well enough to cut into my weekend.' Cyril Connolly declared in *The Unquiet Grave* in 1944 that 'the industrialization of the world, the totalitarian state, and the egotism of materialism have made an end to friendship'. And, there are plenty who have agreed with Connolly that true friendship quietly but definitely expired.

In 1960 in *The Four Loves*, C. S. Lewis lamented that friendship had come to be thought of as 'something quite marginal; not a main course in life's banquet; a diversion; something that fills up the chinks of one's time'. In 2008, like Connolly, John von Heyking and Richard Avramenko wrote as if it were universally understood that friendship has gone for ever. In *Friendship and Politics: Essays in Political Thought* they cry: 'So whither friendship?'

If friendship was killed, who or what dealt the final blow? There has been some vigorous, at times comic, finger-pointing. In *The Four Loves* C. S. Lewis says friendship was ruined by women and the working classes. He maintains that when they got the vote, women and the masses became jealous of upper-class men's friendships, so elbowed in and spoilt them, turning friendship into an 'endless prattling jolly'. He rails against Wordsworth and Coleridge too, saying that they sabotaged friendship with their Romantic movement.

In ancient and medieval times, explains Lewis, 'Affection and Eros were too obviously connected with our nerves, too obviously shared with the brutes.' And so friendship, 'that luminous, tranquil world of relationships freely chosen', predominated. Three hundred years later 'came Romanticism and "tearful comedy" and the "return to nature" and the exaltation of sentiment'. Friendship, he says, 'had not tearful smiles and keepsakes and baby-talk enough to please the sentimentalists. There was not blood and guts enough about it to attract the primitivists.' And thus, says Lewis, after a few more depredations, friendship disappeared from our lives.

Women, the working classes *and* the Romantic movement: that's some trio of villains Lewis drums up. Von Heyking and Avramenko are more specific: 'The hostility – or, at best, the ambivalence – toward friendship among various Protestant thinkers is one of the roots for the ambiguous place of friendship in liberalism.' And they are not alone in suggesting that friendship and religion don't go together. Christianity posits a pure union with God as an ideal. 'God Is My Friend,' sang Marvin Gaye in 1971. One of the hymn-writer Albert Midlane's best-known hymns, written in 1859, reads:

> There's a Friend for little children
> Above the bright blue sky,
> A Friend who never changes,
> Whose love will never die.

With God cast as the supreme friend, others can only be an unhealthy distraction.

Saleem Dhorat's *Friendship and Our Young Generation*, a pamphlet published in 2004 by the Islamic Da'wah Academy, says: 'All friendships and relationships established for the sake of the world are of no avail. Not only are they a waste of time, but on the day of Qiyamah [Judgement], they will be a means of destruction ... Young people are drained of virtue and the chance of a successful future by the scourge of evil friendship.' In Dhorat's text, friends are people who lead away from Allah towards vices, including women, drugs and violence.

Something that crops up again and again as being bad for

friendship is individualism. Indeed, Sandra Lynch and Preston King name the rise of individualism as friendship's biggest single enemy. As Lynch puts it in her book *Philosophy and Friendship* (2005), 'Relations that emphasise individuality and free choice are apt to be confused with or degenerate into relations in which self-interest or self-gratification guide our actions.' If it's all about *me*, *myself*, *I*, friendship becomes an imposition. In *Friendship in Politics* Preston King and Graham M. Smith concur: with individualism, 'the emphasis is upon ego, the individual, in headlong pursuit of desire, stripped of moral inflection. We shall likely infer from such an orientation that amity and fellow-feeling can have little place.'

Religion, materialism, industrialisation, individualism – capitalism too – *all* at work against friendship? That's an awful lot of enemies.

But whether or not friendship really did ever die, a peculiar aversion to it has been evident in some quarters. There are places where 'friendship' is conspicuous for its absence.

The social psychologist Donald Pennington instead talks about 'affiliation motivation', explaining: 'This term reflects our propensity and need to set up, keep and repair, when necessary, good social relationships with others ... to enable us to compare ourselves with others, thereby reducing uncertainty; to obtain the reward of stimulating company; to be valued; and to gain emotional support.' *Affiliation motivation?* Doesn't he just mean the urge towards 'friendship'?

I expected to find the word used regularly in feminist texts. The hundreds of women who lived in the Greenham Common peace camp, set up in 1981 in protest against nuclear missiles and which lasted for the better part of ten years, could not have got through the cold nights and repeated arrests, evictions and vigilante attacks without it. I *know* friendship played a big part in the women's movement. But in many seminal books on the subject friendship features under other names, in other guises.

In her 1972 essay 'Sisterhood', Gloria Steinem talks of 'consciousness sessions' or 'rap groups', which she defines as an attempt to give women what men have always had, 'some place – a neighbourhood, a bar, a street corner, something – where they could get together and be themselves'. It sounds like friendship, but she doesn't call it that. 'Rap groups,' she said, 'were an effort to create something of our own, a free place – an occasional chance for total honesty and support from our sisters.' In 1982, she wrote an essay entitled 'Networking' to describe the new, improved version of 'rap groups'. Once again, she gives us a description of friendship, but with a different label: 'Networks are psychic territory ... A few hours a week or a month of making psychic territory can let us know that we are not alone and affirm a new reality.'

Betty Friedan's *The Feminine Mystique* (1963) was inspired by the results of a questionnaire she gave out to two hundred of her former Smith College classmates during a fifteenth-anniversary reunion. She determinedly talks of them as 'classmates' rather than 'friends'. But nevertheless, their comments helped launch the second wave of feminism.

When Lynch and King talk about individualism as having been bad for friendship, they focus on 'individualism' as being close to synonymous with 'selfish', and on 'selfishness' as bad. If friendship is essentially narcissistic, can it still be good for society? Samuel Mencher points out in his 1967 article 'Social Authority and the Family', that abolitionists and suffragettes as well as feminists and gay rights activists have all fought on the platform of individualism.

Kant argues in his 'Lecture on Friendship' (1770) that we should not be so quick to judge self-love as wrong. If we interpret Aristotle's 'a friend is another self' as meaning that each friend loves the other 'in place of himself', he says, then friendship can be seen as both selfish *and* altruistic. 'If we felt that others would care for our happiness as we for theirs, there would be no reason to fear that we should be left behind. The happiness I gave to another would be returned to me ... This is the Idea of friendship, in which self-love is superseded by a generous reciprocity of love.' And so, he concluded, friendship can stem from egoism yet still gain 'the sanction of the moral rule'.

But friendship involves favouring some individuals over others when in the bigger scheme of things those individuals don't necessarily deserve special treatment. When we talk of 'nepotism', we don't usually mean it as a good thing.

Elizabeth Telfer stretches the argument further, maintaining that it's not only OK if friendship involves narcissism – it's also OK if friendship itself is intrinsically unfair. In her paper 'Friendship' she points out that if you have to choose between helping a friend out and donating money to charity, and you opt for the first, a small measure of unfairness may be involved. But the good that friendship does society overall makes it morally justifiable. 'The understanding developed by [friendship] and the mutual criticism involved in it will improve the way friends deal with people outside the relationship.' It is not just acceptable to focus on friends. It is preferable. 'We may suggest that the general welfare is best served by our regarding friends as having a special claim on us. We may defend this view on the grounds that more happiness overall is produced if each man makes the welfare of a few others his special concern for two reasons: he will be able to be more effective if he concentrates his energies, and he will be able to know more precisely what the needs of a small group are.'

Michael Pakaluk agrees. In *Other Selves: Philosophers on Friendship* (1991) he says that Telfer's argument is watertight. In the field of moral philosophy she contributed something significant: she showed irrefutably that even flawed friendships do society good.

Telfer's essay came out back in 1971. Steinem was still using euphemistic terms such as 'networking' in 1982; a certain queasiness about 'friendship' was oddly persistent. Did something happen that began to change perceptions?

In the mid-1980s, the AIDS epidemic hit. Everyone, homosexual and heterosexual alike, was, if indirectly, affected, by the sheer quantity of deaths. Friends were lost – suddenly, at a young age – and these bereavements sent shock waves through society.

AIDS arrived in the West in gay communities at a time when many had not yet 'come out', either at work or to their families and heterosexual friends. Painful questions were raised about what friends should tell each other. Should 'true' friends have been open about their sexuality? It felt like a betrayal to find out a friend was gay only because they had become ill.

In their *A Global Report: AIDS in the World*, published in 1992, Jonathan Mann, Daniel Tarantola and Thomas Netter state that one reason for compiling the book was the deaths from AIDS of friends and colleagues. Similarly, Andrew Sullivan wrote his 1998 memoir *Love Undetectable: Reflections on Friendship, Sex and Survival* following the death of a close friend from AIDS. He evokes vividly how the devastation seemed to come from nowhere. One minute he was part of a vibrant American gay community, the next they were all struggling to deal with one funeral after another. He describes how mourning a friend was complicated by the response of the person's family. Many parents disapproved of the friends because they disapproved of the lifestyle the deceased had led, or they thought he had led, and the people associated with it. For those excluded by blood relatives, in such a situation other friends were essential.

Sullivan writes: 'I don't think I'm alone in thinking that the deepest legacy of the plague years is friendship.' And, he says, members of the gay community were actually quite well prepared. During the fight for gay rights in earlier years, friendship was important but there had been no reason to confirm it on paper. Now that experience was helping. 'Denied a recognized family, often estranged from their natural one, they had learned in the few decades of their free existence that friendship was the nourishment that would enable them to survive and flourish.'

As Sullivan says, gay men 'are good at friendship not because they are homosexual, but because, in the face of a

deep and silent isolation, they are human. Insofar as friendship was an incalculable strength of homosexuals during the
calamity of AIDS, it merely showed, I think, how great a
loss is our culture's general underestimation of this central
human virtue.'

# 30

# A Friend in Need

These Strangers, in a foreign World,
Protection asked of me –
Befriend them, lest Yourself in Heaven
Be found a Refugee.

The lyricism of this poem by Emily Dickinson distracts from the fact that it advocates a rather pragmatic take on friendship. Her verse champions inclusivity on the grounds that friendship is a good insurance policy. If you befriend people in need while you are comfortable, then later, if you fall on bad times, they will probably help you. The idea that we sometimes have to be persuaded into friendship is built into the poem.

In her life, it seems she held a different view. Dickinson has a reputation as reclusive. Her biographer Lyndall Gordon says in fact she had plenty of friends, and was constantly trying to pull them closer. 'Lassoes of letters went whirling out from the Homestead to more than forty correspondents,' says Gordon. 'With poems copied in her own hand, Dickinson reached out to others. "I grope fast, with my fingers, for all out of my sight I own – to get it nearer – ... *I own*.'" 'Friends are my estate,' she wrote.

The psychologist Abraham Maslow began developing his famous 'hierarchy of needs' in the 1940s. He argued that before any individual can achieve 'self-actualization' his 'belongingness' needs have to be met first. He described 'belongingness' as a state of receiving and giving love, affection, trust and acceptance. Yet, when he named 'belongingness' as critical in works including 'Motivation and Personality', he tended to lump 'family' and 'friends' together, treating them as interchangeable.

Some, on the other hand, when trying to assess what we need for our well-being, miss out friends completely. Authors including Dr Romulo A. Virola and Jessamyn O. Encarnacion linked the 1971 'Philippine Happiness Index' with the Philippine economic index in order to come up with the Philippine Gross National Happiness Index for the country's tenth National Convention on Statistics. In their paper, 'Measuring Progress of Philippine Society', they admitted they didn't put 'friends' on the initial questionnaire at all. To their surprise, 'sex' came very low as a source of happiness, while the participants' responses forced 'friends' on to the Happiness Index – to the top, beside family, health and religion.

So is it friends, or is it family, that we most need? We tend to think that the traditional family has always been at the centre of things, but in his *Mutual Aid: A Factor of Evolution*, published in 1902, the Russian Peter Kropotkin argues that the modern notion of family is a relatively recent construct, and that it is the need for friendship that is natural to us. 'Far from being a primitive form of organization, the family is a very late product of human evolution.' He says friendship, in fact, is key to our existence. He puts a strong case.

Though best known as an anarchist, Kropotkin was also a geographer and had spent time with small, autonomous communities living in the Siberian wilderness. His theory of 'mutual aid' was sparked by Charles Darwin's theory of evolution. He admired Darwin, but thought he had got one thing totally wrong. From his own researches Kropotkin concluded that animals and humans are driven not by ruthless competition, as Darwin suggested, but rather by an innate desire to support each other.

And he presents many examples of 'primitive' societies that were structured around friendship rather than family. He uses palaeo-ethnologists' finds to show that early man moved about in clusters, hunting in groups of friends. Kropotkin notes that, rather than breaking off into rivalrous families fighting each other for control of resources, the 'barbarians' divided up into village communities that 'knew no personal inheritance of property' and kept as a core value the fair sharing-out and common defence of land. 'For thousands and thousands of years, this organization has kept men together, even though there was no authority whatever to impose it.' In their natural state, he says, humans choose to function with 'mutual aid' as their main motivating force.

Kropotkin refers to nineteenth-century missionaries who clearly wanted, and expected, to feel superior when they travelled abroad to convert 'primitive' tribes. But then on arrival, the more open-minded ones were surprised at what they found. The Norwegian ethnographer C. S. Lumholtz, who 'sojourned in North Queensland', reported to the Paris Anthropological Society in 1888 that even though the 'natives' of Australia were so barbaric that they practised cannibalism, they only ever ate strangers. And 'the feeling of friendship is known among them; it is strong. Weak people are usually supported; sick people are very well attended to; they are never abandoned or killed.'

Kropotkin quotes one G. G. Bink, 'who stayed in New Guinea, chiefly in Geelwink bay, from 1871 to 1883', as stating: 'Friendship is relatively strong among persons belonging to different tribes, and still stronger within the tribe. A friend will often pay the debt of his friend, the stipulation being that the latter will repay it without interest to the children of the lender.' Kropotkin points out that the medieval guilds of Europe, like the Russian *druzhestva* and *arteli* or the Turkish *esnaflar*, ensured brotherhood even despite the intense competition that inevitably came with the then boom in commerce. Examining the Teutons, Celts and Slavonians, he gives numerous examples of tribes that practise mutual aid and consequently survive and flourish. It is isolated family units 'fighting each other for the means of subsistence' that are unnatural. Rather, 'sociability and the need of mutual aid and support' are part of our psychological make-up.

So where did our conviction that society should be organised around small family units come from? Kropotkin argues that it was the emergence of states built 'on the pattern of Imperial Rome' that put an end, sometimes violently, to mutual aid. It might seem surprising that he felt able to attribute the birth of the family as we know it to a specific era. But the social scientist Samuel Mencher also pinpoints Imperial Rome as the start of some serious problems with the arrangement of society: 'In ancient Rome, the paterfamilias had almost unlimited power within the family', and he notes that this power was enshrined in law. He suggests that sayings such as 'An Englishman's home is his castle' exemplify to this day the ancient Roman set-up: the father at the head of the family, which is seen as an inviolable unit. Mencher quotes Justice Patrick Devlin, who wrote in 1965: 'In the regulation of marriage and divorce the secular law is bound more closely to the moral law than in any other subject. This is quite natural. The institution of marriage is the creation of morality.'

With the family endorsed in law as a morally superior grouping of individuals, it is not surprising if friendship came to be seen by some as a force that undermined the greater good.

C. S. Lewis, who wrote effusively about friendship, also declared in *The Four Loves*: 'Friendship is unnecessary, like philosophy, like art, like the universe itself (for God did not need to create it). Friendship has no survival value.' According to Kropotkin, as we saw, quite the opposite is true. His *Mutual Aid* aims to convince us that, rather than focusing on family units, we should be organising our societies around friendship. All very well in the personal sphere, perhaps, but 'mutual aid' is not something we usually associate with the trading floor or the board room. Don't places to do with financial success, built on competition and the survival of the fittest, feel much more Darwinian? They certainly have until now (although that could be in the process of changing – a possibility which Chapter 34 explores).

For as long as the human race staggers on, it is hard to prove that by holding friendship in low esteem we threaten our existence. But various historical and geographical studies offer insight. Kropotkin's talk of missionaries and guilds seems fanciful at times, but it is not that hard to find other instances of societies in which mutual aid is practised.

The anthropologist Margaret Mead spent time with the Arapesh tribe of New Guinea. In her book *Sex and Temperament in Three Primitive Societies*, published in 1935, she describes how the Arapesh make a 'socialised treatment of food' central to their society. It is not only that things are shared. Whatever each tribe member catches or grows must be given to another. If food is difficult to come by and a lot of work goes into catching or growing something, it doesn't come naturally to give it away. Mead reports that the Arapesh elders go to some lengths to make sure that tribe members do. Each generation of leaders chooses future leaders from amongst the children. Then, these future leaders are each given a 'buanyin', or exchange partner, from another family. Given that the aim is to turn the boys into calm, sharing adults, the tradition may look counter-intuitive to an outsider: the exchange partners are required to insult each other. 'Was he born head first like a normal human being, or perhaps he came feet first from his mother's womb?' They must taunt mercilessly, to provoke each other to work harder at hunting and cultivating the land. 'Has he no pigs, no yams?'

And the tradition is effective. It ensures that mutual support is embedded in the tribe's culture. A man who eats something he has hunted himself is considered beyond the pale. By the time the young leaders reach adulthood, says Mead, they are unacquisitive and cooperative. Arapesh men wouldn't think of keeping a tally of any gifts, given or received. Each person eats game killed by another, food grown by another and so on. Amongst the Arapesh, if you don't have good 'trade-friends', you might not eat at all.

But perhaps the most pertinent, although horrific, illustrations of the importance of friendship to our survival are the concentration camps of the Second World War, where, because friendship was recognised to be so powerful, it was actively suppressed. Prisoners were regularly moved between barracks; severe penalties were imposed on any who went into other prisoners' quarters. The Austrian-American child psychologist Bruno Bettelheim, incarcerated in Dachau and Buchenwald between 1938 and 1939, says in *The Informed Heart* that the camp officials succeeded in making friendship between prisoners impossible. Far from being essential to survival, Bettelheim suggests, it was one of the first things to go. The lives of all prisoners were precarious. No one wanted to invest in individual relationships. Apart from anything else, there was no energy for friendship, says Bettelheim, only 'steady pressures towards emotional isolation'.

Primo Levi was in Auschwitz from February 1944 until the end of the war. His account of his time there, *If This Is a Man*, at first seems to support Bettelheim's conclusion. He shows that personal gain was central to any relationship. Some prisoners were friendly to guards and camp officials in the hope of winning privileges. One prisoner, Henri, 'cultivated' the English PoWs, from whom he could occasionally get cigarettes; and 'Henri was once seen in the act of eating a real hard-boiled egg.' Few inmates befriended the *Musel-männer* – literally 'Muslims', but here meaning the thinnest and weakest prisoners – because they rarely survived long and because contact with them felt tainting. Levi avoided the *Muselmänner* too.

Did camp life expose friendship as a worthless sham? Even as Levi took care to keep the physical energy he put into any relationship proportionate to the material gain, he couldn't help investing emotionally. A question that he keeps coming back to in *If This Is a Man* is whether the moments that he felt were friendship, and valued as friendship, could really count. Unexpectedly, in Chapter 5, Levi says: 'Alberto is my best friend.' *Best friend.* What does this mean in the context of Auschwitz?

Only twenty-two, Alberto had an excellent 'capacity for adaptation', didn't complain and spoke a bit of French, German and Polish as well as his native Italian. He was a useful person to be friends with.

Often, the conversation Primo Levi and Alberto managed to snatch was about thefts they might undertake. They collaborated on a plan to steal graph paper that could be bartered: and they exchanged ideas. Levi tells how he transported a broom from the yard in bits, the two halves of the handle tied to his thighs under his trousers; Alberto took a large file from the tool store and, swapping it for two smaller ones, gave only one back. And it wasn't only objects that the prisoners acquired via the friendship they formed – indeed, these were less valuable than some of the other benefits. Sometimes what they were able to experience together after the success of a particularly devious scheme was a sense of pride.

The bunks were tiny, and they were shared. '[T]o have a bed-companion whom one can trust, or at least with whom one can reach an understanding, is an inestimable advantage,' says Levi. 'Since we are forced to exchange sweats, smells and warmth with someone under the same blanket, and in a width little more than two feet, it is quite desirable that he be a friend.' For six months Levi shared a bunk with Alberto. For all his skill as a thief, critically, Alberto was 'uncorrupted'. He kept his head high.

Anna Pawełczyńska, who was in Auschwitz between 1942 and 1945, says in *Values and Violence in Auschwitz* that friendship between the prisoners was what made camp life bearable. It's just that it was friendship defined rather differently. '[E]ach of the Ten Commandments required fundamental reinterpretation,' she says. 'Only the most important of the socialist watchwords remained: "*Fraternité*". In practice, the most beautiful motto "Love your neighbour as yourself" would have required the attitude of an early Christian martyr. In the language of a prisoner battling for his values it sounded like "Do not harm your neighbour and, if at all possible, save him."' Those who managed this 'salvaged the highest values'.

Pawełczyńska draws attention to the fact that prisoners pursued friendship despite the risk involved. 'To be accepted by a group of fellow-prisoners, one needed certain traits of character that eased the process of living together: friendliness, readiness to help, patience, tolerance, self-control.' Few may have actively wanted to engage in the risky business of befriending the weak, but prisoners were more likely to be accepted by their fellows if they showed 'boldness and decisiveness in protecting [them]'. The trade-off in such instances was not a cigarette for a hard-boiled egg. Pawełczyńska is clear about the gains that made the expenditure of scarce energy worth it: 'A prisoner whose attitude won the confidence and acceptance of a larger group of inmates gained another weapon. He was bolstered by the collective strengths of the group who gave him support and to whom he gave support.'

After the war, Pawełczyńska became a sociologist. In *Values and Violence in Auschwitz*, when she talks about friendship and its effects on the prisoners, her sociologist's tone lightens. With fellow prisoners, it was possible to effect tiny, invaluable acts of defiance. 'One important weapon of inner resistance that could not be taken away was a prisoner's sense of humour.' Friends could exchange jokes. They could turn hauling sewage into a game. A 'whispered quip could bring release from the paralysis of fear'.

Also, friends could give each other hope. This is something Levi too highlights. He describes how, in the washrooms, the men showed each other chests, buttocks, thighs. These were acts of friendship, to tell each other that they didn't yet look ready for the gas chamber, even if it was a lie: 'Our comrades reassure us: "You are all right, it will certainly not be your turn this time."'

Levi struck up a friendship with Pikolo, an Alsatian student. It was all a bit halting as Pikolo didn't speak much Italian, and Levi spoke only rudimentary French and German. One of the most moving scenes in *If This Is a Man* sees Levi suddenly anxious, during an errand he's on with Pikolo, not just to explain Dante's *Divine Comedy* but to recite as many passages as he can remember and have a go at translating, so that Pikolo can understand them as well. In doing so, he endangers both of them. He delays the completion of their errand, expending much too much emotional energy. But Levi has been able during this short time to forget where he is. His talk with Pikolo has taken them back to a time when conversations like that were not just allowed, but taken for granted. It has given them the idea that it might be possible at some point in the future to take such discussions for granted again.

Bettelheim later admits that there was indeed a need for friendship that the prisoners couldn't shake off. Each prisoner, he says, had between three and five 'comrades' in their quarters, and the basis of their relationship was a willingness to hear complaints and a desire to have their own complaints heard in return. By giving vent to their anger in this way, the men could feel alive.

Pawełczyńska concludes: 'Every prisoner had his own "neighbors". In the midst of the fight against a world of hatred, as a reaction to a degenerate system of terror, a world of friendship came into being.'

# 31

# Cappuccino Comrades

You are more powerful with a friend than on your own.

Just on our street, I see this. If a nightclub that is a bit too close for comfort puts an application in to the council for very late operating hours, for example, a bunch of us residents will get together over a coffee in one of our houses or a local café and decide what we are going to do about it.

Well, perhaps it's not quite that organised. And maybe it's not every time there's a licence application or some equivalent issue. But as residents, we do work very well together. I am certain that we wouldn't if we didn't like each other.

Some of the best business ideas start as unexpected by-products of friends meeting up for a chat. Buttonbag is a small company that makes craft kits. It sells direct to the public and to over four hundred stockists across the country. Two friends, Sara Duchars and Sarah Marks, both with young children, used to meet regularly for coffee, and during their chats discovered that they were both frustrated by the lack of imaginative children's dressing-up clothes in the shops. So Duchars, a professional costumier, and Marks, a keen amateur since childhood, began making their own. This led to a stall in Greenwich Market, and then to their craft-kits idea. And they were off. Lots of twenty-first-century cottage industries start this way.

But friendship can be a force for much bigger changes, too. And this has been true through history.

When Christopher Wren went up to Oxford in 1650, he was already interested in many aspects of science. Critically, the head of his college Dr John Wilkins, who had similar interests, made sure he had friends to pursue them with. Wilkins gave Wren and Seth Ward, then Savilian Professor of Astronomy, their own room in which they could set out telescopes, thermometers, lenses and other equipment, and pursue hypotheses and build models at their leisure. Wilkins, Wren, Ward and other like-minded scientists founded what was known by its members as 'the Greate Clubbe' and would evolve to become the Royal Society.

The Greate Clubbe had serious aims. If a member's attendance wasn't regular, he was expelled. Each week the group set out to make 'inquisitive experiments', with the aim, as Ward put it in 1652, that 'out of a sufficient number of such experiments, the way of nature in workeing may be discovered'.

There was a level at which science offered an escape. As Wilkins's biographer Barbara Shapiro notes, it is easy to see why science was so appealing in the 1650s. At a time of political and religious upheaval, it could be neutral: it offered 'a respite, a non-controversial topic of conversation and joint endeavour'. Their pursuit of science allowed the men to share their ideas and to interact. The Greate

Clubbe members gave each other invaluable encouragement, and their friendship allowed their 'inquisitive experiments' to flourish.

The club's meetings were held in one of the friends' lodgings, initially in William Petty's rooms, which were, handily, above an apothecary shop. So it wasn't too hard for them to get hold of some of the necessary materials. There was a substantial membership fee, and the members managed to fit out an entire laboratory, conservatory and library. By pooling resources, as time went on they could afford to buy more equipment.

In 1650 John Wallis wrote admiringly to a friend: 'Besides divers and other fine inventions and contrivances, [Wren] hath found out a way to measure the moistnesse and dryness of the air exactly.' This 'weather clock' took Wren one step closer to helping perfect the barometer.

Significant inventions came out of the Greate Clubbe. Wren certainly couldn't have achieved all he did on his own. Indeed, his biographer Adrian Tinniswood suggests it was Wren's Wadham friendships that turned 'a precocious teenager' into one of the leading figures of the seventeenth century. Of the fifty or so men who were members of the Great Clubbe in its early years, twelve were from Wadham. Individually, they would have been unable to entertain such a grand ambition as to discover the 'way of nature in workeing'. Together, their potential was incalculable.

Two centuries later, in London, the young Royal Academy graduates John Everett Millais, William Holman Hunt and Dante Gabriel Rossetti were similarly buoyed by friendship. They met one day in 1848 in Millais's parents' house on Gower Street, and concluded that they didn't have to be outcasts, even though they disagreed with the main artistic principles of the reigning Academicians. They held that their contemporaries' works, and indeed all works since Raphael, were mechanistic. They drew up rules: any artist in their group should look to nature and to medieval painting for inspiration, and must have genuine, heartfelt ideas to express. They gave themselves a name – the Pre-Raphaelite Brotherhood.

The pre-Raphaelites are considered unfashionably romantic now. But at the time they made quite an impact. The Royal Academy had a stranglehold on the British art world, and the pre-Raphaelites broke it. The movement still has its own section in the main national art collections, from the Walker Gallery in Liverpool to the Kelvingrove in Glasgow and the Victoria and Albert Museum in London.

Friendship can steel people to fight the statute books too.

In the 1840s, early on in her work as a reformer, Elizabeth Cady Stanton, at the time a member of the abolitionist movement, had been refused the right to speak at meetings because of her gender. At first, in her fight for suffrage, Stanton allied herself with a fellow abolitionist and social reformer, Lucretia Mott. It was they who organised the first women's rights convention, which took place at Seneca Falls in 1848. But it wasn't until Stanton met Susan B. Anthony, then a Temperance worker, that the women's movement in America began to gain real momentum. Stanton and Mott had worked efficiently enough together, but between Stanton and Anthony there was the spark of friendship.

In 1850 they launched the magazine *Revolution*. They

petitioned Congress together, they campaigned all over the country. They suffered innumerable setbacks, but together they felt indefatigable. In 1869 they founded the National Woman Suffrage Association. In the same year, Wyoming Territory granted women suffrage, and state after state followed suit until in 1920 the Nineteenth Amendment granted all American women the right to vote.

'In thought and sympathy we are one,' wrote Stanton, 'and in the division of labor we exactly complemented each other.' They even did something as intimate as write together. And in writing, said Stanton, 'we did better work than either could alone. While she is slow and analytical in composition, I am rapid and synthetic. I am the better writer, she the better critic. She supplies the facts and statistics, I the philosophy and rhetoric.' Neither could take more credit than the other, she concluded. 'Our speeches may be considered the united product of our two brains.'

Stanton and Anthony's publications include *History of Woman Suffrage*. The project was vast. The first volume was published in 1881, and the last in 1922 after the authors' deaths; volumes 4 to 6 were by other writers, but the first three were by Stanton and Anthony.

In the continued fight for the women's cause, a hundred years later, Susie Orbach, psychotherapist and social critic, and Luise Eichenbaum believed that established psychotherapy wasn't sufficiently meeting women's needs. In their book *Between Women: Love, Envy and Competition in Women's Friendships* (published in 1987), they describe their first encounter as 'risky and electrifying'. It was 1969. Orbach was giving a lecture at Richmond College in New York, where

Eichenbaum was a student. Orbach was twenty-five, Eichenbaum nineteen. Luise was captivated, she remembers, by Susie's long suede skirt and high purple boots. They each had long-held ideals that they cherished. Together, as friends, they felt ready to take on the establishment. In 1976, they founded the Women's Therapy Centre in London to give therapy to women who couldn't otherwise afford it. The charity is still going strong three and a half decades later; its sister organisation, the Women's Therapy Centre Institute in New York, recently celebrated its thirtieth anniversary.

Such endeavours take a huge amount of hard graft. These kinds of intense friendships are not without problems. There can be a considerable cost to one or other of the individuals concerned: one party may start to feel that they've been dumped with the boring bits. Irritation and resentment can easily set in.

Stanton describes her work with Anthony on *History of Woman Suffrage* emphatically as joint. But it required Anthony regularly to look after her friend's seven children so that Stanton could lock herself away to write in silence. In Orbach and Eichenbaum's case, they fell out so badly that the Women's Therapy Centre nearly didn't survive. They describe it all in *Between Women* – wincingly at times. But they managed to turn their unhealthily 'merged attachment' into a 'separated' but still 'significant' one. Stanton and Anthony, too, kept feelings of envy and competition from ruining their friendship.

However, it is not only morally upright citizens who are helped by friendship to realise big ideas. Friends who occupy the moral low ground can fortify each other too.

\*

In the late 1800s in America, Butch Cassidy was a small-time crook in Utah before he drew together friends including Elzy Lay and Harry 'the Sundance Kid' Longabaugh to form the Wild Bunch. They lived on the 'outlaw trail', stealing tens of thousands of dollars from banks and trains in Utah and Wyoming. In between, they hid out in Robbers' Roost, a place in the hills where, the 1969 film *Butch Cassidy and the Sundance Kid* suggests, even the rock formations colluded to protect the rebels' friendship. In the famous black and white photograph of Cassidy and the Wild Bunch, the men have their hats at rakish angles and their hands firmly on each other's shoulders.

In Britain in 1963, 'the Great Train Robbery' was pulled off by friends Gordon Goody, Bruce Reynolds, Ronald 'Buster' Edwards, Ronnie Biggs and others, who between them got away with £2.5 million in mailbags from a Glasgow night train. Unfortunately for them, it was friendship that proved their undoing as well. Evidence including fingerprints left on a game of Monopoly they'd been playing in their hideout beforehand contributed to their capture.

There are other complications. Friendship is appealing because it pulls people together, but it feels especially potent if it also excludes.

It emerged in 1997 that the Tory leader David Cameron had been a member of the exclusive Oxford University Bullingdon Club while he was a student. The press was delighted to be able to report that membership was (and still is) by invitation only, and barely feasible unless you have independent wealth. Doing well enough in your A levels and at your interview to get to Oxford certainly isn't enough to

get you into the Bullingdon. It isn't merely the price of the
food that members have to cover. There's also the outfit,
running into thousands of pounds these days. Some members of the Bullingdon have given dinners that have got so
rowdy, with so much drink flowing and restaurants badly
smashed up, that damages have had to be paid on the spot.

Jobs for the boys and old boy networks? Not all right, surely.
But because friendship often not only involves inequity but
sanctions it too, should it be rigorously kept out of business and
politics? A great deal would be lost, if so. Groups of friends can
achieve things that would be well-nigh impossible for strangers.

In the Second World War the Germans started making
'heavy water' (deuterium oxide), a substance that can be used
to make nuclear weapons, at the Norsk Hydro plant in Norway.
Between 1940 and 1943 the Allies devised a series of sabotage
actions, including Operation Freshman, which sent thirty-four
commandos in Halifax gliders to target the plant. Freshman
was ill conceived in every way. After having been deposited by
the gliders, the commandos were supposed to make their way
to the Norsk Hydro plant on fold-up bikes across one of the
biggest wildernesses in Europe. Temperatures were well below
zero, the snow was waist-high, and the plant was situated
halfway up a gorge. The gliders crashed, and before they'd got
anywhere near the plant the survivors were rounded up and
killed on the spot by Nazi forces.

In February 1943, nine friends undertook the same mission. In Operation Gunnerside they destroyed the Norsk
Hydro plant without firing a single shot, in a raid so daring
that in 1965 it was made into a film, *The Heroes of Telemark*,
starring Kirk Douglas.

Knowledge of the terrain had made a big difference. The Operation Freshman commandos weren't familiar with it, or with the icy, treacherous conditions, whereas the nine men of Operation Gunnerside were Norwegians; they knew the mountains, they had grown up in the county of Telemark together. But their success rested on much more than local knowledge. The heroes of Telemark were friends before they undertook Operation Gunnerside, and this undoubtedly made a huge difference to the success of their mission. They were all clear that they wanted to come out of the raid with no casualties on either side (while they were in the plant, they advised one of the workers to open his mouth so he would not be made deaf when the dynamite went off). Before the raid, four of the men lived for three months on the remote Hardanger Plateau in a hut made of planks. The temperature was minus 20, the ice inside the hut covered the ceiling and stretched halfway down the walls. The radio operator, Knut Haugland, often had trouble transmitting because he was shivering so badly. At one point things got so desperate they had to scrape moss off the rocks as food to survive.

The hardship they endured together was extreme. But the fact is that most men, if forced to live together in a hut for three months, would have worked something out. If the members of Operation Gunnerside hadn't been friends before, they would have had to develop reasonable relations pretty quickly.

There is one particular group that puts friendship at the centre of their lives that is especially interesting in the context of friendship as a force for change. The Quakers.

Founded in the 1640s, the group was called the Society of Friends. The name 'Quakers' came later (it's said, because members 'quaked' when the spirit filled them), but they are known today simply as 'Friends'. A main tenet of the movement is that there is no hierarchy – everyone's on an equal footing.

At the start, members called each other 'thou', regardless of rank. No decisions were taken at meetings until everyone had agreed. And with friendship as their starting point, the Quakers brought much positive change in the wider community.

In *An Intimate History of Humanity*, Theodore Zeldin notes: 'Quakers set up the first anti-slavery society, which led to the first law challenging slavery: any slave who set foot in England became a free person. They were the first to organise a boycott, in the eighteenth century, against products originating from slave-owning countries ... They were the first people in the world to plead for the abolition of the death penalty. In the eighteenth century, John Belley proposed a free national health service, as well as a study of Indian and American medicine to complement that of Europe. Elizabeth Fry (1780–1845) [also a Quaker] was one of the earliest instigators of prison reform.'

Zeldin's list goes on. 'They invented the idea of offering humanitarian help to civilians devastated by war: in 1870–1 they brought food, clothing and medicine to both sides in the Franco–Prussian War. They went to jail in 1914 to establish the rights of conscientious objectors.'

Because Quakers are pacifists, it is often assumed that they are in the final analysis ineffectual. This is certainly not the case. Yet while Zeldin celebrates Quakers as social activists, he dismisses them as real political players.

And it's true, Quakers have never made a big splash in politics. Zeldin says that's because it became clear early on that 'friendship and the giving of orders were incompatible, and that friendship was not a system for large groups of people'.

'To be brought up among Friends is to be brought up to quiet ways of working,' says Harold Loukes in his account of the history of Quakerism. Politics, with its 'violent back-slapping, baby-kissing, and boisterousness', is fundamentally at odds with the Quakers' natures. But individually, the Quaker nature didn't necessarily have much to do with it because for most of the first two hundred years of the movement's existence, Friends were not allowed to participate in politics.

The movement was founded during the Civil War by George Fox. Through the early years of Quakerism, religious intolerance was rife. He and his followers were ostracised for refusing to attend church or take the sacrament, and were often imprisoned, Fox spending a total of about six years incarcerated. In 1656, the year after he and his followers refused to take the Oath of Abjuration – whereby they would have agreed to permanent exile – nearly a thousand of them were behind bars.

Quakers couldn't stand for Parliament in Britain until 1828. And when Joseph Pease did stand, and was elected MP for South Durham in 1832, he couldn't take his place until a special committee had been convened to confirm that instead of swearing on the Bible, which no Quaker would do, he could instead make a 'solemn affirmation' – and so, finally, become the first Quaker Member of Parliament.

It is also often thought that Quakerism and business don't go together. Accounts such as Zeldin's and Loukes' certainly give that impression. If Quakers' sensitivity and 'quiet ways of working' make them ill-suited to politics, running a factory, surely, must be impossible for any upstanding Friend. In fact, Quakers became active in commerce, and their businesses flourished in judicious alliances that combined profit-making with a fair deal for employees and customers alike. Friendship and profits could, and did, go together. I only have to look at the shelves in my kitchen cupboard to see that some of the best-known names in biscuits are those of originally Quaker firms: Carr, Jacob's and Huntley & Palmer's, for instance. The English chocolate business was dominated throughout the nineteenth century by Quaker firms, most famously Cadbury, Rowntree and Fry. The Friends did particularly well in the iron and textile industries and in mining and banking. Lloyds and Barclays were both founded by Quakers. Edward Pease, the father of Joseph, started the Stockton to Darlington railway line and collaborated with George Stephenson to employ steam traction. Indeed, Edward Milligan found no shortage of Friends to include in his *Biographical Dictionary of British Quakers in Commerce and Industry 1775–1920*, which runs to 2,800 entries.

As non-conformists, in the early days Friends were barred from the major universities. Their refusal to swear oaths meant that they were also excluded from the 'learned professions', notably the law and medicine. Commerce was their best option. But it wasn't that the Quakers did well in business *despite* their principles of friendship. In *Quaker Enterprise in Biscuits: Huntley and Palmers of Reading 1822–1972*, T. A. B. Corley shows that the beliefs of fellow Quakers Thomas Huntley and George Palmer were embedded in factory life. As teetotallers they came down hard on employees caught drinking in work hours. And they wanted to eliminate swearing in the factory as well. But they managed to give even their punishments a friendly edge. Misdeeds such as drinking and swearing incurred fines that went into a benevolent 'sick fund box'.

And, it wasn't just individual Quakers who worked to make commerce and friendship congruent. Good business practice was a main topic at local meetings. Quakers were advised to keep regular accounts, pay debts promptly and avoid any dishonest practice 'which endangers peace of mind'. Furthermore, they were invited to keep checks on each other, and to answer questions at their preparative meetings, such as, 'Are Friends just in their dealings and punctual in fulfilling their engagements?' And as Quaker communities were generally small, if one person disapproved of another, that disapproval 'exercised a powerful conditioning effect,' notes Corley.

Even before Friends were allowed into politics, they were moulding it. 'Four of the five leaders of the feminist movement in nineteenth-century America were Friends,' acknowledges Zeldin, 'a third of the pioneers of prison reform, 40 per cent of the abolitionists. They wrote the Equal Rights Amendment.'

In fact, friendship is absolutely compatible with politics and business, and perhaps we need more of it in both – which is not to say that everyone must convert to Quakerism. But there's a good case for arguing that the principles of friendship that featured in the commercial and political lives of Quakers should be adopted more widely. Indeed, in *Friendship in Politics*, King and Smith say that we should make 'friendly networks' central to governance. Friendship makes society stronger precisely because such networks are 'less like a pile of marbles, pebbles or coins, and more like a chain. The chain, in which A links with B and B in turn with C and C in turn with etc., is a set of serial connections. Each of its links is distinctive in that the rapport of A to B is not that of B to C. Thus there is strength to the whole in that each member is both bound and free, committed yet independent, caught up in a chain but not overwhelmed by a mass.'

'Friendships,' argue King and Smith, 'give citizens confidence and (paradoxically) independence.'

# 32

# Loss

The death of a friend is more than the physical loss of a person. The opportunities to continue building your store of shared experiences are gone too. Suddenly the truth, longevity and memory of that friendship is one-sided.

While you are both alive, free will is central to friendship. And that is one reason the death of a friend is so particularly unsettling. Even if you met initially because your parents brought you together as toddlers, if you went on to stay in touch as adults that was because you both decided to. You wanted to spend time together. You *chose* each other. The news that a friend is dead or dying attacks our sense that we have control over anything. By dying they betray us. They remind us we are all mortal. It is not uncommon to feel cross and let down.

And if there was actually little real friendship in a person's life, that becomes horribly clear at their funeral. They may have been genial and gregarious, but picked the wrong people to associate with. Or perhaps they were befriended by others for the wrong reasons. F. Scott Fitzgerald gives a poignant description in *The Great Gatsby* of Jay Gatsby's vast numbers of New York socialite friends, who all adore his generous parties, falling away rapidly when he gets involved in a sordid scandal. His funeral is attended by the novel's narrator Nick Carraway, Gatsby's father and just one of the people who used to come to his parties – who seems, anyway, to have turned up by mistake.

Nico was known the world over through the 1960s and 1970s as fashion model and singer with the Velvet Underground. When she died in a bike accident in 1988 she was a confirmed heroin addict, whose attempt to revive her career as a singer from a base in Manchester had been a resounding flop. James Young played keyboards on the last tour. As he describes it in *Songs They Never Play on The Radio: Nico, the Last Bohemian*, Nico had two funerals. At the one in Yorkshire, her Mancunian music manager Dr Demetrius 'read poetry to a captive congregation of me, Eric Random, a couple of Goths and a fellwalker in an anorak and bobble-hat'. And the funeral in Germany, her homeland, was still more desolate. The fell-walker didn't stop by. Nico didn't know who turned up at her funerals, of course. The pain was Young's.

Mark Finch was a film promoter, so it was his job to know a lot of people. He ran London's Piccadilly Film Festival in the 1980s and then the San Francisco International Lesbian and Gay Film Festival from 1992 to 1994. His death in 1995 was sudden and tragic. He was in his early thirties. His funeral service at St James's Church, Piccadilly, was full to overflowing. There was a clear sense at the service that mourners were competing – with their positioning in the pews, with their weeping – each jostling to show that they had been his particularly close friend. And I suspect the reason I felt this jostling so keenly was because I was doing it too. We can only be sure of the depth of *our* feelings for a friend – we can't know if those feelings were reciprocated. A lot of self-doubt gets stirred up. One way of managing grief following the death of a friend is to decide that you are, in fact, the central figure in the whole drama.

I was one of Mark's friends – not his best, I knew that – but quite close, I'd thought. Mark was fantastically good at making each friend feel like the only person in the world who mattered to him. At his memorial service, I suspect I resented the other mourners because their sheer numbers suggested that in fact I wasn't special at all. With their hankies and bawling they made me feel like an interloper, when I wanted to feel like the protagonist in a Shakespearean tragedy.

The Roman statesman and writer Seneca told us too much grief is only a parade. In his essay *On Grief for Lost Friends* he says: 'Let not the eyes be dry when we have lost a friend, nor let them overflow. We may weep, but we must not wail.' If the quantity of grief displayed is the measure of the depth of feeling for your lost friend, then you can't even smile wanly, as it will suggest you have forgotten them already. 'The most shameful cure for sorrow, in the case of a sensible man, is to grow weary of sorrowing.' But Seneca's stoicism can be very hard to muster.

Montaigne's celebrated essay 'On Friendship' was triggered by the death of his friend the writer Étienne de la Boétie, in 1563. They'd only known each other for five years, but in the essay Montaigne is keen to show that the brevity of the relationship in no way diminished it. He gives us long, lovelorn descriptions. He says his friendship with la Boétie was brought about by 'some decree of heaven'. Such a friendship as this 'has no model but itself, and can be compared only to itself'.

Much of Montaigne's essay is beautiful. It is great to hear someone declare unreservedly that friendship is both wonderful and wonderfully important. It is particularly refreshing to hear it from someone who experienced periods of scepticism. But at times he sounds almost petulant. He expresses rage that something has been taken from him.

When the German film director Werner Herzog heard in 1974 that his friend the film historian Lotte Eisner was dying in Paris, he didn't jump on a plane and rush to be with her, or even telephone her. He packed a compass in his duffel bag and set off to walk to Paris from Munich – 'in full faith,' he says, 'believing that she would stay alive if I came on foot'. Later, he published the notes from his three-month-long journey as *Of Walking in Ice*. On page 25 he asks, 'Lotte Eisner, how is she?' On page 45, 'Is our Eisner still alive?' But she's hardly mentioned in the rest of the text. He seems not to be interested in recalling either the good or the bad times they spent together; he doesn't analyse her importance to the film world; he doesn't think about the characteristics that attracted him. The journey is meant to be for her. But his focus is almost entirely on himself and what he sees and experiences along the way. He pays close attention to frost-bitten earthworms stranded on asphalt and cigarette packets on the roadside that take on corpse-like qualities. Especially, we learn the minutiae of Herzog's own privations; how, for instance, he has to scrabble meals together and break into an abandoned house to grab a few hours' sleep. And when he does finally get to Paris, as he reports it, he doesn't so much as ask how his friend is feeling. Indeed, she has to push a chair over so he can put his feet up.

Was Herzog's response to his friend's illness, in making his trip to see her into an expedition, self-centred? In any event Eisner welcomed him, and perhaps his plan did work – she went on to live for another nine years.

In earlier times, it has sometimes been judged better to have friends than family at your deathbed.

In the classical world it was taken as read that women and children would be too upset to be present when a loved one approached death; *they* would be the ones demanding sympathy. In Greece in 399 BC, Socrates was condemned to death for 'impiety' and 'corrupting the youth'. On his last day, his wife and sons were sent from his cell early on, as a matter of course. In his essay 'Of Friendship' Francis Bacon argued that it is better to have friends at your deathbed than family members, who can be disabled by grief, or distracted by avarice if an inheritance is at stake. If a man about to die is surrounded by blood relatives, second wives, cousins and so on, he'll suspect that after his death his wishes will be forgotten, argues Bacon. That is, unless he has a true friend, in which case he can feel almost certain that the things he cares about most – his children or 'the finishing of a work' – will be attended to properly.

In Graham Swift's novel *Last Orders* (1996), the south London butcher Jack doesn't want his wife by his side as he lies in hospital dying of cancer, but rather his old friend Ray, or 'Raysy'. In Ray's presence, Jack can make lewd jokes about the attractive young nurse. With his mate, he can feel virile again even as he's attached to the hospital bed by tubes and drips, a plastic name-tag round his wrist.

We are moving into an era when more and more people will find themselves far away from family as they approach death, or, as the divorce rate mounts, estranged; or, as more people decide against procreation, with no family at all. Reflecting on the 1980s AIDS epidemic, Andrew Sullivan notes in *Love Undetectable*: 'The duties demanded in a plague, it turned out, were the duties of friends: the kindness of near strangers, the support that asks the quietest of acknowledgments, the fear that can only be shared with someone stronger than a lover.'

In Swift's novel, Jack's last request is to have his remains scattered from Margate pier. His wife doesn't understand it, she's angry and so she refuses. But Jack's wartime buddies Ray, Lenny and Vic get in the car with Jack's adopted son Vince and drive to the coast. During the drive, a variety of infidelities and betrayals emerge. Accusations fly, and at one point on a hill near Faversham, fists too. When the men arrive at Margate pier, it's to find a sign saying, 'THIS LAND IS PRIVATE – TRESPASS AT YOUR OWN RISK.' They climb over anyway.

In reality, not every friend is as indefatigable as Ray, Lenny or Vic. All sorts of excuses can be presented for not going to the hospital ward or venturing into the bedroom, where the curtains will undoubtedly be closed, the bedlinen infused with the smells of illness, and the patient will want to talk about nothing but his or her pain. The effects of terminal illnesses are generally frightening to see. Like Herzog, if we learn that someone is dying, we don't necessarily rise to the occasion. And unlike Eisner, neither, necessarily, does the person who is soon to depart.

Socrates' friends might well have been glad if he had been in clear distress about his forthcoming execution. Instead, there in his cell, he wanted to chat to his visitors as if everything was fine. He was visited every day by different friends, and they found his calm enormously disturbing.

According to Plato in *The Last Days of Socrates*, when the philosopher's friend Crito came to see him in gaol he was desperate. The authorities had made it easy for Socrates to escape, but most Athenians didn't know that he had turned down opportunities to flee, so Crito's fear was that they would all assume that Socrates' friends had been too mean to put up the money. 'I shall not only lose a friend whom I can never possibly replace,' wailed Crito, 'but besides a great many people who don't know you and me very well will be sure to think that I let you down, because I could have saved you if I had been willing to spend the money; and what could be more contemptible than to get a name for thinking more of money than of your friends?' The man facing imminent death had to put a lot of energy into soothing his visitor, explaining that taking poison was his only honourable option. He took the time to help Crito even though he was the one facing execution.

But Socrates was healthy and sure of his decision. If the person facing death is suffering physical pain, patience can be in short supply.

When he was on his deathbed in October 1855, the philosopher Kierkegaard called his old friend Emil Boesen to him. Boesen was a pastor, so Kierkegaard must have known Boesen would think he wanted spiritual comfort. Sure enough, on 17 October Boesen wrote to his wife excitedly: 'I have come here almost to be his father confessor.'

At one point during his friend's visit, Kierkegaard said he felt as if he could be lifted up like an angel, straddle a cloud and sing, 'Hallelujah! Hallelujah! Hallelujah!' Boesen asked, 'And all that, of course, is because you believe in Christ and take refuge in him in God's name?'

'Yes, of course,' snapped Kierkegaard, 'what else?'

Boesen asked if he would change anything he'd said in his life, and Kierkegaard demanded: 'Why do you want to bother me with this!'

Boesen asked Kierkegaard again and again if he would pray with him. But Kierkegaard seemed more interested in the question of whether or not he would be famous after his death. 'I will gladly die,' he declared. 'Then I will be certain that I accomplished the task. Often people would rather hear what a dead person has to say than someone who is alive.'

His biographer Alastair Hannay describes Kierkegaard as 'mischievous'. This is to put it kindly. As he neared the end, Kierkegaard said to Boesen: 'Things have certainly been pretty hot for you because of your association with me, haven't they?', clearly enjoying the discomfort he was causing.

Boesen asked: 'Won't you take Holy Communion?'

'Yes, but not from a pastor, from a layman,' declared Kierkegaard. This would be difficult to arrange, Boesen told him.

'Then I will die without it.'

In his last hours Kierkegaard was contradictory, manipulative, capricious. He didn't want spiritual guidance from his childhood friend – rather, a last chance to be human.

Socrates too seemed suddenly to get fed up with his friend's demands for reassurance. 'It is about time that I took my bath,' he said abruptly, towards the end.

Crito demanded: 'But how shall we bury you?'

'Any way you like,' said Socrates, 'that is, if you can catch me and I don't slip through your fingers.'

# 33

# Google Grief

Until recently, when someone died family gathered round largely to the exclusion of friends, who were informed much later by telephone, or via a notice in the newspaper. Of course this generally happens because the family's grief is so intense they can't think about anybody else's. But a friend's grief can be intense too. And it can be tough to feel that you are being informed as an afterthought, perhaps mainly to bulk out the numbers at the funeral. Or maybe your surname begins with W so you're at the end of the deceased's address book, or despite all your years playing bridge together you'd just never met the family. Whatever the reason, if you are quite far down the list to be told, there can be a feeling that your grief should be scaled down accordingly. A best man or maid-of-honour or friend from nursery might get an early call and be forgiven for mourning loudly. But if you not only get the sense of being superfluous to requirements, but fear you'll be considered melodramatic if you show too much emotion, that makes the hurt still harder to bear.

However, this no longer has to be the case. Technology

has democratised the process. With a round-robin email or a Facebook posting, everyone can know immediately that a friend has died or that they are dying.

One friend, Rose, was close to someone who was diagnosed with terminal cancer. Rose's friend, Jane, was young and very popular. She had a wide circle of friends, but her physical health deteriorated so quickly that soon after the diagnosis she wasn't able to do much. Jane was in London and her family was based in Northumberland, so her friends were essential to her. But lots of visitors at once was too tiring. Rose and a few other intimate friends were able to manage the situation through Jane's Facebook site, making sure that visitors came in a regular trickle. They gave updates on other ways in which friends could help, for example with gifts of meals – laborious to prepare, but they made Jane feel physically more comfortable.

Of course, there are down sides to the way the new technology alters our experience of friends' illnesses and deaths. And some of them are major.

More and more, people get their news through the Web, and increasingly young people get it through social networking sites. The morning after Michael Jackson died I was on a commuter train at 7.30 a.m. It became clear that a dozen or so A-level students on the train had all heard through Facebook. Few were really affected – the news had been received primarily as shocking gossip. But what if, while rushing between putting your make-up on and grabbing some breakfast and yelling at a younger sibling, the news is of the death of a close friend? What if, when a teenager gets home drunk at 1 a.m., having just been dumped by her boyfriend – only he hasn't yet told her in person – she logs on and hears the news then?

Since Facebook can be accessed at any time of the day or night, there's a bigger chance that a death or other bad news will be heard when a user is vulnerable.

I once learned in a school assembly that two boys had died the previous day after diving into the River Wharfe. Presumably the headmaster took advice beforehand. Certainly, I could see that he chose his words carefully to comfort his pupils and help make the news manageable. I knew the boys vaguely, but I did not consider them my friends. Had Facebook been around, I almost certainly would have. Even if I rarely spoke to them in person, I could have known which football team they supported and the name of their favourite pop band. Social networking sites lend an air of unreality to friendships, and they can turn death into a commodity.

Between 2007 and 2009, twenty-four people aged between fifteen and twenty-eight in the County Borough of Bridgend in Wales committed suicide, almost all of them by hanging. The press leapt on the fact that they were all, through social networking sites, friends with at least one other Bridgend suicide victim. The suggestion was that the existence of such sites had exacerbated the situation; that without the Internet, there would not have been so many suicides. A main point of friends, for teenagers, is that often they provide an escape from home. In situations like this, parents and siblings may be able to offer little consolation. When bad news comes from sites like Myspace, Friends Reunited, Facebook or Bebo, it throws the young person back into cyber space to memorial sites, devising their own tribute.

In an interview for *The Times* the author of *Suicide Clusters*, Loren Coleman, said there's no doubt that social networking sites such as Facebook glamorise death. 'Reality TV means young people are constantly bombarded with instant fame and instant success. A young person in a deprived area sees this and it's psychologically destructive. They think: if I'm a nobody but I commit suicide, I'll be a somebody. I'll get my photo in the papers, I'll have a memorial on the internet. How can I be a celebrity? Well, if I don't get onto *Big Brother*, an alternative is death. My friends are doing it.'

It is important to remember that suicide clusters are not new, but they are still rare. That is why the Bridgend suicides became a media phenomenon. And it is not only young people who find themselves badly affected when news of a friend's death hits them from cyberspace. It is such a common experience that in 2003 it prompted the *Observer* journalist Michele Kirsch to coin the term 'Google grief'. With its alliteration and its overtones of illicit coffee-break Internet searches, the term suggests that Google grief is silly and should not happen. If we are only hearing about an old classmate's death through a website, Kirsch points out, they probably weren't really our friend anyway. And if that's the case, she asks, are we being forced, via Dr Elisabeth Kübler-Ross's grief cycle model – denial, anger, bargaining, depression, then acceptance – to grieve for people who never really mattered to us? When a friend we really care about dies, will we find that we've had so much practice that we know just how to deal with grief, or, on the other hand, that we've grown numb?

Needless to say, fame played tricks before the World Wide Web. In her memoir of Winifred Holtby, *Testament of Friendship*, Vera Brittain wrote of her friend's funeral in 1935: 'A recent volume of popular psychology puts to its readers, as a test of their ability to win affection: "If you died to-morrow, how many people would come to your funeral?" In Winifred's case, we know the answer. Midday on Tuesday in London is a busy hour and St Martin-in-the-Fields is a large church, but at Winifred's funeral service it was crowded to the doors. Half the congregation were people who hardly knew her, but many of them wept as bitterly as though they were mourning the best friend they had ever lost.'

Brittain doesn't address the possibility that some of those near-strangers may have gone to the funeral to see and be seen. Holtby was a prolific journalist, writing for *Time and Tide* and many other publications. She knew some pretty high-profile people. For the year before the journalist Ruth Picardie died, she wrote a weekly column for the *Observer* in which she described the progression of her breast cancer, published after her death as *Before I Say Goodbye*. Half the country could feel they knew everything about her, her children and her husband. It wasn't only the close friends of Picardie who spilled out of her memorial service into Holborn's Red Lion Square.

Google grief is still quite new, perhaps in a way exciting. Holtby and Picardie were both young when they died. For many at those funeral services, it must have been their first experience of the death of a contemporary: some were no doubt curious, trying on for size how it feels to lose a friend.

I suspect that Google grief is something we will all get floored by a couple of times in our lives. But we will quickly get it into proportion, as we realise that we must protect our emotions. For when we learn that a friend we really love has died or is dying, new technology will do little to alleviate the pain.

# 34

# Tapping In

Friendship is an extraordinary social – and business – resource. In *How to Win Friends and Influence People* Dale Carnegie says it brings 'dollars, many dollars every day'. He meant for individuals, but his rule applies to society as a whole. It is no wonder politicians want to tap into it.

In his article 'A Matter of Respect' (2005), the sociopolitical scientist David Halpern looked at neighbourhoods in Britain and the US in which people consider themselves as 'getting along' and being 'close knit', and found that 'children who go to schools in areas with higher levels of civic engagement attain significantly higher grades at 16'. He cites econometric modelling to show that social trust has a considerable impact on a country's growth rates. If trust decreases, as Halpern notes it did in America from 44 per cent in 1981 to 33 per cent in 2001, the economy becomes less stable. 'Social capital and trust oil the wheels of an economy, speeding the flow of information and lowering transaction costs.'

Halpern's close-knit communities have lower crime rates,

too. Neighbourhoods where people *don't* get along incur calculably higher insurance, policing and prison costs.

The UK government's 2008 Foresight Report shows that social exclusion translates into breakdowns, medication and hospitalisation. Exploring the financial implications, the report concludes: 'There is evidence that mental health costs £77bn a year in England alone, with direct costs to the economy approaching £49bn.' So it would seem that a lack of friendship can destabilise markets and inflate the NHS bill, while the presence of friendship, through reducing crime and helping our children get better grades at GCSE, gives them the prospect of better jobs and more lucrative futures. There is massive financial incentive, billions of pounds' worth, for Western governments to try and use it. Mark Vernon suggests in *The Philosophy of Friendship* that in the corridors of power, 'the idea of civic friendship is ... gaining ground. Here the thought is that modern democracy can be revivified by a notion of citizenship that includes a concern for others' wellbeing.' Politicians, he says, are starting to view friendship as 'the new social glue to paste over networked lives.'

But as countless stories in this book show only too clearly, friendship can be confusing and unpredictable. It certainly doesn't come with a nice neat applicator nozzle. How can politicians take control of this 'glue'?

There has been a striking shift in the language of politics. Barack Obama used grassroots support to secure the presidency of the United States in 2008. His speeches were dominated by talk of friends pulling together. He called on Americans to 'share the burdens and the benefits'; he spoke of 'the responsibilities we have to one another'. On becoming the first African-American to win the White House, he attributed his success partly to a campaign 'built by working men and women who dug into what little savings they had to give five dollars and ten dollars and twenty dollars to this cause'. An extraordinary seven million contributed. A relative newcomer, Obama won 52 per cent of the popular vote. 'I believe,' he said on 28 May 2008 in Thornton, Colorado, 'it's time to lead a new era of mutual responsibility.'

A few days before the UK's general election in 2010, the Conservative Party put up posters declaring, 'Social Responsibility Not State Control'. The platform that took them to power that May as the Conservative–Liberal Democrat coalition was the 'Big Society', a 'process' David Cameron described in a speech on 19 July 2010 as being about 'pushing power down and seeing what happens. It's about unearthing the problems as they come up on the ground and seeing how we can get round them. It's about holding our hands up saying we haven't got all the answers – let's work them out, together ... The rule of this government should be this: if it unleashes community engagement – we should do it.' The Opposition leader Ed Miliband accused the government of 'cynically attempting to dignify its cuts agenda by dressing up the withdrawal of support with the language of reinvigorating civic society'.

Terms like 'mutual responsibility' and 'neighbourhood army' are beautifully vague. They make me think of the pop song 'Why Can't We Be Friends?' by the 1970s band War. The song is buoyant and makes you feel Yes, let's do that! But when you listen to the words, it's an endless repeat of the title with inane interjections about not having seen you around for a long time and remembering the time you drank my wine. It may sound lovely, but it doesn't mean much.

Can politicians actually legislate their way into capitalising on friendship? Elizabeth Telfer talks of friendship involving an unofficial contract, not one written down on paper but one that evolves of its own accord and is agreed by both parties. I know I have quite a range of policies, each of them unique to a particular friendship. While I might accept with mild amusement that one friend will be five or ten minutes late every time we meet, I might find a lack of punctuality in another intolerable. In Aire in Flanders in 1188 the townspeople 'confirmed by faith and oath that they will aid each other as brethren in whatever is useful and honest'. In Elizabethan times, the residents of Swallowfield in Berkshire signed a contract promising to live together 'in good love and lykinge one another'. But the people of the Flemish town all lived in one place, the residents of Swallowfield too. My own friendship 'policies' now extend to people around the world, and some of those individual policies have inevitably changed over time. The duties and corresponding rights that were tacitly agreed when we lived in the same house or city can't remain unchanged if we now live two or three hundred miles apart.

Surely such contracts are just too nebulous for politicians to get a grip on?

In 2001, when he was re-elected prime minister, Tony Blair made a concrete attempt to get friendship on to the statute books. He installed David Halpern as Chief Analyst in his Strategy Unit. Author of the book *Social Capital* (a

term he devised), Halpern's concern is how to measure, label
and then harness the positive effects of friendship for society. He was up against a powerful tradition: in political
philosophy, pronouncements such as Machiavelli's that you
have to be ruthless, that no one can be trusted, and Jean-
Jacques Rousseau's belief that it is 'the weakness of man
which renders him social', still clung. A lot of people still
didn't like using the 'f' word.

It was a pretty left-of-field appointment for Blair to make.

And perhaps that was part of the problem. Halpern couldn't
just say, *We need to encourage friendship, it is good for us indi-*
*vidually and for society*. Any recommendations came cloaked
in complicated language. All the same, his thinking informed
Blair's 'respect' agenda, which pushed initiatives including
Antisocial Behaviour Orders to the fore. The ground rule the
government came up with to deter antisocial behaviour was
this: ASBOs could be ordered in response to 'conduct which
caused or was likely to cause alarm, harassment, distress, or
harm to one or more persons not of the same household as
him or herself and where an ASBO is seen as necessary to
protect relevant persons from further anti-social acts by the
Defendant'.

ASBOs got a very mixed reception. They were meant to
make people feel safer, to help them get on better with each
other. But they were all stick, no carrot. Writing in the
*Guardian*, criminal defence solicitor Matt Foot noted that
ASBOs had been put in place to stop a young boy from
playing football and an eighty-seven-year-old great-grand-
father from being sarcastic. Furthermore, 'even some victims
of antisocial behaviour are aware that they have not been

served well by Asbos,' said Foot, citing a woman who'd admitted that the ASBO she'd brought against young people in her area had only divided the community.

ASBOs were perhaps proving a rather blunt instrument. But friendship is an invaluable resource. Politicians looked for other ways of harnessing it.

In October 2007, speaking at Kew Royal Botanic Gardens, the Labour minister Hilary Benn introduced the notion of friendship as an aid in reducing Britain's $CO_2$ emissions. Instead of talking about enforcement through penalties, he spoke of initiatives such as 'You, Me and the Climate' whereby 'across London, a group of young people are committing to change their lives to live more sustainably, and to encourage others to join them'. If eleven million of us turned the thermostat down by 1 degree centigrade, we'd be 1 per cent closer, he said, concluding: 'On our own, our actions might seem small. But together, we can make more progress than any of us might expect. We just need to look each other in the eye, and say: "I will if you will."'

In 2009, a global pandemic of swine flu was declared. In another attempt to throw a net around friendship, the government decided 'flu friends' were the answer. The Ministry of Health put leaflets through people's doors and adverts everywhere telling the public they should not go to their doctor if they started suffering flu-like symptoms. Instead the MoH advised, in the biggest health campaign of its kind for twenty years: 'Confirm your "flu friends" – these are friends and neighbours who can help you if you become ill; they could get your medication or food for you so that you don't have to leave the house – this will help stop the virus from spreading.'

Organisations and institutions other than government are seeing friendship as a force for change, too.

In March 2009, in an attempt to reduce the number of teenagers killed or maimed in road accidents, Transport for London devised a set of posters with the strapline, 'Don't let your friendship die on the road.' TfL describes the posters as 'stark', and they are. In one, a young man appears to be leaning against a wall; look again, and you see he's lying on the road dead, hit by a car. 'The message is a clear call to action, "Think! Look out for your mates",' says TfL, adding in its explanatory literature that the campaign 'is based on the insight that friendship is one of the most important things in young people's lives'.

The celebrity chef Jamie Oliver, alarmed by this country's obesity figures, looked to friendship. Government initiatives such as the 'five a day' campaign were clearly not working, so in 2008 for his Channel 4 television series *Jamie's Ministry of Food*, Oliver went to Rotherham to see if, using friendship, he could succeed in halting the rise in obesity where government campaigns had failed. Incongruously, perhaps, a key part of the idea came from a campaign mounted in Soweto in the 1980s, when people in the black townships refused to send their children to school because educational institutions were considered part of the state apparatus. But they still wanted their children to learn to read, so local civic associations such as the United Democratic Front came up with the idea of 'Each One Teach One'. The theory was that if each child who could read taught a friend, and those friends taught more friends, and so on, literacy would spread efficiently and fast even during political turmoil.

Oliver's version was called 'Pass It On'. If each person he taught a healthy recipe to passed it on to two of their friends, and two of their friends passed it on to two more and so on, the programme's makers calculated, within six months all Rotherham would have learnt at least one good recipe. And it was heart-warming to see coalminers, single mothers and call-centre staff all teaching each other how to fry onions or make omelettes, until in one programme dozens of blokes were standing at table after table in a football stadium, all tenderising clingfilm-wrapped chicken breasts with rolling pins.

But politicians' interventions, and even Jamie Oliver's flamboyant TV efforts, start to look trifling in the face of changes that are happening globally. Friendship is not the same as collaboration, but perhaps collaboration and community grow out of the same roots: shared likes and dislikes, shared goals, and shared ideals.

Fairtrade is about social conscience. Buying Fairtrade products is about making at least a friendly gesture to people leading tough lives in countries such as Kenya, the Dominican Republic, Belize and Ghana. The organic food business has done well over the last decades, but Fairtrade has done better. Data analysts Nielsen reported that the monthly sales growth of organic food in the US dropped from 24 per cent in March 2008 to 1 per cent in March 2009. The UK experienced a similar shrink in the growth of 'organics'. By contrast, according to the UK's Fairtrade Foundation, Fairtrade sales have just kept going up, from £16.7 million in 1998 to £493 million in 2007. Between 2008 and 2009, at the height of a worldwide recession, the sales of Fairtrade food in the UK rose by another £100 million. In May 2011, the Foundation announced that 'sales of Fairtrade products soared by 40% in 2010 to an estimated retail value of £1.17bn,' adding, 'UK shoppers are ... showing no downturn on ethical values despite the tough economic times.'

In their book *Wikinomics: How Mass Collaboration Changes Everything*, Don Tapscott and Anthony D. Williams suggest that Web 2.0 applications, which allow Internet users to share information (sites such as Wikipedia and Facebook depend on Web 2.0 technology), are forcing a complete rewrite of the business rule book. *Wikinomics* explains why those in charge of the great corporations must change their approach to business. It highlights a fundamental shift in how sections of the business world are having to operate already. 'We are talking about deep changes in the structure and modus operandi of the corporation and our economy.'

Web 2.0 has made it possible for peer-to-peer recommendations to impact on companies globally almost instantly. If a friend of a friend tells you via Facebook about a product by clicking 'Like' and so activating a thumbs-up icon, for example, their opinion is likely to have significantly more impact on you than an advertisement. The advertiser just wants to *sell*. Your friend, or Facebook acquaintance, is presumably just telling you honestly what they think, one mate to another. The new 'competitive principles' which Tapscott and Williams speak of include 'openness, peering, sharing and acting globally'.

'Peering' is a great new word. After all, it is not frivolous or by-the-by to tell a friend that a new movie is brilliant. In passing on my opinion, I am doing something much more grand: I am 'peering'.

But the point is, peer-to-peer recommendation has always carried more weight than any advert or government edict. It's just that the modes of communication that were available to us – Royal Mail, for example – meant that those recommendations couldn't reach very many very fast.

It is delightful to hear from Tapscott and Williams that corporations are being encouraged to include a degree of openness and sharing in their 'new competitive principles'. Except, the manager who buys *Wikinomics* is likely to be motivated not so much by the desire to be a better 'friend' himself but, rather, by the hope that he'll be able to profit from others' friendships. He wants in on the massive friendship group that his business will hopefully forge with consumers.

However, there's only so much manipulation of customers' relationships with each other that managers can effect. Businesses are largely on the back foot. There may be downsides to the World Wide Web. But it is also bringing friendship in like a tidal wave.

# 35

# Our Chariot Awaits

We are at a strange juncture. It is thanks to new technology that friendship, buoyed by email, twitter and social networking sites, has become highly visible. It is being propelled with fresh energy into the world. Politicians and corporations are all busy trying to harness this new wave, some of them making fools of themselves in the process while others exploit friendship networks with sophistication.

Yet simultaneously friendship is under threat. Individually, we often feel too busy and fraught to commit proper time to it. With new technology comes the risk that social networking sites and online games will trivialise your friendships or even lead you to reject real friendships altogether. Carl Jung wrote: 'The meeting of two personalities is like the contact of two chemical substances: if there is any reaction, both are transformed.' Real friendship is dynamic *and* reactive.

Its reactiveness is being compromised in other ways too. Plastic surgery and certain 'non-surgical interventions' promote faces that are uniform and barely mobile. Roaring laughter and blazing rows don't sit easily with blepharoplasty, pinnaplasty or dermabrasion. People have eyebrows, notes Mick O'Hare of *New Scientist*, to express emotions, most significantly 'to telegraph friendly intentions from a safe distance' – something that 'would have had obvious survival value for our ancestors'. We're barely conscious of these minute declarations of warm feeling, they're so swift. But they guide us before words are spoken. An Australian *New Scientist* reader, Alison Venugoban, commented: 'The importance of eyebrow position as a guide to mood was brought home to me when a friend had Botox injections in the lines on her forehead and couldn't raise or lower her eyebrows. Talking to her became a disconcerting experience – the bottom half of her face remained mobile but her eyebrows did not move. I couldn't deduce her mood accurately by looking at her expression, and needed to use other cues such as her actions and speech.'

Social networking websites such as Facebook and Bebo also introduce a certain flatness to our interactions. It's possible to have private conversations and make some messages available only to a select few, but a main point of Facebook is to have everything accessible to everyone. Holiday snaps and music choices go up as if each user is an online gallery. There's no intimacy – no physical contact, no sofa to sit on, no eye-to-eye contact, no *smelling*.

The smell of one's friends may seem like an odd thing to raise. But smell is a very important, if subtly sensed, part of close social interaction. I am very fond of some friends' perfumes. They signal happy times. Scents connected with activities with friends can bring back good memories: a game of French cricket in a field on a bright spring day, the grass freshly cut; or in winter, the smell of crumpets toasting on a log fire.

The importance of friendly intimacy is perhaps best demonstrated by its absence: at its worst, being apart from others can cause real damage. For its 2010 report *The Lonely Society?*, the Mental Health Organisation carried out a UK-wide survey of 2256 adults and found that half of us think people are getting lonelier. Only one in five said they never felt lonely, while one in three said they would be too embarrassed to admit to loneliness. Something has to be done, and the MHO gives solid recommendations. It might sound funny, but the MHO hails with absolute seriousness an Age Concern project in Cheshire called 'Men in Sheds', an idea originally from Australia that brings older men together, in sheds, to practise carpentry.

Group activity can be the start of real community and real friendships. Bingo, for example, comes out very well on the MHO scale of local amenities that foster friendship. '"Eyes Down": A Study of Bingo' by Rachael Dixey which involved collecting data from 7166 players between 1981 and 1982, is a delicate exploration of how bingo helps some women find companionship. Only 44 per cent of her respondents cited 'winning some money' as the main reason for playing. The gatherings are not regimented, and that is critical to bingo's appeal. Often housed in old cinemas, bingo allows players to arrive early and sit on the edge for a while if they're tired, or if they don't know anyone. Once the game starts, the small tables help them get to know each other quickly. 'It is possible to argue that in an age where caring networks have failed, the bingo club provides the focus for a "moral community". In many clubs the management takes its welfare role very seriously, sending flowers to members when widowed or ill, asking after members' health and so on,' writes Dixey. 'Many of the elderly women would arrive up to two hours before the afternoon session started, to eat, talk, knit, read or play cards with others in a warm place.'

Aristotle's and Plato's friendships of virtue blossomed in aesthetically pleasing wrestling schools in the Mediterranean sunlight. These philosophers knew, as do bodies like the Mental Health Organisation two thousand years later, that friendship and the companionship, community and happiness it fosters make a better society. The MHO report singles out post offices, suggesting that instead of closing the smaller village ones, governments should be opening more of them, because important friendships are often nurtured while people wait to buy stamps and collect pensions. Similarly, rather than cutting the funding for adult education, governments should be pumping money in because the pottery and stained-glass and flower-arranging classes at further education colleges provide people with invaluable opportunities to 'establish new social connections'. Such provision can stave off loneliness, which in turn reduces the cost to the Exchequer of treating mental illness.

But as David Halpern says, 'Behavioural norms are rarely held in place by laws and formal sanctions alone.' The government can't order lonely people to go to bingo sessions and expect them to comply. The MHO recommends subtler interventions. It wants the government to commission programmes to 'map' local sports clubs and library book groups, for example, so that GPs, mental health workers, occupational therapists, schools, colleges and youth workers can quickly direct people they identify as being in need to places where friendships are fostered.

The drama of the sacrifices made by Achilles and Patroclus on the battlefield during the Trojan War, for each other and for their fellow soldiers, is wonderful to read. Today we admire the commitment to each other of those who daily risk their lives in Afghanistan and elsewhere. At the other end of the spectrum, we should also be treasuring the banter that Bert and Fred engage in over a game of bowls, the laughter and stimulation that Imogen and Daisy enjoy during badminton, the confidences exchanged during the coffee break at the a cappella class that comfort Beverley and Joe. Our need for community and friends runs deep. It's how we're made. Friendship helps us reach a better understanding of ourselves. It might be hard to find sometimes. But we crave it.

In twelfth-century Yorkshire, to prove that God sanctions friendship, Aelred wrote: 'What soil or river produces one single stone of one kind? Or what forest bears but a single tree of a single kind? ... [Animals] run after one another, play with one another, so eagerly and happily do they enjoy their mutual company, that they seem to prize nothing else so much.' Seven hundred years later, Nietzsche wrote to his sister Elisabeth: 'My poor soul is so sensitive to injury and so full of longing for good friends, "who are my life". Get me a small circle of men who will listen to me and understand me – and then I shall be cured!' To his friend Erwin Rohde he wrote: 'Think what life would be like without a friend. Could one, would one, have borne it?' Twenty-eight years after the essays which were so negative about friendship were published, in a complete volte face Francis Bacon wrote in 1625: 'Without true Friends the world is but a wilderness.'

In July 2006 the New Economics Foundation (NEF) and Friends of the Earth launched the 'Happy Planet Index'. With low consumption and high satisfaction as the main measures of contentment instead of gross domestic product, out of the 178 countries surveyed the UK and the US came 108th and 150th, whereas Honduras and Guatemala featured in the top ten and the South Pacific island of Vanuatu came top. How could the residents of tiny Vanuatu be happier than those of the richest nations in the world? Marke Lowen, who lives there, told the *Guardian*: 'Life here is about community.'

In *Friends: Making and Keeping Them in Today's Busy World* Geoff Baker, an American pastor, describes how, when he suffered a breakdown, he found that his belief in God could not help him but his friends could. They gave him a glimpse of who he could be again. 'As we and they look back,' writes Baker, 'we can see God's hand at work powerfully during those difficult times ... but he chose to use fragile people as his hands and feet. It is difficult to overestimate the value of friendship in our walk with God.' King and Smith conclude simply: 'If a good society – meaning civil society – has a constitution, then friendship is it.' Moral philosophers and churchmen, politicians and political philosophers, sociologists and mental-health organisations are looking to friendship to pull us through in the twenty-first century.

In Disney's 1967 cartoon *The Jungle Book*, Mowgli the man-cub is cheeky and engaging. But the characters that the closing credits stay with are the big-hearted if querulous friends Baloo and Bagheera – their differences now pushed aside, the director decided that it would be the sight of the bear and the panther going back into the jungle to negotiate its dangers together that would bring the big smiles. In Carrol Reed's musical *Oliver!* (1968), it is not the squeaky-clean hero that the camera lingers on in the end, but the Artful Dodger and the old moneylender Fagin. Despite having lost everything they've cheated and thieved for, we see the friends crossing the bridge arm in arm, even breaking into a little dance.

'Without the juice of friendship, I would not be even what I seem to be,' wrote Zora Neale Hurston in her autobiography, *Dust Tracks on the Road*. 'So many people have stretched out their hands and helped me along my wander. With the eye of faith, some have beheld me at Hell's dark door, with no rudder in my hand, and no light in my heart, and steered me to a peace within. Some others have flown into that awful place west and south of old original Hell and, with great compassion, lifted me off the blistering coals and showed me trees and flowers.' All these are the powers and privileges of friendship.

It is clear from *Dust Tracks* that friendship saved Hurston from suicide. She doesn't pinpoint a specific moment when a friend pulled her back from the edge – half the time, her friends probably didn't even know they were helping her. Small acts and gestures accumulate. Friendship can, as she puts it, 'throw light back on a day that was so dark, that even the sun refused to take responsibility for it'. Friends make a difference when we feel bad – if life is good, with friends it can feel still better.

Make new ones. Work at your existing ones. At your allotment, set the hoe and the dibber aside and talk to your fellow plot-holder. Start that game of online Scrabble. Get out a pen and paper and write a letter to your oldest friend.

# 36

# Golden Oldies

'What can be more encouraging than to find the friend that was welcome of one age, still welcome at another?' asked Robert Louis Stevenson. For years, Samuel Johnson thought this a rare event: 'No expectation is more frequently disappointed,' he wrote, 'than that which naturally arises in the mind from the prospect of meeting an old friend after a long separation.'

In 'The Decay of Friendship' he explained at length why friendships cannot last. If friends meet again after a gap, 'The first hour convinces them that the pleasure which they have formerly enjoyed is forever at an end.' If friends are too different, their interests will gradually separate them; if too alike, they will be in competition. Small disputes begun in jest can be 'continued by the desire of conquest, till vanity kindles into rage, and opposition rankles into enmity'. You like the same things, you want the same things; it won't be long, says Johnson, before you fight each other for the same things.

Johnson is very convincing in his argument that over time,

friendships will inevitably sour or fade. Stevenson is just as adamant in his belief:

It's an owercome sooth for age an' youth
And it brooks wi' nae denial,
That the dearest friends are the auldest friends
And the young are just on trial.

'The Decay of Friendship' came out in 1758, when Johnson was forty-nine, at a time when he was still striking out and forging his career. He was keenly competitive. His *Dictionary* had been published three years earlier. He was still working on his eight-volume edition of Shakespeare, which came out in 1765. By the 1770s, his reputation was secure. When he was sixty-eight, in a letter dated 1 September 1777, he confided to his friend James Boswell:

When I came to Lichfield, I found my old friend Harry Jackson dead. It was a loss, and a loss not to be repaired, as he was one of the companions of my childhood. I hope we may long continue to gain friends, but the friends which merit or usefulness can procure us, are not able to supply the place of old acquaintances, with whom the days of youth may be retraced, and those images revived which gave the earliest delight.

As we grow older, friends who remind us of when we were young become increasingly important. Just the sound of a Yorkshire accent can relax me. Although, since Yorkshire is much bigger than most British counties – the distance between

Whitby in the north-east and Sheffield in the south-west is getting on for a hundred miles – if I am feeling picky, I'll feel less relaxed if the accent is Yorkshire Wolds as opposed to Dales. But generally, the moment I hear that Yorkshire twang I assume that the speaker knows 'nowt' means 'nothing', 'mardy' means 'sulky', and Eccles cakes are gorgeous. I feel they have a hold of some of the things that make me who I am.

One friend lives in Singapore now. I have a memory from when I was eleven of walking with her down to a place that everyone called the Fairy Dell. I was troubled. I can't remember the details, but I do remember that something my friend said made me feel understood. There were pines round the edge of the dell, bluebells over every inch of ground, it seems now, the sun was shining. That moment underpins every email and Christmas card exchange with her, every conversation.

When two friends who I have known since I was eighteen were round for dinner a few years ago, a shift in the conversation prompted them to burst into song. They were in the school choir together. I can hold a tune, but I have an unusual mid-range pitch. I'm not a *good* singer, but I do enjoy singing immensely. The next year when we met up again, those same friends brought some song sheets. And a few Christmases in a row now, they've come round and we've sung carols. Just the thought of belting out 'The Holly and the Ivy' with them gives me a glow. Because we're old friends, we don't worry about looking foolish. I can goof every other note and feel sure that nobody will mind.

I think again of Dr Johnson: 'We cannot tell the precise moment when friendship is formed,' he told Boswell on 19 September 1777. 'In a series of kindnesses there is at last the one which makes the heart run over.' The location may change. One or both of you may move, from a flat in Clapham to a house in Islington or from a room in Brixton to a farm near Lancaster. But at each new place, when you meet, it is with those kindnesses already there. In time, the vessel overflows to become a well, the well a reservoir which remains in place even after major life changes.

People whose fortunes alter dramatically often stick with special vigour to friends who knew them before it all began to happen. Andréa Bendewald and Jennifer Aniston met in the late 1980s while they were still at high school in New York, before the runaway success of the TV series *Friends* in the mid-1990s made Aniston a star. 'What's so great with Andréa is that I'm still the same person I always was,' she says. 'It's been wonderful to have a best friend who knew me before this whirlwind. Somebody I can go home to. Somebody who knows what's real.'

If things go wrong, old friends are particularly welcome. When the political philosopher Hannah Arendt had to flee Nazi Germany and arrived in New York in 1941, she was still only in her thirties. She soon gained plenty of acquaintances. She built up a vibrant social life. But she didn't get close to many Americans. She remained shy, as her biographer Elisabeth Young-Bruehl puts it, except in the presence of those she had known in her youth, 'or in an atmosphere that evoked her youth, an atmosphere of German culture where the right quotation from Goethe was always at hand'.

The value of old friends can be precisely the fact that there is no need to go over the past. They understand exactly.

In Amy Tan's novel *The Joy Luck Club*, Suyuan Woo has fled the Chinese civil war and in 1949 arrives in San Francisco, having lost her husband and twin daughters. She decides in advance the kind of people she will want as old friends. At events hosted by the Refugee Welcome Society, she looks for three women who are 'young like me'. She picks out An-mei Hsu, Lindo Jong and Ying-ying St Clair because their expressions show that they have also left 'unspeakable tragedies' behind in China. They don't need or necessarily even want explanations from each other. Over the years, as they forge new lives as exiles, as their children grow up, Suyuan Woo and the other three women do become old friends. Each week, they treat themselves to food they hope will bring good fortune: 'dumplings shaped like silver money ingots, long rice noodles for long life, boiled peanuts for conceiving sons'. It is all part of the ritual of forgetting. After eating, they play mah-jong, only breaking the silence to say '*Pung!*' or '*Chr!*' when taking a mah-jong tile. These women's need for each other sets the pattern of their lives.

In my life, a couple I've known for some time have over the years on birthdays and other occasions given me presents including a carry-all, a chef's knife, a set of glasses and two duck-feather pillows. Another has given me two sets of fully lined curtains. These gifts occupy places around the house. They are an important part of what makes the place I live my home. They are talismans. Old friends often can't remember the details of the curveballs life has pitched in your direction, but they remember enough. Perhaps a scene in a film hits a nerve or a stranger at a party says something tactless. Your old friend can cover for you. If you've had to rush out of the cinema in tears he may arrive outside with tissues, then steer you to a bar; at the party, she may inconspicuously divert the conversation and keep it going in a more neutral direction until you feel comfortable.

And just as old friends can protect you from other people, they can protect you from yourself too. They can be honest when new friends wouldn't dare. Perhaps you have one friend in particular you go to to find out if a new outfit looks rubbish. Maybe sometimes you can't help it – you slip into being pompous or a bit snide, and you're really grateful for the old friend who gives you a sobering look, or laughs.

Because of her tendency to launch into sweeping political statements based on what she herself said was scanty knowledge, the novelist Mary McCarthy lost a lot of friends during the Cold War and the Nixon presidency. In 1968 at the time of the Vietnam War, she visited Hanoi, then wrote about her experience almost as if she was writing a travel article. Hannah Arendt didn't like the approach her friend had taken. She felt McCarthy had 'over-indulged in the pleasures of intellectual detachment in a time of crisis'. But the women had been close since 1944 and had already survived a number of disagreements. In 1975, the year Arendt travelled to Copenhagen to collect the prestigious Sonning Prize, the friend she chose to take as her guest was McCarthy.

Jennifer Aniston says of Andréa Bendewald: 'I trust her with parts of myself I don't trust with anybody else, and I can be honest about confessing things to her – even when it doesn't feel good.'

I asked one friend for help with a surprise for my partner. I needed an old and trusted friend because putting up bunting – the surprise – involved drilling into walls that my partner had only recently plastered, papered and painted. The friend had particular technical skills that made him the perfect accomplice. And as he knelt there, rifling through my partner's tin of nails and sundry items, our old friend suddenly picked something out and held it up.

'Look,' he said, eyes alight, 'he's got an ammonite in with his drill bits.'

Cradled in a Draper hole cutter sat a tiny, curling pyrite ammonite from a trip to Staithes we had made, two families together, searching for fossils. No one else would have understood the significance of the fact that my partner keeps a couple of fossilised molluscs in his tin of DIY accessories.

Instantly I was taken back to that trip from several years ago. And it wasn't just the trip to Staithes that we'd all made together that came back with the discovery of the ammonite. It was also a walk along Welsh cliffs to catch the tail-end of a sunlit Regatta, a twilit barbecue on a camping holiday in Devon, a New Year's Eve with children falling asleep on the sofa.

Indeed, with old friends the memories unfold, then string out, rather like bunting. Singly, none of them would necessarily amount to much. But these scraps of the past, old, often incomplete, when strung together make a whole that is comforting and beautiful.

# Bibliography

Abbey, Ruth, 'Circles, Ladders and Stars: Nietzsche on Friendship', in *The Challenge to Friendship in Modernity*, ed. Preston King and Heather Devere (Frank Cass, 2000)

Abrams, Dominic, and Rutland, Adam, 'The Development of Subjective Group Dynamics', in *Intergroup Attitudes and Relations in Childhood through Adulthood*, ed. Sheri R. Levy and Melanie Killen (Oxford University Press, 2008)

Ackroyd, Peter, *Dickens* (Sinclair Stevenson, 1990)

Addington Symonds, Mrs John (ed.), *Recollections of a Happy Life: Being the Autobiography of Marianne North*, vols 1 and 2 (Macmillan & Co., 1892)

Addison, Joseph, 'We Two Are a Multitude', *Spectator* no. 68 (18 May 1711)

Aelred of Rievaulx, *Spiritual Friendship*: Book I: *The Origin of Friendship*, trans. Eugenia Laker (Cistercian Publications, 1974)

Alcott, Louisa May, *Little Women* (Blackie, 1979)

Allen, Alexandra, *Travelling Ladies: Victorian Adventuresses* (Jupiter, 1980)

Amory, Mark (ed.), *The Letters of Evelyn Waugh* (Weidenfeld & Nicolson, 1980)

Anzai, Nobuyuki, *MÄR*, vol. 5 (Viz Media, 2005)

Angier, Carole, *Jean Rhys* (André Deutsch, 1990)

Aquinas, Thomas, *Summa contra Gentiles*, trans. Anton C. Pegis et al. (University of Notre Dame Press, 1975)

Atwood, Margaret, *The Handmaid's Tale* (Virago, 1987)

—— *Cat's Eye* (Virago, 1990)

Austen, Jane, *Emma*, ed. James Kinsley, intro. by Terry Castle (Oxford University Press, 1995)

Auster, Paul (trans. and intro.), *The Notebooks of Joseph Joubert* (New York Review Books, 2005)

Bacon, Francis, *Essays* (Geoffrey Cumberlege/Oxford University Press, 1947)

Baden-Powell, Robert, *Scouting for Boys: A Handbook for Instruction in Good Citizenship*, ed. Boehmer, Elleke (Oxford University Press, 2005)

Bailey, Jenna, *Can Any Mother Help Me?* (Faber & Faber, 2007)

Baker, Geoff, *Friends: Making and Keeping Them in Today's Busy World* (Inter-Varsity Press, 1999)

Batchelor, Susan, 'Discussing Violence: Let's Hear It from the Girls', *Probation Journal*, vol. 48 (1 Jan. 2001)

Beckman, Heidi; Regier, Nathan; and Young, Judy L., 'The Effect of Workplace Laughter Groups on Personal Efficacy Beliefs', *Journal of Primary Prevention*, vol. 28, no. 2 (2007), pp. 167–82

Behn, Aphra, *Oroonoko: or, the Royal Slave*, ed. Joanna Lipking (W. W. Norton, 1997)

Benson, L. D. (ed.), *The Riverside Chaucer* (Oxford University Press, 1988)

Berkman, Lisa, and Breslow, Lester, *Health and Ways of Living: The Alameda County Study* (Oxford University Press, 1983)

Bettelheim, Bruno, *The Informed Heart: The Human Condition in Modern Mass Society* (Thames & Hudson, 1960)

*Bible: New Revised Standard Version* (Oxford University Press, 1995)

Bickel, Mary E., *Geo W. Trendle: Creator and Producer of The Lone Ranger, The Green Hornet, Sgt. Preston of the Yukon, The American Agent and Other Successes: An Authorized Biography* (Exposition Press, 1971)

Bjørnvig, Thorkild, *The Pact: My Friendship with Isak Dinesen*, trans. Ingvar Schousboe and William Jay Smith (Louisiana State University Press, 1983)

Bland, Susan; Winkelstein, Warren; Krogh, Vittorio; and Trevisan, Maurizio, 'Social Network and Blood Pressure: A Population Study', *Psychosomatic Medicine*, 53: pp. 598–607, http://www.psychosomaticmedicine.org/content/53/6/598.full.pdf (1991)

Blunden, Edmund, *Leigh Hunt: A Biography* (Archon Books, 1970)

Blythe, Ronald (ed.), *Hazlitt: Selected Writings* (Penguin English Library, 1982)

Bostridge, Mark, *Florence Nightingale* (Penguin Books, 2008)

Bourne, Randolph, 'The Excitement of Friendship' (*Atlantic Monthly*, December 1912)

Bowen, Elizabeth, *Seven Winters* (Longman & Co., 1943)

—— *The Mulberry Tree*, ed. Hermione Lee (Harcourt Brace Jovanovich, 1986)

Bradbury, Malcolm, *The History Man* (Arrow, 1980)

Brightman, Carol (ed.), *Between Friends: Correspondence of Hannah Arendt and Mary McCarthy 1949–1975* (Secker & Warburg, 1995)

Brinton, Howard, *Friends for 300 Years: The History and Beliefs of the Society of Friends since George Fox Started the Quaker Movement* (Harper & Brothers, 1952)

Brittain, Vera, *Testament of Friendship* (Fontana/Virago, 1981)

Buell, Laurence, *Emerson* (Belknap Press, 2003)

Burke, Peter, *Popular Culture in Early Modern Europe* (Scolar Press, 1994)

Burman, Michele, with E. K. Tisdall, *A View from the Girls: Exploring Violence and Violent Behaviour* (Economic and Social Research Council, 2001)

Byrne, Paula, *Mad World: Evelyn Waugh and the Secrets of Brideshead* (HarperCollins, 2009)

Calvino, Italo, *If on a Winter's Night a Traveller* (Vintage, 1988)

Campbell, Robin (ed. and trans.), *Letters from a Stoic: Epistolae Morales ad Lucilium* (Penguin Classics, 2004)

Carnegie, Dale, *How to Win Friends and Influence People* (Ebury/Vermillion, 1981)

Cassirer, E., *Kant's Life and Thought* (Yale University Press, 1981)

Castro, Ginette, *American Feminism* (New York University Press, 1990)

Chapman, R. W., et al. (eds), *Boswell's Life of Johnson* (Macmillan & Co., 1929)

Charters, Ann (ed.), *Jack Kerouac, Selected Letters 1940–1956* (Penguin, 1995)

Chitty, Susan, *Gwen John: 1876–1939* (Hodder & Stoughton, 1981)

*Life of Frances Power Cobbe: As Told by Herself* (Swan Sonnenschein & Co., 1904)

Collodi, Carlo, *The Adventures of Pinocchio*, trans. 1944, Estate of E. Harden (MDS Books/Mediastat, 2003)

Compton-Burnett, Ivy, *Pastors and Masters* (Hesperus Press, 2009)

Connolly, Cyril, *The Unquiet Grave* (Hamish Hamilton, 1973)

Coolidge, Susan, *What Katy Did* (Children's Press, 1974)

Corey, Peter, *Coping with Friends* (Scholastic Press, 1996)

Corley, T. A. B., *Quaker Enterprise in Biscuits: Huntley and Palmers of Reading 1822–1972* (Hutchinson, 1972)

Daniels, Walter, *Life of Ailred of Rievaulx*, intro. F. M. Powicke (Thomas Nelson, 1950)

Darnton, Robert, *The Kiss of Lamourette: Reflections in Cultural History* (Norton, 1990)

Darton, Harvey, *Children's Books in England*, preface Brian Alderson (Cambridge University Press, 1982)

Davies, Martin L., *Identity or History? Marcus Herz and the End of the Enlightenment* (Wayne State University Press, 1995)

Defoe, Daniel, *Robinson Crusoe* (Oxford University Press, 1981)

Dhorat, Shaykh Muhammad Saleem, *Friendship and Our Young Generation* (Islamic Da'wah Academy, 2004)

Dickens, Charles, *Our Mutual Friend* (Bounty Books, 1978)
—— *Hard Times* (Oxford Classics, 2008)

Diehl, Joanne Feit, *Elizabeth Bishop and Marianne Moore* (Princeton University Press, 1993)

Diener, Ed, *Culture and Subjective Well-being* (MIT Press, 2000)

Dillon, Millicent, *A Little Original Sin: The Life and Work of Jane Bowles* (Virago, 1988)

Dinnage, Rosemary, *Alone! Alone!: Lives of Some Outsider Women* (New York Review Books, 2004)

Disraeli, Benjamin, *Coningsby, or The New Generation* (Nelson, 1844)

Dixey, Rachael, '"Eyes Down": A Study of Bingo', in *Relative Freedoms: Women and Leisure*, ed. Erica Wimbush and Margaret Talbot (Open University Press, 1988)

Doyle, Arthur Conan, *The Memoirs of Sherlock Holmes* (Penguin Books, 2008)

Dumas, Alexandre, *The Three Musketeers*, trans. David Coward (Oxford University Press, 1991)

Durkheim, Emile, *The Elementary Forms of the Religious Life: A Study in Religious Sociology*, tr. J. W. Swain (George Allen and Unwin, 1915)

Elliott, Anthony, *Contemporary Social Theory* (Blackwell, 1999)

Emerson, Ralph Waldo, *On Love and Friendship* (Peter Pauper Press, 1982)

Enright, D. J., and Rawlinson, David (eds), *The Oxford Book of Friendship* (Oxford University Press, 1991)

Epstein, Joseph, *Friendship: An Exposé* (Houghton Mifflin, 2006)

Everitt, Anthony, *Cicero: A Turbulent Life* (John Murray, 2001)

Falconer, William Armistead (trans.), *Cicero: De Senectute, de Amicitia, de Divinatione* (William Heinemann, 1922)

Ferris, Paul (ed.), *Dylan Thomas: The Collected Letters* (J. M. Dent, 1985)

Fielding, Helen, *Bridget Jones's Diary* (Picador, 1996)

Fitzgerald, F. Scott, *The Great Gatsby* (Penguin Books, 1981)

Fitzgerald, Penelope, *The Blue Flower* (Flamingo, 2002)

Foley, Alice, *A Bolton Childhood* (Manchester University Extramural Department, 1973)

Ford, Richard, *The Sportswriter* (Collins Harvill, 1986)

Foresight Mental Capital and Wellbeing Project, 'Mental Capital and Wellbeing: Making the Most of Ourselves in the 21st Century', Final Project Report – Executive Summary (The Government Office for Science 2008), http://www.bis.gov. uk/assets/biscore/corporate/migratedD/ec_group/116-08-FO_b

Forster, E. M., *Two Cheers for Democracy* (Edward Arnold, 1951)

Foucault, Michel, 'Friendship as a Way of Life,' (first published in *Gai Pied* (1981)), in *Foucault Live (interviews 1961–1984)*, ed. Sylvère Lotringer, trans. Lysa Hochroth and John Johnston (Semiotext(e), 1989)

French, Nicci, *Complicit* (Michael Joseph, 2009)

Friedan, Betty, *The Feminine Mystique* (Victor Gollancz, 1963)

Fromm, Erich, *To Have or to Be?* (Abacus, 1988)

Gee, Sue, *Reading in Bed* (Headline Review, 2007)

Geraghty, Christine, *Women and Soap Opera* (Polity Press, 1991)

Glendinning, Victoria, *Vita: The Life of Vita Sackville-West* (Weidenfeld & Nicolson, 1983)

Golding, William, *Lord of the Flies* (Faber & Faber, 1978)

Goldsmith, Barbara, *Other Powers: The Age of Suffrage, Spiritualism, and the Scandalous Victoria Woodhull* (Granta Books, 1998)

Gordon, Lyndall, *Lives like Loaded Guns: Emily Dickinson and Her Family's Feuds* (Virago, 2010)

Gowing, Laura; Hunter, Michael; and Rubin, Miri (eds), *Love, Friendship and Faith in Europe 1300–1800* (Palgrave Macmillan, 2005)

Grahame, Kenneth, *The Wind in the Willows* (Methuen, 1971)

Grant, Linda, *We Had It So Good* (Virago, 2010)

Grayling, A. C., *The Quarrel of the Age: The Life and Times of William Hazlitt* (Weidenfeld & Nicolson, 2000)

Grenfell, Joyce; Grenfell, Reggie; and Garnett, Richard, *Joyce by Herself and Her Friends* (Macmillan, 1980)

Griffin, Jo, *The Lonely Society?*, report for the Mental Health Organisation, http://www.mentalhealth.org.uk/content/assets/PDF/publications/the_lonely_society_report.pdf (2010)

Grunberger, Richard, *A Social History of the Third Reich* (Penguin Books, 1991)

Gummere, R. M. (trans. and ed.), *Seneca: Epistolae Morales* (Harvard Press, 1917)

Halpern, David, *Social Capital* (Polity Press, 1995)

—— 'A Matter of Respect', *Prospect Magazine*, no. 112 (July 2005), http://www.prospectmagazine.co.uk/2005/07/amatterofrespect/

Hammond, J. L., and Hammond, Barbara, *The Bleak Age* (Penguin Books, 1947)

Hannay, Alastair, *Kierkegaard: A Biography* (Cambridge University Press, 2001)

Hanson, Lawrence, *Mountain of Victory: A Biography of Paul Cézanne* (Secker & Warburg, 1960)

Hardy, Thomas, *Tess of the d'Urbervilles*, intro. A. Alvarez and ed. David Skilton (Penguin Books, 1978)

Hart, Roger, *Children's Experience of Place: A Developmental Study* (Irvington, 1978)

Hemingway, Ernest, *A Moveable Feast* (Jonathan Cape, 1964)

Herzog, Werner, *Of Walking in Ice*, trans. Marje Herzog and Alan Greenberg (Jonathan Cape, 1991)

Heyking, John von, and Avramenko, Richard (eds), *Friendship and Politics: Essays in Political Thought* (University of Notre Dame Press, 2008)

Hinton, S. E., *The Outsiders* (Puffin Classics, 2007)

Hodgson Burnett, Frances, *A Little Princess*, intro. Adeline Yen Mah (Puffin, 2008)

Hollingdale, R. J., (trans. and ed.), *A Nietzsche Reader* (Penguin Books, 1977)

Holtby, Winifred, *South Riding* (Virago, 1988)

Homer, *The Iliad*, trans. E. V. Rieu (Penguin Books, 1976)

Houlbrooke, Ralph A., *The English Family, 1450–1700* (Longman, 1984)

Howkins, Chris, and Sampson, Nick, *Searching for Hornbeam: A Social History* (Chris Howkins, 2000)

Hughes, Kathryn, *George Eliot: The Last Victorian* (Fourth Estate, 1998)

Hughes, Thomas, *Tom Brown's Schooldays* (Puffin Books, 1974)

Hurston, Zora Neale, *Dust Tracks on the Road: An Autobiography*, intro. Maya Angelou (Library of America, 1995)

Huxley, Elspeth, *Florence Nightingale* (Chancellor Press, 1975)

Ireland, A. (ed.), *Selections from the Letters of Geraldine E. Jewsbury to Jane Welsh Carlyle* (Longman, 1892)

James, Oliver, *Affluenza* (Vermilion, 2007)

Johnson, Samuel, 'The Decay of Friendship', *The Idler* no. 23 (23 Sept. 1758)

Jordan, W. K., *Edward VI: The Threshold of Power* (George Allen & Unwin, 1970)

Kalstone, David, *Becoming a Poet: Elizabeth Bishop with Marianne Moore and Robert Lowell* (Farrar, Straus and Giroux, 1989)

Kane, Bob, *Batman: Archives*, vol. 1 (DC Comics, 1990)

Kant, Immanuel, 'Lecture on Friendship', in *Lectures on Ethics*, trans. Louis Infield (Methuen & Co., 1930)

Kaufmann, Walter (trans. and ed.), *Friedrich Nietzsche: The Gay Science* (Random House, 1974)

Kelly, Fergus, *All Things Spice: The Complete, Unofficial Story of The Spice Girls* (Puffin, 1997)

Kenyon, Olga (ed.), *Eight Hundred Years of Women's Letters* (Sutton Publishing, 1997)

Kerouac, Jack, *On the Road* (André Deutsch, 1958)

Kierkegaard, Søren, 'You Shall Love Your Neighbour', in *Works of Love*, trans. Howard and Edna Hong (Harper & Row, 1962)

King, Preston, and Smith, Graham M. (eds), *Friendship in Politics* (Routledge, 2007)

Kingsley, Charles, *The Water Babies: A Fairy-tale for a Land-baby* (J. M. Dent, 1966)

Kirmmse, Bruce H., *Encounters with Kierkegaard* (Princeton University Press, 1996)

Kropotkin, Peter, *Mutual Aid: A Factor of Evolution*, intro. Paul Avrich (Penguin Books, 1972)

La Gaipa, John L., 'The Negative Effects of Informal Support Systems', in *Personal Relationships and Social Support*, ed. Steve Duck with Roxane Cohen Silver (Sage, 1990)

Larson, Reed, and Bradney, Nancy, 'Precious Moments with Family Members and Friends', in *Families and Social Networks*, ed. Robert M. Milardo (Sage, 1989)

Laurence, Anne; Bellamy, Joan; and Perry, Gillian (eds), *Women, Scholarship and Criticism: Gender and Knowledge, c. 1790–1900* (Manchester University Press, 2001)

Le Roy Ladurie, Emmanuel, *Montaillou: Cathars and Catholics in a French Village 1294–1324* (Penguin Books, 1980)

Lee, Hermione, *Virginia Woolf* (Chatto & Windus, 1996)

—— *Edith Wharton* (Chatto & Windus, 2007)

Levi, Primo, *If This Is a Man* and *The Truce*, trans. Stuart Woolf (Abacus, 1987)

Lewis, C. S., *The Four Loves* (Collins, 1960)

Locke, John, *Some Thoughts Concerning Education*, ed. John W. Yolton (Oxford University Press, 1989)

Loukes, Harold, *The Discovery of Quakerism* (George C. Harrap, 1960)

Lovell, Terry, *British Feminist Thought* (Basil Blackwell, 1990)

Lynch, Sandra, *Philosophy and Friendship* (Edinburgh University Press, 2005)

Lyon, James K., *Bertolt Brecht in America* (Methuen, 1982)

Mann, Jonathan; Tarantola, Daniel; and Netter, Thomas (eds), *A Global Report: AIDS in the World* (Harvard University Press, 1992)

Marx, Groucho, *Memoirs of a Mangy Lover* (Futura, 1975)

Maslow, Abraham, 'A Theory of Human Motivation', *Psychological Review*, Vol. 50 (July 1943)

—— *Motivation and Personality* (Harper & Row, 1970)

Mathews, Nieves, *Francis Bacon: The History of a Character Assassination* (Yale, 1996)

McCarthy, Mary, *The Group*, intro. Candace Bushnell (Virago, 2010)

Mead, Margaret, *Sex and Temperament in Three Primitive Societies*, intro. Helen Fisher (Perennial, 2001)

Mencher, Samuel, 'Social Authority and the Family', *Journal of Marriage and the Family*, vol. 29, no. 1 (Feb. 1967)

Mill, John Stuart, *Autobiography*, preface Harold J. Laski (Oxford University Press, 1958)

—— *On the Subjection of Women*, foreword Fay Weldon (Hesperus Press, 2008)

Milligan, Edward, *Biographical Dictionary of British Quakers in Commerce and Industry 1775–1920*, vol. 8 (William Sessions, 2007)

Mitchell, Sally, *Frances Power Cobbe* (University of Virginia Press, 2004)

Montaigne, Michel de, *Essays*, trans. J. M. Cohen (Penguin Books, 1984)

Moore, Jane, *Mary Wollstonecraft* (Northcote House, 1999)

Murray, Gail Schmunk, *American Children's Literature and the Construction of Childhood* (Twayne Publishers, 1998)

Negra, Diane, 'Quality Postfeminism? Sex and the Single Girl on HBO', *Genders Journal*, no. 39 (2004), http://www.genders.org/g39/g39_negra.html (University of Colorado)

—— *What a Girl Wants? Fantasizing the Reclamation of Self in Post-feminism* (Routledge, 2009)

Némirovsky, Irène, *Suite Française* (Knopf, 2006)

Nichols, J. G. (ed.), *Literary Remains of King Edward the Sixth*, vol. 1 (Roxburghe Club, 1857)

Nietzsche, Friedrich, *Human, All Too Human: A Book for Free Spirits*, trans. R. J. Hollingdale, intro. Erich Heller (Cambridge University Press, 1986)

Niffenegger, Audrey, *The Time Traveller's Wife* (Vintage, 2005)

*The North London Collegiate School 1850–1950: A Hundred Years of Girls' Education: Essays in Honour of the Frances Buss Foundation* (Oxford University Press, 1950)

Obama, Barack, *Change We Can Believe In: Barack Obama's Plan to Renew America's Promise* (Canongate, 2008)

O'Connor, Pat, *Friendships between Women* (Harvester Wheatsheaf, 1992)

O'Hare, Mick (ed.), *Does Anything Eat Wasps? and 101 Other Questions* (Profile Books, 1995)

Olivier Bell, Anne (ed.), assisted by Andrew McNeillie, *The Diary of Virginia Woolf*, vol. 2, *1920–1924* (Penguin Books, 1981)

Orbach, Susie, and Eichenbaum, Luise, *Between Women: Love, Envy and Competition in Women's Friendships* (Arrow Books, 1994)

Orwell, George, *Nineteen Eighty-four* (Penguin Books, 1983)

Otto, Whitney, *How to Make an American Quilt* (Picador, 1991)

Ozment, Steve (ed.), *Three Behaim Boys: Growing Up in Early Modern Germany* (Yale University Press, 1990)

Pakaluk, Michael, *Other Selves: Philosophers on Friendship* (Hackett, 1991)

Parini, Jay, *John Steinbeck: A Biography* (William Heinemann, 1994)

Pawełczyńska, Anna, *Values and Violence in Auschwitz: A Sociological Analysis*, trans. Catherine S. Leach (University of California Press, 1979)

Pearson, Roberta E., and Uricchio, William (eds), *The Many Lives of Batman: Critical Approaches to a Superhero and His Media* (Routledge, 1991)

Pennington, Donald; Gillen, Kate; and Hill, Pam, *Social Psychology* (Hodder Headline, 1999)

Picardie, Ruth, *Before I Say Goodbye* (Penguin, 1998)

Pitts, John, *Reluctant Gangsters: Youth Gangs in Waltham Forest* (University of Bedford Press, February, 2007)

Plato, *The Last Days of Socrates*, trans. and intro. Hugh Tredennick (Penguin Classics, 1979)

— 'Lysis: A Dialogue on Friendship', trans. Stanley Lombardo, in Michael Pakaluk, *Other Selves: Philosophers on Friendship* (Hackett, 1991)

Pointer, Larry, *In Search of Butch Cassidy* (Constable, 1979)

Public Health Agency of Canada, 'Young People in Canada: Their Health and Well-being, http://www.phac-aspc.gc.ca/hp-ps/dca-dea/publications/hbsc-2004/chapter_4-eng.php(October2004)

Purvis, June, *A History of Women's Education in England* (Open University Press, 1991)

Pym, Barbara, *Excellent Women* (Penguin Books, 1983)

Rabb, Theodore K., *Renaissance Lives: Portraits of an Age* (Pantheon Books, 1993)

Raikes, Elizabeth, *Dorothea Beale of Cheltenham* (Archibald Constable and Co., 1908)

Rawson, Beryl, *The Politics of Friendship: Pompey and Cicero* (Sydney University Press, 1978)

Rewald, John, *Paul Cézanne*, trans. Margaret H. Liebman (Spring Books, 1965)

—— (ed.), and Hacker, Seymour (trans.), *Paul Cézanne: Letters* (Hacker Art Books, 1984)

Rhys, Jean, *Good Morning, Midnight* (Penguin Books, 1980)

Richardson Jr, Robert D., *Emerson: The Mind on Fire* (University of California Press, 1995)

Ricks, Christopher, *Tennyson* (Collier Books, 1972)

Roberts, Michèle, *Paper Houses: A Memoir of the 70s and Beyond* (Virago, 2007)

Rochefoucauld, François, Duc de la, *Reflections; or Sentences and Moral Maxims*, trans. J. W. Willis Bund and J. Hain Friswell (1871)

Romulo,Virola A. and Encarcion, Jessamyn, O. (eds), 'Measuring Progress of Philippine Society: Gross National Product or Gross National Happiness?' 10 National Convention on Statistics (NCS) (October, 2007) http://www.nscb.gov.ph/ncs/10thNCS/papers/invited%20papers/ips28-03.pdf

Rousseau, Jean-Jacques, *The Social Contract*, trans. and intro. Maurice Cranston (Penguin Books, 1988)

Rowe, Christopher (trans. and historical intro.), and Broadie, Sarah (philosophical intro. and commentary), *Aristotle: Nicomachean Ethics* (Oxford University Press, 2002)

Rowe, Dorothy, *Friends and Enemies* (HarperCollins, 2000)

Rutherford, Mark, *Last Pages from a Journal and Other Papers* (BiblioBazaar, 2009)

St Just, Maria (commentary), *Five o'Clock Angel: Letters of Tennessee Williams to Maria St Just* (André Deutsch, 1991)

Salinger, J. D., *Catcher in the Rye* (Penguin, 1994)

Schom, Alan, *Émile Zola: A Bourgeois Rebel* (Queen Anne Press, 1987)

Schulz, Charles M., *I Need All the Friends I Can Get* (Determined Productions, 1964)

Sewell, Elizabeth M., *Principles of Education: drawn from nature and revelation and applied to female education in the upper classes*, vols 1 and 2 (1865)

Shapiro, Barbara, *John Wilkins, 1614–1672: An Intellectual Biography* (University of California Press, 1969)

Showalter, Elaine (ed.), *Daughters of Decadence* (Virago, 1993)

Sias, Patricia M., and Bartoo, Heidi, 'Friendship, Social Support, and Health', in *Low-cost Approaches to Promote Physical and Mental Health* (Springer, 2007)

Skidmore, Chris, *Edward VI: The Lost King of England* (Weidenfeld & Nicolson, 2007)

*Stevie Smith: A Selection*, ed. Hermione Lee (Faber & Faber, 1983)

Spark, Muriel, *The Prime of Miss Jean Brodie* (Penguin Classics, 2010)

Spencer, Liz, and Pahl, Ray, *Rethinking Friendship: Hidden Solidarities Today* (Princeton University Press, 2006)

Spender, Stephen, *World Within World* (Faber & Faber, 1977)

The Spice Girls, *Forever Spice* (Little, Brown, 1999)

Stanton, E. C.; Anthony, S. B.; Gage, M. J.; and Harper, I. H. (eds), *History of Woman Suffrage* (Fowler & Wells, 1881)

Steegmuller, Francis, *A Woman, A Man, and Two Kingdoms: The Story of Madame d'Épinay and the Abbé Galiani* (Secker & Warburg, 1992)

Steinem, Gloria, *Outrageous Acts and Everyday Rebellions* (Holt, Rinehart & Winston, 1983)

Stern-Gillet, Suzanne, *Aristotle's Philosophy of Friendship* (State University of New York Press, 1995)

Stevenson, Robert Louis, *The Meaning of Friendship* (Edward Osgood Grover, 1909)

Stewart, John (ed.), *Kierkegaard and His Contemporaries: The Culture of Golden Age Denmark* (Walter de Gruyter, 2003)

Stone, Lawrence, *The Family, Sex and Marriage in England 1500–1800* (Penguin Books, 1990)

Sturgis, Matthew, *Walter Sickert: A Life* (HarperCollins, 2005)

Sturt, George, *Change in the Village* (Cambridge University Press, 2010)

Sullivan, Andrew, *Love Undetectable: Reflections on Friendship, Sex and Survival* (Chatto & Windus, 1998)

Swift, Graham, *Last Orders* (Picador, 1996)

Sykes, Christopher, *Evelyn Waugh: A Biography* (Collins, 1975)

Tadmor, Naomi, 'Friends and Neighbours in Early Modern England', in *Love, Friendship and Faith in Europe 1300–1800*, ed. Laura Gowing, Michael Hunter and Miri Rubin (Palgrave Macmillan, 2005)

Tan, Amy, *The Joy Luck Club* (Vintage, 1998)

Tapscott, Don, and Williams, Anthony D., *Wikinomics: How Mass Collaboration Changes Everything* (Portfolio, 2006)

Tartt, Donna, *The Secret History* (Knopf, 1992)

Telfer, Elizabeth, 'Friendship', in *Proceedings of the Aristotelian Society*, vol. 71 (1971)

Thompson, D., and LoBianco, L. (eds), *Jean Renoir: Letters*, trans. Craig Carlson, Natasha Arnoldi and Michael Wells (Faber & Faber, 1994)

Thompson, Michael, and O'Neill Grace, Catherine, with Cohen, Lawrence J., *Best Friends, Worst Enemies: Children's Friendships, Popularity and Social Cruelty* (Michael Joseph, 2002)

Thomson, David, *England in the Nineteenth Century* (Penguin Books, 1991)

Thoreau, Henry, *A Week on the Concord and Merrimack Rivers* (Houghton Mifflin, 1961)

Thurman, Judith, *Isak Dinesen: The Life of Karen Blixen* (Penguin Books, 1986)

Tinniswood, Adrian, *His Invention So Fertile: A Life of Christopher Wren* (Jonathan Cape, 2001)

Tomalin, Claire, *The Life and Death of Mary Wollstonecraft* (Penguin Books, 1992)

Toplis, Grace (ed.), *Leaves from the Note-books of Frances M. Buss: being selections from her weekly addresses to the girls of North London Collegiate School* (Macmillan, 1896)

Townsend, John Rowe (ed.) *Trade and Plumb-cake for Ever,*

*Huzza! The Life and Work of John Newbery 1713–1767* (Colt Books, 1994)

Tracy, Kathleen, *Sacha Baron Cohen: The Unauthorised Biography* (RBooks, 2008)

Trevelyan, G. M., *English Social History: A Survey of Six Centuries* (Penguin Books, 1986)

Triandis, Harry, 'Cultural Syndromes and Subjective Well-being', in *Culture and Subjective Well-being*, ed. Ed Deiner and Eunkook M. Suh (MIT Press, 2000)

Twain, Mark, *The Adventures of Tom Sawyer* and *The Adventures of Huckleberry Finn* (Wordsworth Editions, 1992)

Uglow, Jenny, *George Eliot* (Virago, 1987)

Veenhoven, Ruut, *World Database of Happiness: Correlates of Happiness* (Erasmus University of Rotterdam, 1994)

Verghese, Abraham, *The Tennis Partner* (Vintage, 1999)

Vernon, Mark, *The Philosophy of Friendship* (Palgrave Macmillan, 2005)

Vizetelly, Ernest Alfred, *Émile Zola: novelist and reformer; an account of his life and work* (Bodley Head, 1904)

Völker, Beate; Flap, Henk; Mollenhorst, Gerald, 'Changing Places: The Influence of Meeting Places on Recruiting Friends', in *Contexts of Social Capital: Social Networks in Markets, Communities and Families*, ed. Ray-May Hsung, Nan Lin and Ronald L. Breiger (Routledge, 2009)

Watson, Kathy, *The Devil Kissed Her: The Story of Mary Lamb* (Bloomsbury, 2004)

Waugh, Evelyn, *Men at Arms* (Penguin Books, 1965)
—— *Brideshead Revisited* (Penguin Books, 1979)

Yolton, John W. (ed.), *The Locke Reader: Selections from the Works of John Locke* (Oxford University Press, 1977)

Wharton, Edith, *A Backward Glance* (Century Hutchinson, 1987)
—— 'The Valley of Childish Things', in *Daughters of Decadence:*

*Women Writers of the Fin-de-Siècle*, Elaine Showalter (ed.) (Virago, 1993)

White, E. B., *Charlotte's Web* (Puffin Books, 2002)

Williams, Perry, 'Pioneer Women Students at Cambridge, 1869–81', in *Lessons for Life: The Schooling of Girls and Women, 1850–1950*, ed. Felicity Hunt (Basil Blackwell, 1987)

Wilson, A. N., *C. S. Lewis: A Biography* (HarperCollins, 2005)

Winnicott, D. W., *The Child, the Family and the Outside World* (Pelican, 1964)

—— *Deprivation and Delinquency*, ed. Clare Winnicott, Ray Shepherd and Madeleine Davis (Tavistock Publications, 1984)

Wodehouse, P. G., *Right Ho, Jeeves* (Penguin Books, 1973)

Wohlmuth, Sharon J., and Saline, Carol, *Best Friends* (Doubleday, 1998)

Woolf, Virginia, *The Waves* (Penguin Books, 1968)

World Health Organization, 'Mental Well-being in School-aged Children in Europe: Associations with Social Cohesion and Socioeconomic Circumstances', http://www.euro.who.int/_data/assets/pdf_files/0010/76483/Hbsc_Forum_2007_mental-well-being.pdf (2007), *The Waves*

Yolton, John, W. (ed.), *The Locke Reader: Selections from the Works of John Locke* (Oxford University Press, 1977)

Young, James, *Songs They Never Play on the Radio: Nico, the Last Bohemian* (Bloomsbury, 1992)

Young-Bruehl, Elisabeth, *Hannah Arendt: For Love of the World* (Yale University Press, 1982)

Zagorin, Perez, *Francis Bacon* (Princeton University Press, 1998)

Zeldin, Theodore, *An Intimate History of Humanity* (Vintage, 1998)

Zola, Émile, *Germinal*, trans. Roger Pearson (Penguin Books, 2004)

# Acknowledgements

With thanks to Lennie Goodings, Judith Murray and Richard Beswick. Thanks for reading sections and/or the whole in draft form to John Barnard, Jane Chamberlain, Juliet Gardiner and Steve Masterson. And thanks of course to my friends, old and new, near and far; to family members and individuals who have been friends to me in ways that have proved transformative; to friends I've seen on a regular basis since my youth; to friends I've seen very recently and to friends I may not have seen for some time but whom I hold in my heart. You know who you are. I love you all.